MW00678516

Critical Issues in Cross Cultural Management

Jessica L. Wildman · Richard L. Griffith
Brigitte K. Armon
Editors

Critical Issues in Cross Cultural Management

 Springer

Editors
Jessica L. Wildman
Institute for Cross Cultural Management
Florida Institute of Technology
Melbourne, FL
USA

Brigitte K. Armon
Organizational Effectiveness
Cox Communications
Atlanta, GA
USA

Richard L. Griffith
Institute for Cross Cultural Management
Florida Institute of Technology
Melbourne, FL
USA

ISBN 978-3-319-42164-3   ISBN 978-3-319-42166-7   (eBook)
DOI 10.1007/978-3-319-42166-7

Library of Congress Control Number: 2016946001

© Springer International Publishing Switzerland 2016
This work is subject to copyright. All rights are reserved by the Publisher, whether the whole or part of the material is concerned, specifically the rights of translation, reprinting, reuse of illustrations, recitation, broadcasting, reproduction on microfilms or in any other physical way, and transmission or information storage and retrieval, electronic adaptation, computer software, or by similar or dissimilar methodology now known or hereafter developed.
The use of general descriptive names, registered names, trademarks, service marks, etc. in this publication does not imply, even in the absence of a specific statement, that such names are exempt from the relevant protective laws and regulations and therefore free for general use.
The publisher, the authors and the editors are safe to assume that the advice and information in this book are believed to be true and accurate at the date of publication. Neither the publisher nor the authors or the editors give a warranty, express or implied, with respect to the material contained herein or for any errors or omissions that may have been made.

Printed on acid-free paper

This Springer imprint is published by Springer Nature
The registered company is Springer International Publishing AG Switzerland

Preface

The Value of Alternate Lenses to Leverage Culture

It has become somewhat of a tradition for my family to hire a professional photographer for the holidays or other special occasions. While it wasn't intentional, it became a way of documenting just how much my son has changed over the years.[1] The photographer that we hire is amazing. I find it hard to reconcile the images that I see from her photographs and the experience of being in the photo session. What seemed to be just an average day looks stunning in the pictures. Again and again, our photographer captures the perfect moment at the perfect time.

Being somewhat of a nerd, I became curious as to how she was able to capture such perfect photographs. I bought a SLR camera and tried to read some books and websites, but found it difficult to replicate the outcomes. After asking our photographer some questions, she shared one of the key elements of her success. She told me that the choice of lens had a great deal to do with her ability to get just the perfect shot.

The choice of lens allows one to gain a different perspective and to have a view of the world that would be invisible to the naked eye. So, while I was in the same physical space during the photo session, I could not see what our photographer could see.

Culture can operate in a similar fashion. Culture allows us to interpret and make sense of our world, and those who come from a similar culture share this interpretive framework. Just like the lens, some cultures focus on events that are close, while other cultures take the telescopic lens's perspective of the distant future.

In the modern world, it is becoming increasingly common to work and interact with people from very different cultures. Globalization brings us closer together, either physically or virtually through the means of electronic communication. English has been adopted as the international language of business. Thus, even though we may be from different cultures, we may speak the same language. Yet,

---

[1]Story courtesy of the first author.

this common language may be deceiving. Its adoption doesn't mean that we have perfect understanding. What makes perfect sense to you may not make sense to your international partner, your international supplier, or your international market. We view the world through different lenses; our perspectives may not align, which can lead to miscommunication, misunderstanding, and lost opportunities.

To share key elements of success in understanding culture, we convened the first Cross-Cultural Management Summit in the spring of 2014. The Summit was hosted by the Institute for Cross-Cultural Management at Florida Tech, and this book is a product of that summit. Culture and organizational effectiveness was the theme that brought the Summit participants together. Each of the participants saw culture impacting their profession, and they gathered to learn more about culture from each other. For our participants from the corporate world, culture was an unknown variable that could impact their bottom line and add risk to their business. For participants from the military, knowledge regarding culture could improve the intelligence they gathered and make sure that our men and women in uniform came home alive. For our participants from academia, a better understanding of the context of cultural dilemmas may be a piece of an intellectual puzzle in a long a productive research career. So while our interest in culture was common ground, the background of the participants was quite varied. We feel that is the real strength of the Summit.

If we all came from the same background and had the same problems, the solutions available to us would be fixed and expertise more limited. However, the participants didn't have the same background, which gives us the opportunity to create and claim value. A quick examination of the summit participants revealed participants flew from China, Europe, Africa, and South America and represented equally diverse professional fields. Included in the participants was a former foreign area officer who used his cultural experienced gained in Indonesia to facilitate the success of a Marine Expeditionary Unit in Cambodia, the first US Marine back in that country since the last battle of the Vietnam War. Another participant was the Vice President of Nortel, who used her understanding of the value of family in Latin cultures to build business in Bolivia, not through the traditional gifts of liquor and cigars, but through family gifts that led to an invitation into the home of her future partners. Yet another participant was a cultural anthropologist who worked with the king of Tonga to improve the quality of life of people on the islands.

The goal of the Summit was to leverage these different vantage points to solve each other's problems, to gain a new perspective, and re-focus on our work. With the aid of a different lens, we might find a solution to our problem that wasn't apparent from our own point of view. In fact, one person's problem may actually be another person's solution. There is an old idiom "One man's trash is another man's treasure," and our hope was that through networking and sharing with other professionals, the participants of the Summit might stumble across just such a treasure.

While the collective wisdom in the room provided the potential for deep learning and problem solving, all of that potential needed to be unlocked before it could be shared. Because the participants of the Summit came from such varied backgrounds, they often spoke different professional "languages." Luckily, the staff of

ICCM often found themselves acting like interpreters, facilitating conversations by helping to translate language and keep conversations on track. With a just little help, we were able to unlock a lot of that hidden expertise through probing questions and explicit clarifications.

By no means was this process easy for any of the Summit participants. It took a lot of effort, patience, and perseverance. Lugging a camera bag full of lenses around is hard work. It is much easier to stick with our same old lens and same old habits. We asked participants of the Summit not only to lead discussions, but to follow tangents down a rabbit hole or two. We encouraged them to look for opportunities to share, question, and translate across professions and contexts. Luckily, the participants were up for the challenges. What resulted was a high energy exchange of thoughts, ideas, questions, and perspectives that lasted the duration of the Summit.

Reflecting on all we learned at the Summit, it would a shame if the lessons we learned weren't spread to a wider audience. The outcome of that sentiment is the book that you're now reading. Our goal for this edited volume was a wider dissemination of the lessons of the Summit so that the value created at the event could be claimed by other professionals with similar challenges.

The 2014 Cross Cultural Management Summit was an enjoyable and memorable event for us. We hope this book will be an enjoyable read for you, and allow you to borrow the lenses of some of thought leaders at the Summit. Perhaps with a change of perspective, your challenges may be drawn into sharper focus and the improved view offer new insights.

Melbourne, USA   Richard L. Griffith
                                                                                   Brigitte K. Armon

Contents

Editors and Contributors

About the Editors

Jessica L. Wildman Ph.D. is an Assistant Professor in the Industrial Organizational Psychology program and the Research Director of the Institute for Cross Cultural Management at the Florida Institute of Technology. She has co-edited two books, co-authored over 30 publications, and presented over 20 times at professional conferences. Her current research interests include trust dynamics across cultures, multicultural work performance, and global virtual team processes.

Richard L. Griffith Ph.D. is the Executive Director of The Institute for Cross Cultural Management at Florida Tech. He has authored over 100 publications, presentations, and chapters, and is the co-editor of "Internationalizing the Organizational Psychology Curriculum" and "Leading Global Teams". His work has been featured in Time magazine and The Wall Street Journal.

Brigitte K. Armon Ph.D. has presented and published on intercultural topics, including: expatriate feedback and adjustment, intercultural competence, and internationalizing the Industrial/Organizational Psychology curriculum. She received her Ph.D. from Florida Institute of Technology in I/O Psychology with a concentration in Cross-Cultural I/O.

Contributors

Meghan W. Brenneman Ed.D. is a Research Manager at Educational Testing Service in Princeton, NJ. Her research focuses on the development and assessment of noncognitive skills for students, teachers and employees.

Tara (Rench) Brown Ph.D. is a Scientist in Aptima's Applied Cognitive Training Systems Division, with expertise in the areas of unobtrusive measurement, team dynamics, training, and adaptability. Dr. Brown holds a Ph.D. and M.A. in

Organizational Psychology from Michigan State University and a B.S. in Psychology from Wright State University.

C. Shawn Burke Ph.D. is a Professor (Research) at the Institute for Simulation and Training, University of Central Florida. She is currently investigating issues surrounding team leadership, cultural diversity in teams, team adaptation, and team roles in mission critical environments. She has published over 80 works related to the above topics.

Jeremy Burrus is a Principal Research Scientist in ProExam's Center for Innovative Assessments, New York. His main research interests are in developing innovative assessments of noncognitive constructs, cognitive biases, and cross-cultural competence. He has over 40 journal articles, book chapters, research reports, and books either published or in press.

Jasmine Duran has an M.S. in Applied Psychology from Arizona State University. Her research interests include training for adaptive performance in novel situations. As a research associate with Global Cognition, Ms. Duran assisted in the validation of a model of culture-general competence to support U.S. Department of Defense service members.

Julianna Fischer is a first-year graduate student in the International Industrial/Organizational Psychology program at the Florida Institute of Technology in Melbourne, FL. She is a research associate for the Institute for Cross Cultural Management and an associate consultant for The Center for Organizational Effectiveness. She earned her B.A. in both psychology and anthropology from Southern Methodist University in 2014. Her research interests include the importance of cross-cultural competence, work-related flow, emotions, and humanitarian work psychology.

Harris Friedman Ph.D. is Professor of Counseling Psychology at University of Florida, Fellow of the American Psychological Association, and holds the diploma in Organizational/Business Consulting Psychology from the American Board of Professional Psychology. He has consulted extensively both domestically and internationally and has over 200 professional publications, many in the area of culture and culture change. Currently he is co-authoring a book on transcultural competence for the American Psychological Association Press.

Sharon Glazer Ph.D. President of Healthy Organization, Professor and Chair of the Division of Applied Behavioral Sciences at the University of Baltimore, Research Professor at UMD Center for Advanced Study of Language and Psychology Department, IACCP Treasurer, and Co-Editor of Culture, Organizations, and Work, specializes in cross-cultural organizational psychology, conducting primary research, engaging in consulting, teaching at universities world-wide, and training for corporate and government organizations. Dr. Glazer was a Fulbright, Erasmus Mundus, International Studies, and Global Studies

Fellow, has over 40 published works, worked and lived on three continents, and speaks six languages.

Jerry Glover Ph.D. is Professor of Organizational Change and Culturally Adaptive Leadership at Hawaii Pacific University. He is a Cultural Anthropologist (University of Florida) who has over 30 years of working with culture change and cultural competence projects. In the 1990s, he led a decade-long international research study of the cultures of 34 corporate, military, educational, and government organizations. In recent years he has worked on 3C projects sponsored by the Department of Defense, including an applied DEOMI study of cultural dilemmas experienced by Warfighters in international missions. He is a Director and Board Member of the International Society for Organizational Development and Change and a Peer Review Editor for the Organizational Development Journal. He has been affiliated with the Trompenaars Hampden-Turner Group (Amsterdam) since 1997. A recent publication is titled "The Cultures of People Who Study Culture" in the Organizational Development Journal (Spring Issue, 2014). He is currently co-authoring a book on transcultural competence for the American Psychological Association Press.

Zachary Horn Ph.D. is the Manager of Quantitative Psychology at Stitch Fix. His background in applied research spans areas of leadership, teamwork, adaptability, and cross-cultural competencies. He received his Ph.D. in Industrial-Organizational Psychology from George Mason University, and serves in multiple leadership positions within the Society for Industrial-Organizational Psychology.

Jennifer Klafehn Ph.D. is an Associate Research Scientist at the Educational Testing Service in Princeton, NJ. Her research focuses on the assessment of noncognitive constructs, particularly the development of tools and systems to measure cross-cultural skills and performance. She also conducts research on factors related to cross-cultural performance, such as metacognition, as well as cross-cultural adaptation and training.

Jonathan Kochert Ph.D. is a Research Psychologist, at the U.S. Army Research Institute. His responsibilities is the development of the Cross Cultural Competence Assessment System and research in unit command climate. Prior to joining ARI, he has served in the U.S. Army and Indiana National Guard as an Infantry non-commissioned officer.

William S. Kramer MS is a doctoral candidate in the I/O Psychology program at Clemson University. He has co-authored over ten publications and book chapters and has been technical lead for a variety of different grants and contracts (e.g. NASA, ARL). His research interests include culture, teams, leadership, and situational context

Borislava Manojlovic Ph.D. is the Director of Research and Adjunct Professor at the School of Diplomacy and International Relations, Seton Hall University. She is an expert in international relations, conflict analysis and resolution, dealing with the past, education in post-conflict settings and atrocities prevention. Borislava received her doctoral degree at the School for Conflict Analysis and Resolution, GMU and her MA at Brandeis University.

Julio C. Mateo is a Senior Research Scientist with 361 Interactive, LLC. His research focuses on the development of cognitive models, assessment tools, and training programs to enhance the cross-cultural competence of the U.S. Armed Forces. Mr. Mateo received a Bachelor's degree in Psychology from the Universidad Pontificia de Salamanca (Spain) and a Master's degree in Human Factors Psychology from Wright State University (USA).

Michael J. McCloskey is President and Chief Scientist of 361 Interactive, LLC. His primary interests center on the study and support of cross-cultural competence and the promotion of expertise in intelligence analysis through the development of decision-centered training, automated aids, and organizational designs. Mr. McCloskey received a Bachelor's degree in Mechanical Engineering and a Master's degree in Human Factors Psychology, both from the University of Dayton (USA).

Kyi Phyu Nyein is currently a doctoral student in Industrial/Organizational Psychology at Florida Institute of Technology. She earned her B.Sc. in Psychology from Davidson College in 2013 and her M.A. in Organizational Sciences with Human Resources Management concentration from George Washington University in 2015. Her current research interests include teams and groups, trust development, violation, repair, and restoration, women's leadership, and gender discrimination and prejudice.

Louise Rasmussen is a principal scientist at Global Cognition, a research and training development organization located in Yellow Springs, Ohio. Her research aims to characterize effective cognition and performance in intercultural situations to inform cultural training and education. She received her Ph.D. in human factors psychology from Wright State University.

Krista Ratwani Ph.D. is a Senior Scientist and Director for the Advanced Cognitive Training Systems Division at Aptima. She has expertise in leader development, team processes, and performance measurement. She holds a Ph.D. and M.A. in Industrial-Organizational Psychology from George Mason University and a B.A. in Psychology from Monmouth University.

Richard D. Roberts Ph.D. is Chief Scientist, Center for Innovative Assessments, ProExam, New York. His main area of specialization is measurement, with a special emphasis on developing innovative new item types for the assessment of both cognitive and noncognitive skills. Dr. Roberts has published about a dozen books and 200 peer-review articles on these topics, with nearly 400 presentations across the globe.

Gregory A. Ruark Ph.D. is the team leader for the Basic Research Program, Foundational Science Research Unit, for the U.S. Army Research Institute for the

Behavioral and Social Sciences. He is a member of SIOP and APA's Division 19. Dr. Ruark holds a Ph.D. in Industrial/Organizational Psychology from University of Oklahoma.

Craig Runde is the Director of the Center for Conflict Dynamics at Eckerd College. Craig is the co-author of several books on workplace conflict management including Becoming a Conflict Competent Leader. Craig received his B.A. from Harvard University, an M.L.L. from the University of Denver, and a J.D. from Duke University.

Winston Sieck is president and principal scientist at Global Cognition, an education research and development organization. His cultural research aims to shed light on general-purpose cognitive skills and mindsets that help professionals to quickly adapt and work effectively in any culture. He received his Ph.D. from the University of Michigan.

Marissa Shuffler Ph.D. is an Assistant Professor of Industrial/Organizational Psychology at Clemson University. Her areas of expertise include team and leader training and development with an emphasis on high risk and complex environments (e.g., virtual, distributed). Her work to date includes an edited book, over 45 publications, and over 100 presentations.

Marinus van Driel Ph.D. is an Industrial/Organizational Psychologist and cross-cultural competence scholar. He has wide-ranging consulting experience with organizations both in the private and government contexts. Among his most notable accomplishments as a scholar are contributing to the institutionalization of cross-cultural competence as an important skillset within the United States Department of Defense and constructing various measures including an organizational-level measure of cross-cultural competence. Marinus has also provided talent management consultation internationally to financial, mining, telecommunications, and aviation organizations. Marinus obtained his doctorate from Florida Institute of Technology and baccalaureate degree from Furman University.

Chapter 1
#TeamLeadership: Leadership for Today's Multicultural, Virtual, and Distributed Teams

Marissa L. Shuffler, William S. Kramer and C. Shawn Burke

Organizations today are increasingly reliant upon technology to bring together diverse teams of individuals from around the globe who can solve the challenges that are beyond the capabilities of a single person (Connaughton and Shuffler 2007). However, while such collaborations may bring together the expertise needed to solve problems, this does not mean that the team members are also experts in teamwork. Failures in communication, coordination, performance monitoring, and other teamwork processes due to issues of working across cultural, temporal, and digital boundaries have plagued teams for years, often with disastrous results (Salas et al. 2008). For example, the Mars Climate Orbiter was lost in 1999 when the engineering team, comprised of members from different countries, failed to coordinate effectively and used the wrong measurement system (meters vs. feet) to construct software, causing the orbiter to disintegrate when it entered the atmosphere at an incorrect angle (Sauser et al. 2009). Thus, in addition to possessing content area expertise, there may be other functions critical to effectively facilitating the necessary processes that enable subsequent team effectiveness when working across time, space, and cultures (Salas et al. 2009).

While the ability for teams to be distributed in numerous regions of the world and connected via virtuality does offer benefits, such contextually driven interactions can also pose a variety of challenges to critical team processes. Certainly,

M.L. Shuffler (✉) · W.S. Kramer
Psychology Department, Clemson University, 418 Brackett Hall, Clemson, SC 29634, USA
e-mail: mshuffl@clemson.edu

W.S. Kramer
e-mail: wskrame@g.clemson.edu

C.S. Burke
Institute for Simulation and Training, University of Central Florida, 3100 Technology
Parkway, Orlando, FL 32826, USA
e-mail: sburke@ist.ucf.edu

© Springer International Publishing Switzerland 2016
J.L. Wildman et al. (eds.), *Critical Issues in Cross Cultural Management*,
DOI 10.1007/978-3-319-42166-7_1

1

while virtuality offers the opportunity of being able to bring together teams of qualified individuals no matter what their geographic location (Maynard et al. 2012), it is important to note that this distribution of members and types of virtual tools utilized may impact how social presence—or a lack thereof—is conveyed in teams, which can in turn inhibit team processes and effectiveness (Kirkman and Mathieu 2005). This impact on social presence interacts further with the composition of the team, both in terms of deep and surface-level diversity issues which may challenge the norms and interactions of team development and teamwork itself (Burke et al. 2010).

Given these complexities that such teams may face, it is important to understand what factors may be able to help improve their performance and reduce the likelihood of critical errors such as those experienced by the Mars Orbiter team. One proposed avenue for effectively facilitating teamwork in complex environments is that of team leadership (Bell and Kozlowski 2002; Burke et al. 2011; Kayworth and Leidner 2001). The purpose of leadership in any given team is to establish goals and set direction that will lead to the accomplishment of these goals (Zaccaro et al. 2001). From a functional leadership perspective, this means performing a range of behaviors, both those specific to the task at hand as well as those behaviors aimed at enhancing the social climate of the team (Zaccaro et al. 2009). Previous research suggests that team leadership is a critical component of ensuring effective team processes and team outcomes (Burke et al. 2006; Salas et al. 2005; Zaccaro 2007).

However, team leadership does not necessarily have to rely solely upon a single individual, as is often the assumption (Pearce and Conger 2003). Indeed, there may be multiple leaders on a team, with different members sharing leadership responsibilities or rotating leadership to ensure effectiveness, referred to as collective leadership (Zaccaro and DeChurch 2011). While still a relatively new area of study, there have been promising findings supporting the idea that collective leadership—whereby multiple members participate in leading—can facilitate effective teamwork and enhance team performance (Balkundi and Harrison 2006; Carson et al. 2007; Mehra et al. 2006; Pearce and Conger 2003). Collective leadership in virtual, distributed, and multicultural environments may be even more effective than traditional vertical leadership, as having multiple team members step up to take on leadership needs can aid in ensuring specific team needs are being met across the team lifecycle (Day et al. 2006).

Thus, the purpose of the current paper is to explore existing research as it may contribute to our understanding of how to best utilize collective team leadership as a mechanism for effectively working in the multicultural, distributed, and virtual environments of today. We first briefly focus on defining the characteristics of complex multicultural, virtual, and distributed environments in terms of their impact on teamwork and team performance, then turn to examining the existing science regarding collective leadership. We then propose several recommendations regarding how such collective leadership may be best incorporated into teams facing these complexities of virtuality, multiculturalism, and distribution, including a discussion of the actionable strategies as well as future research directions. It is hoped that this white paper will serve as a starting point to further the discussion regarding collective leadership as a potential avenue for enhancing teams facing the challenges and complexities of the twenty-first century.

Summary of the Science

Complexities in the Twenty-First Century: Multiculturalism, Virtuality, and Distribution

Today, global organizations are no longer the exception, but the norm (Burke et al. 2010). The resulting multicultural workforce can have tremendous benefits as talent and resources are no longer geographically constrained. Indeed, multicultural teams have rapidly increased in their prevalence across a range of organizations. Multicultural teams are defined as those whose members have diverse values and beliefs based on their cultural orientation (Von Glinow et al. 2004). In seeking to provide guidance to organizations there has been a fair amount of work conducted which examines multicultural differences in group or team-based work. For example, research has shown cultural differences have implications for cooperation (e.g., Kirkman and Shapiro 2001), communication (Conyne et al. 1999), feedback (Earley et al. 1999), conflict type (Elron 1998; Mortensen and Hinds 2001), efficacy (Gibson and Krikman 1999), adaptation (Harrison et al. 2000), decision-making (Kirchmeyer and Cohen 1992), and team performance (Gibson and Krikman 1999; Matveev and Nelson 2004).

Furthermore, given advances in technology and communication, such teams may operate in distributed locations, requiring them to collaborate through virtual media such as videoconferencing or teleconferencing (Connaughton and Shuffler 2007; Martins et al. 2004). Indeed, virtuality and distribution have become the norm in most team situations, with it no longer being a question of whether or not teams are virtual and distributed, but instead the degree to which teams are virtual and distributed (Kirkman and Mathieu 2005). Virtuality therefore has come to be viewed on a continuum, with low virtuality teams being those whose synchronous communications are rich in task information and social cues (e.g., videoconferencing) and high virtuality teams being those whose asynchronous communications are weaker in providing relevant task and social information (e.g., email, instant messaging). Distribution, while in research often dichotomized into full distribution or collocation, can also be viewed along a similar continuum, with teams capable of being partially distributed (e.g., half the team collocated, other members isolated) in many different possible configurations.

While this environment seems to be built for success, there is an ever-growing debate regarding whether multiculturalism, distribution, and virtuality in teams are in fact opportunities or instead crippling challenges to organizations (Stanko and Gibson 2009). If there are cultural differences in teamwork when looking intra-culturally across cultures, the challenges they pose are compounded when multiple cultures are placed within a single team. However, it has been argued that these teams can be effective to the degree to which they are able to manage the need for consensus versus the need for diversity (Argote and McGrath 1993). While the diversity in skills and perspectives may benefit multicultural teams, the team also needs a degree of common ground in order to facilitate coordinated action and the understanding that leads to that coordination (Argote and McGrath 1993). Thus, as organizations increasingly rely on multicultural teams, a debate emerges regarding the challenges and opportunities of merging vastly different backgrounds, traditions, motivations, and concerns (Dinwoodie 2005). From one viewpoint, multiculturalism can challenge teams by making communication difficult and miscommunication more likely (Von Glinow et al. 2004). However, differences in culture can also bring together individuals whose unique experiences and expertise can be of great benefit to enhancing teamwork (Connaughton and Shuffler 2007). Therefore, it is critical to understand how to best leverage these unique qualities of multicultural teams.

Certainly, distribution and virtuality may be viewed as either advantages or disadvantages as well, depending on the context. Distribution of members can serve as a boundary, leading to lowered levels of interaction from both a task and a social perspective (Kraut et al. 2002; O'Leary and Cummings 2007). Less interaction means that team members will be less likely to convey that they have the necessary knowledge, skills, and abilities needed to be successful as a team, causing other members to potentially ignore or misinterpret their attempts at influence (Zaccaro et al. 2012). Indeed, Kerr and Jermier (1978) note the role of physical distance creating conditions whereby effective teamwork may be challenging or altogether impossible. From a virtuality standpoint, teams that maximize the opportunities that are provided by virtuality can greatly benefit, such as the use of synchronous collaboration tools that can allow for simultaneous idea generation across space and time (Kirkman and Mathieu 2005). However, much like multiculturalism, the incorporation of virtuality can also impede teamwork, often due to a lack of social cues or difficulty sharing information (Mesmer-Magnus et al. 2011). In sum, it is critical to not only understand how to best leverage culture and maximize it to the fullest extent possible, but also to create environments whereby teams are provided with the support needed to function effectively in virtual and distributed environments.

Collective Leadership: A Means for Enhancing Today's Teams?

Given these complexities that teams today face, one avenue that may provide a source of support is that of leadership, particularly leadership at the collective team level (Pearce 2004). In looking at the literature on the leadership of collectives, the predominant amount of work that has been conducted, both conceptually and empirically, examines leadership as a vertical influence process. While vertical leadership has a long history and is indeed important, it is but one type of leadership. Moreover, in the complex environments of the twenty-first century often it is impossible for one individual to have the requisite knowledge and skill to successfully enact vertical leadership to the exclusion of other forms of leadership. Others have also acknowledged that the sharing of leadership and responsibility within organizations is now critical to survival (Merkens and Spencer 1998).

The notion of leadership being shared among individuals in collectives is not a new concept (e.g., Gibbs 1954); however, its focused study is a relatively new phenomenon across a range of disciplines (Yammarino et al. 2005). But, what does it mean to collectively lead? While there have been several conceptualizations put forth across disciplines (Carson et al. 2007), the common theme running throughout the various conceptualizations is that collective leadership involves the distribution of the leadership responsibilities throughout the team (Lambert 2002; Jackson 2000; Pearce and Conger 2003) and does not negate vertical leadership. In examining the literature on collective leadership what seems to differ among researchers is the manner in which the responsibilities are shared and the exact nature of what constitutes 'leadership.' For example, while some researchers explicitly view collective leadership as an emergent phenomenon that occurs within the team (Day et al. 2004), others do not disallow the possibility that shared leadership can be formally prescribed (Pearce and Sims 2002). In relation to form, the argument is that collective leadership is the "serial emergence of multiple leaders over the lifespan of the team" (Pearce and Sims 2002, p. 176) as compared to the notion of co-leadership. In a similar notion, Day et al. (2004) talk about leadership capacity which is a form of collective leadership conceptualized as an emergent state whereby social capital is built within the team. In sum, collective leadership involves both the delineation of who is leading, as well as the degree to what and how different leadership behaviors are distributed, rotated, or simultaneously shared among members (Zaccaro and DeChurch 2011).

Work on collective leadership recognizes the complexity present within organizational settings and relies on the underlying tenet that "those who are doing the job are [often] in the best position to improve it" (Jackson 2000, p. 16). This form of leadership has been argued to be most useful when tasks are interdependent and complex (Pearce 2004). Thus, collective leadership may be well suited for the demands of multicultural, virtual, and distributed environments. Further, collective leadership should be effective at facilitating the processes that comprise teamwork, which in turn should lead to enhanced team performance, as the relationship between teamwork and team performance has been well established (LePine et al. 2008; Marks et al. 2001). By having multiple team members fulfilling leadership needs as they arise, teams should have all necessary resources needed to ensure that all teamwork processes and emergent states develop and operate smoothly (Marks et al. 2000).

Indeed, a number of studies have illustrated the link between collective leadership and team outcomes (e.g., Avolio et al. 2009; Carson et al. 2007;

Kukenberger et al. 2011; Pearce and Sims 2002, 2002). Research has illustrated the impact of leadership as a collective team property on team outcomes, as it is proposed that contributing leadership both meets the needs of the team as well as increasing the commitment of members offering such leadership (Mathieu et al. in press). In addition to the work previously discussed by Pearce et al. (2001), Carson et al. (2007) found in their study of shared leadership, teams with more dense leadership networks (i.e., higher levels of shared leadership) were associated with higher levels of team performance as rated by clients. Other studies have offered support for the link between team leadership and team member satisfaction and overall effectiveness (e.g., Avolio et al. 2009; Ensley et al. 2006; Erez and Gati 2002). From a virtual context, Muethel et al. (2012) offered empirical support for the link between shared leadership and team performance in dispersed teams. Thus, while research in this area is still growing, there appears to be initial support to the idea that collective leadership does in fact have a positive influence for teams operating in complex environments.

Bridging the Gap: Evidence-Based Practices

Certainly, leadership has been argued to play a pivotal role in determining team effectiveness (Burke et al. 2006). Within multicultural, virtual, and distributed teams, leadership actions become even more important given the likelihood of the team exhibiting degradations in team coherence, which in turn, promotes the coordinated action indicative of effective teams. Promoting collective leadership may therefore help teams adapt to difficulties in execution and process loss. Drawing from several existing bodies of literature, we next offer several evidence-based practices that may aid practitioners in determining how to best promote collective leadership efforts within their teams.

First, organizations utilizing team members who are distributed should take the form of media that they use to communicate into consideration, particularly if those team members are to be involved in collective leadership. Social influence is a key defining factor of leadership, and without appropriate media to convey such social presence, leadership may suffer or fail to exist at the collective level (Hoch and Kozlowski in press). While text-based virtual tools such as instant messaging may offer benefits for enhancing other aspects of teamwork, in order to convey social presence needed for influence, teams would benefit from the use of richer media such as teleconferencing or videoconferencing (Mesmer-Magnus et al. 2011). However, this does not mean that all organizations must acquire the richest media possible, as there were not distinct differences for videoconferencing and teleconferencing. Therefore, it may be perfectly suitable for teams to continue to use teleconferencing in order to successfully convey the social presence needed for influencing others. Thus, it is important from a collective leadership standpoint that teams utilize appropriate media for conveying social presence.

Furthermore, using the appropriate media based upon a team's life cycle will also have implications for creating effective virtual, multicultural teams. For instance, Staples and Zhao (2006) found that virtual teams with a culturally heterogeneous composition were likely to run into problems and exhibit low levels of cohesion and increased conflict amongst team members. This was found to be due to the fact that the teams, upon first observing surface-level differences between the members, were more likely to create subgroups which, in turn, generated faultlines. However, research has shown that this negative aspect of virtual, culturally heterogeneous teams can be reduced, if not avoided completely by starting with the use of a virtual tool with reductive capabilities (Huang et al. 2004). Specifically, with tools that take away the ability to see the other team members, surface-level diversity can be minimized initially, resulting in fewer subgroups (Watson et al. 1993).

A second practical recommendation for organizations is to encourage the development of all team members in terms of leadership, not just a single vertical leader. Results of multiple previous studies show value in having multiple team members step up and take on leadership responsibilities as team needs for leadership emerge (Hoch and Kozlowski in press; Pearce and Conger 2003; Pearce 2004). Thus, moving toward the development of leadership in all team members may provide a distinct advantage for organizations who utilize collective leadership (Day et al. 2004). Furthermore, as traditionally the focus of leadership development has remained at the individual level, it may be necessary to refine existing programs in order to encourage and reward leadership at the team level.

Third, it may be worthwhile to consider the role of both assigned and emergent leadership in these types of teams. As noted by Pearce and Conger (2003), having members of a team share in leadership responsibilities does not negate the role of formal, assigned vertical leaders. Instead, it may be better to consider such formal leaders as team coaches, whereby the role of such coaches is to help facilitate the active involvement of team members in the leadership process (Hackman 2002). Indeed, Hackman and Wageman (2005) argue that team coaching involves "those interventions that inhibit process losses and foster process gains" (p. 273). If, as argued previously, successful leadership is beyond the capability of a single individual in a team, perhaps the most effective role of a formal leader is to enable and motivate other team members to step up and take on leadership functions as needs arise. Drawing upon the findings of the present study, this may mean helping the team understand how to collectively lead for a single behavior (e.g., who needs to step up at what time), and when members should be specialized in particular leadership roles.

Finally, organizations must take into consideration attitudes toward leadership from a cultural perspective when attempting to implement collective leadership structures. Given that some cultures may be very hierarchical in nature, not all cultures may be accepting of the idea of multiple individuals leading, which may discourage the implementation of such collective structures (Bienefeld and Gorte 2014). For example, Hiller et al. (2006) found that teams whose members were more strongly collectivistic were more likely to accept and enact collective leadership than those with more individualistic members. However, those teams who enacted collective leadership were in fact more successful in terms of team performance. Thus, a clear understanding of cultural perspective on leadership may serve as an important foundation for ascertaining the degree to which collective leadership will be accepted, enacted, and even encouraged in multicultural environments.

Due to fundamental differences in cultures such as acceptance of lateral influence, research tends to point to the idea that cultural diversity is negatively related to collective leadership (Pearce and Conger 2003; Ramthun and Matkin 2012). This is be coupled by the fact that culturally diverse teams can be less cohesive and effective if the cultural differences are salient (Elron 1998; Lau and Murnighan 1998). For instance, in a recent meta-analysis, it was shown that when teams had salient subgroups, cultural diversity was negatively related to overall communication (Greer et al. 2012). Based on these findings, while it might appear that there is no room for collective leadership in culturally diverse teams, that is not the case. A team that is culturally competent is more likely to have intrinsic motivation to learn from those who are different and, in turn, engage in collective leadership behaviors (Hooker and Csekszentmihalyi 2003). Additionally, as will be discussed in detail in the following section, the development of a hybrid culture has the ability to even the playing field so that everyone on the team shares mutual values regarding collective leadership.

Actionable Implementation Strategies

Given the existing empirical evidence regarding collective leadership, particularly in relation to the environmental complexities team face today, there are several actionable implementation strategies that may serve to promote effective collective leadership structures. These strategies may also serve well as a starting point for further research in this area. Table 1.1 offers a summary of these recommendations, and a discussion of each follows. First, before teams begin to work together, it is important to understand how technology, training, and individual cultural differences may all affect subsequent teamwork and team performance. Thus, in order to facilitate effective collective leadership, team technology choices should be carefully matched appropriately to anticipated needs for leadership. This may in fact mean utilizing a range of media tools that can be combined to effectively create environments whereby both social influence and task-related information can be conveyed. For example, teams may need to utilize videoconferencing or teleconferencing software for initial and check in meetings in order to ensure that team members can establish relationships with one another that will facilitate social influence. This may be particularly important in teams that are partially distributed or contain isolated members, in order to provide all members a fair chance of being involved in the leadership process (O'Leary and Mortensen 2005). However, less rich media such as chat or email may prove very useful in providing records of

Table 1.1 Collective leadership implementation strategies

Strategies for utilizing collective leadership in twenty-first century teams
Before performance
• Marry technology with leadership needs—utilize interactive, media rich technologies as appropriate for managing social relationships, but also leverage text-based communications as a means for task-based leadership
• Train and develop leaders to think about leadership collectively in order to leverage collective leadership's benefits in practice
• Determine team openness to collective leadership—given cultural differences, is collective leadership a viable idea? If so, what might it look like?
During performance
• Create a third culture for leadership—set leadership norms based on a mix of the cultural values, beliefs of team members
• Clearly define leadership roles and structure, especially as they emerge/change over time
• Proactively incorporate distributed team members into leadership structures to strengthen team member buy in
After performance
• Debrief teams regarding leadership strengths and weaknesses to determine how structure may need to be adjusted for future performance

information that can be used for task-based leadership behaviors such as monitoring progress toward goals.

In addition to this focus on media selection, before performing teams should also receive training and development that will open them up to the idea of collective leadership, particularly if it is not something that they may typically utilize given their cultural norms and beliefs. This should involve providing potential leaders with training that will not only cultivate a psychologically safe environment whereby members can feel open to influencing and being influenced by others, but also provide a foundation regarding what collective leadership structures may look like, and how to leverage this structure of leadership to achieve the specific team goals. Relatedly, it may also be a necessary strategy to examine if the team members are actually willing and capable of supporting collective leadership structures. Assessing openness to collective leadership is a critical and necessary step for multicultural teams, and can provide an understanding of the degree to which team members may want or need to focus on developing a collective leadership structure. If team members are not open to collective leadership, it may not be worth the effort and time to develop it, especially in complex work environments.

After teams begin performing, a few additional implementation strategies for developing collective leadership may be useful. As team members may bring in their own unique cultural beliefs and perspectives regarding their perceptions of leadership, creating a hybrid culture for leadership may be an effective strategy. This type of hybrid culture has proven effective in terms of establishing other team norms (Burke et al. 2010), and involves the team gaining an understanding of their similarities and differences regarding leadership in order to create new, team level norms and values related to leadership. For example, if some members of the team are open to collective leadership while others prefer traditional vertical leadership, it may be possible to leverage a combined approach given prior research exhibiting the benefits of both collective and vertical leadership performed together.

In preparation for the establishment of a hybrid culture within a multicultural team, it is important for the organization to carefully consider the critical differences in the cultural makeup of the team and identify where potential conflicts might arise. Getting these differences out in the open will serve to reduce their impact and help team members understand not only how they are different from one another, but also the same. While research shows that, based on culture, there might be resistance to working in a multicultural team (Janssens and Brett 2006), if the organization is careful to create a supportive environment and ensure that the hybrid culture is working for the team, it is likely possible to minimize this apprehension and create shared values and beliefs surrounding behaviors important to collective leadership and the team as a whole.

Two additional strategies that can be implemented once teams begin to perform are the clear definition and redefinition of who is leading the team at any given point in time, as well as the proactive incorporation of distributed team members in collective leadership. First, one of the primary benefits of collective leadership lies in the ability of different team members to take on leadership responsibilities based on team needs. As team needs change over time due to task or relationship needs, the leadership structure of the team may also change. Team members must therefore also keep one another on the same page in regards to the existing leadership structure at any given time. This may involve regular briefings that include updates on who is leading, or a defining of leadership structure changes at the launch of the team in anticipation of leadership role changes based on expertise or other individual characteristics (Morgeson et al. 2010; Zaccaro and DeChurch 2011). Overall, a clear understanding of leadership responsibilities can help reduce confusion over who is leading at any given point, and can ensure that team needs are being met completely. Related to this establishment of leadership, teams should also be proactive in seeking and accepting leadership from members who are physically distributed from one or more team members. The involvement of distributed team members aids not only in their own "buy in" in terms of team commitment, but can also dually serve to utilize their leadership skills and expertise as teams face challenging situations.

After a team has performed, a final implementation strategy for ensuring collective leadership success is that of debriefing. Debriefing has been utilized in a range of environments, and can be particularly helpful in identifying team strengths and weaknesses in order to enhance future performance episodes (Tannenbaum and Cerasoli 2013). Conducting debriefs regarding the strengths and weaknesses in terms of leadership structure may help to uncover unique team member contributions and skills regarding leadership that may help to facilitate future interactions, as well as to recognize ways in which collective leadership may be better implemented to encourage future successes. Or, it may be necessary to recognize when collective leadership may not be the most advantageous approach, as well as how it might be better facilitated using different media selections.

Conclusion

While traditionally viewed as an individual variable, collective leadership appears to have a unique contribution on the effectiveness of teams. Furthermore, as working in multicultural, physically distributed teams via the use of virtual tools becomes the norm of organizations, it is important that the impact of these contextual factors are accounted for when determining what effective leadership structures should be put into place in teams. Given the previous discussion, science focused upon understanding collective leadership is sorely needed, yet the existing body of research does offer a starting point for how organizations may best incorporate leadership as a collective entity into regular practices through the aforementioned actionable strategies. However, first and foremost, an organization interested in implementing collective leadership must decide if such a structure fits within their current organizational norms, beliefs, and practices. Only the acceptance of such a structure at the organizational level will promote its incorporation from the top down. It is hoped that the proposed ideas and strategies serve to advance our current understanding of leadership as a collective construct and begins to push researchers and practitioners to think more specifically about how to develop teams to meet the contextual challenges they face every day.

Acknowledgments The views in this work are those of the authors and do not necessarily reflect official Army policy. This research was supported by the United States Army Research Laboratory and the United States Army Research Office under Grant W911NF-08-1-0144.

References

Argote, L., & McGrath, J. E. (1993). Group processes in organizations: Continuity and change. *International Review of Industrial and Organizational Psychology, 8*, 333–389.
Avolio, B., Walumba, F., & Weber, T. (2009). Leadership: Current theories, research, and future direction. *Annual Review of Psychology, 60*, 421–449.
Balkundi, P., & Harrison, D. A. (2006). Ties, leaders, and time in teams: Strong inference about network structure's effects on team viability and performance. *Academy of Management Journal, 49*(1), 49–68.
Bienefeld, N., & Grote, G. (2014). Shared leadership in multiteam systems how cockpit and cabin crews lead each other to safety. *Human Factors: The Journal of the Human Factors and Ergonomics Society, 56*(2), 270–286.
Bell, B. S., & Kozlowski, S. W. J. (2002). A typology of virtual teams: Implications for effective leadership. *Group and Organization Management, 27*, 14–49.
Burke, C. S., DiazGranados, D., & Salas, E. (2011). Team leadership: A review and look ahead. In A. Bryman, D. Collinson, K. Grint, B. Jackson, & M. Uhl-Bien (Eds.), *The Sage handbook of leadership* (pp. 338–351). London: Sage.
Burke, C. S., Shuffler, M. L., Salas, E., & Gelfand, M. (2010). Multicultural teams: Critical team processes and guidelines. In K. Lundby (Ed.), *Going global: Practical applications and recommendations for HR and OD professionals in the global workplace* (pp. 46–82). San Francisco: Wiley.

Burke, C. S., Stagl, K. C., Klein, C., Goodwin, G. F., Salas, E., & Halpin, S. (2006). What types of leadership behaviors are functional in team? A meta-analysis. *The Leadership Quarterly, 17*, 288–307.

Carson, J. B., Tesluk, P. E., & Marrone, J. A. (2007). Shared leadership in teams: An investigation of antecedent conditions and performance. *Academy of Management Journal, 50*(5), 1217–1234.

Connaughton, S. L., & Shuffler, M. (2007). Multinational and multicultural distributed teams: A review and future agenda. *Small Group Research, 38*(3), 387–412.

Conyne, R. K., Wilson, F. R., Tang, M., & Shi, K. (1999). Cultural similarities and differences in group work: Pilot study of a US–Chinese group comparison. *Group Dynamics: Theory, Research, and Practice, 3*(1), 40.

Day, D. V., Gronn, P., & Salas, E. (2004). Leadership capacity in teams. *Leadership Quarterly, 15*, 857–880.

Day, D. V., Gronn, P., & Salas, E. (2006). Leadership in team-based organizations: On the threshold of a new era. *The Leadership Quarterly, 17*(3), 211–216.

Dinwoodie, D. L. (2005). Solving the dilemma: A leader's guide to managing diversity. *Leadership in Action, 25*(2), 3–6.

Earley, P. C., Gibson, C. B., & Chen, C. C. (1999). "How did I do?" versus "How did we do?" Cultural contrasts of performance feedback use and self-efficacy. *Journal of Cross-Cultural Psychology, 30*(5), 594–619.

Elron, E. (1998). Top management teams within multinational corporations: Effects of cultural heterogeneity. *The Leadership Quarterly, 8*(4), 393–412.

Ensley, M. D., Hmieleski, K. M., & Pearce, C. L. (2006). The importance of vertical and shared leadership within new venture top management teams: Implications for the performance of startups. *The Leadership Quarterly, 17*, 217–231.

Erez, M., & Gati, E. (2004). A dynamic, multi-level model of culture: from the micro level of the individual to the macro level of a global culture. *Applied Psychology, 53*(4), 583–598.

Gibb, C. A. (1954). Leadership. In G. Lindzey (Ed.), *Handbook of social psychology* (Vol II). Cambridge, Massachusetts: Addison-Wesley.

Gibson, C. B., & Kirkman, B. L. (1999). Our past, present, and future in teams: The role of human resource professionals in managing team performance. *Evolving practices in human resource management: Responses to a changing world of work*, 90–117.

Greer, L. L., Homan, A. C., De Hoogh, A. H., & Den Hartog, D. N. (2012). Tainted visions: The effect of visionary leader behaviors and leader categorization tendencies on the financial performance of ethnically diverse teams. *Journal of Applied Psychology, 97*(1), 203.

Hackman, J. R. (2002). *Leading teams: Setting the stage for great performances*. Boston: Harvard Business School Press.

Hackman, J. R., & Wageman, R. (2005). A theory of team coaching. *Academy of Management Review, 30*(2), 269–287.

Harrison, D. A., Johns, G., & Martocchio, J. J. (2000). Changes in technology, teamwork, and diversity: New directions for a new century of absenteeism research. *Research in personnel and human resources management, 18*, 43–92.

Hiller, N. J., Day, D. V., & Vance, R. J. (2006). Collective enactment of leadership roles and team effectiveness: A field study. *The Leadership Quarterly, 17*, 387–397.

Hooker, C., & Csekszentmihalyi, M. (2003). Flow, creativity, and shared leadership. *Shared leadership: Reframing the hows and whys of leadership*, 217–234.

Huang, R., Carte, T., & Chidambaram, L. (2004). Cohesion and performance in virtual teams: An empirical investigation. *AMCIS 2004 Proceedings*, 161.

Jackson, S. (2000). A qualitative evaluation of shared leadership barriers, drivers, and recommendations. *Journal of Management in Medicine, 14*(3/4), 166–178.

Janssens, M., & Brett, J. M. (2006). cultural intelligence in global teams: A fusion model of collaboration. *Group and Organization Management, 31*(1), 124–153.

Kayworth, T., & Leidner, D. (2001). Leadership effectiveness in global virtual teams. *Journal of Management Information Systems, 17*, 7–40.

Kerr, S., & Jermier, J. M. (1978). Substitutes for leadership: Their meaning and measurement. *Organizational behavior and human performance, 22*(3), 375–403.

Kirchmeyer, C., & Cohen, A. (1992). Multicultural groups their performance and reactions with constructive conflict. *Group & Organization Management, 17*(2), 153–170.

Kirkman, B., & Mathieu, J. (2005). The dimensions and antecedents of team virtuality. *Journal of Management, 31*, 700–718.

Kirkman, B. L., & Shapiro, D. L. (2001). The impact of cultural values on job satisfaction and organizational commitment in self-managing work teams: The mediating role of employee resistance. *Academy of Management Journal, 44*(3), 557–569.

Kraut, R. E., Fussell, S. R., Brennan, S. E., & Siegel, J. (2002). Understanding effects of proximity on collaboration: Implications for technologies to support remote collaborative work. *Distributed Work*, 137–162.

Kukenberger, M., Mathieu, M. J., D'Innocenzo, L., & Reilly, G. (2011) Shared leadership in teams: An investigation of the impact of team composition and performance. *Academy of Management Meetings*. San Antonio, TX.

Lambert, L. (2002). A framework for shared leadership. *Educational Leadership*, 37–40.

Lau, D. C., & Murnighan, J. K. (1998). Demographic diversity and faultlines: The compositional dynamics of organizational groups. *Academy of Management Review, 23*(2), 325–340.

LePine, J. A., Piccolo, R. F., Jackson, C. L., Mathieu, J. E., & Saul, J. R. (2008). A meta-analysis of teamwork processes: Tests of a multidimensional model and relationships with team effectiveness criteria. *Personnel Psychology, 61*(2), 273–307.

Marks, M. A., Mathieu, J. E., & Zaccaro, S. J. (2001). A temporally based framework and taxonomy of team processes. *Academy of Management Review, 26*(3), 356–376.

Marks, M. A., Zaccaro, S. J., & Mathieu, J. E. (2000). Performance implications of leader briefings and team-interaction training for team adaptation to novel environments. *Journal of Applied Psychology, 85*(6), 971.

Martins, L. L., Gilson, L. L., & Maynard, M. T. (2004). Virtual teams: What do we know and where do we go from here? *Journal of Management, 30*(6), 805–835.

Matveev, A. V., & Nelson, P. E. (2004). Cross cultural communication competence and multicultural team performance perceptions of American and Russian managers. *International Journal of Cross Cultural Management, 4*(2), 253–270.

Maynard, M. T., Mathieu, J. E., Rapp, T. L., & Gilson, L. L. (2012). Something (s) old and something (s) new: Modeling drivers of global virtual team effectiveness. *Journal of Organizational Behavior, 33*(3), 342–365.

Mehra, A., Smith, B. R., Dixon, A. L., & Robertson, B. (2006). Distributed leadership in teams: The network of leadership perceptions and team performance. *The Leadership Quarterly, 17* (3), 232–245.

Merkens, B. J., & Spencer, J. S. (1998). A successful and necessary evolution to shared leadership: a hospital's story. *Leadership in Health Services, 11*(1), 1–4.

Mesmer-Magnus, J. R., DeChurch, L. A., Jimenez-Rodriguez, M., Wildman, J., & Shuffler, M. (2011). A meta-analytic investigation of virtuality and information sharing in teams. *Organizational Behavior and Human Decision Processes, 115*(2), 214–225.

Morgeson, F. P., DeRue, D. S., & Karam, E. P. (2010). Leadership in teams: A functional approach to understanding leadership structures and processes. *Journal of Management, 36*, 5–39.

Mortensen, M., & Hinds, P. J. (2001). Conflict and shared identity in geographically distributed teams. *International Journal of Conflict Management, 12*(3), 212–238.

Muethel, M., Siebdrat, F., & Hoegl, M. (2012). When do we really need interpersonal trust in globally dispersed new product development teams?. *R&D Management, 42*(1), 31–46.

O'Leary, M. B., & Cummings, J. N. (2007). The spatial, temporal, and configurational characteristics of geographic dispersion in teams. *MIS quarterly, 31*(3), 433–452.

O'Leary, M. B., & Mortensen, M. (2005). Subgroups with attitude: Imbalance and isolation in geographically dispersed teams. *In Presented at the Academy of Management Conference*. Honolulu, Oahu, HI.

Pearce, C. L. (2004). The future of leadership: Combining vertical and shared leadership to transform knowledge work. *Academy of Management Executive, 18*(1), 47–57.

Pearce, C. L., & Conger, J. A. (2003). All those years ago: The historical underpinnings of shared leadership. In C. L., Pearce & J. A. Conger (Eds.), *Shared leadership: Reframing the hows and whys of leadership* (pp. 1–18). Thousand Oaks, CA: Sage.

Pearce, C. L., & Sims, H. P. (2002). Vertical versus shared leadership as predictors of the effectiveness of change management teams: An examination of aversive, directive, transactional, transformational and empowering leader behaviors. *Group dynamics: Theory, Research, and Practice, 6*, 172–197.

Pearce, C. L., Perry, M. L., & Sims, H. P. (2001). Shared leadership: Relationship management to improve nonprofit organization effectiveness. In T. D. Conners (Ed.), *The nonprofit handbook: Management* (pp. 624–641). New York: Wiley.

Ramthun, A. J., & Matkin, G. S. (2012). Multicultural shared leadership a conceptual model of shared leadership in culturally diverse teams. *Journal of Leadership & Organizational Studies, 19*(3), 303–314.

Salas, E., Cooke, N. J., & Rosen, M. A. (2008). On teams, teamwork, and team performance: Discoveries and developments. *Human Factors: The Journal of the Human Factors and Ergonomics Society, 50*(3), 540–547.

Salas, E., Rosen, M. A., Burke, C. S., & Goodwin, G. F. (2009). The wisdom of collectives in organizations: An update of the teamwork competencies. *Team effectiveness in complex organizations: Cross-disciplinary perspectives and approaches*, 39–79.

Salas, E., Sims, D. E., & Burke, C. S. (2005). Is there a "Big Five" in teamwork? *Small Group Research, 36*(5), 555–599.

Sauser, B. J., Reilly, R. R., & Shenhar, A. J. (2009). Why projects fail? How contingency theory can provide new insights–A comparative analysis of NASA's mars climate orbiter loss. *International Journal of Project Management, 27*(7), 665–679.

Stanko, T. & Gibson, C. B. (2009). The role of cultural elements in virtual teams. In R. S. Bhagat & R. M. Steer (Eds.), *Handbook of culture, organizations, and work* (pp. 272–304). Cambridge, UK: Cambridge University Press.

Staples, D. S., & Zhao, L. (2006). The effects of cultural diversity in virtual teams versus face-to-face teams. *Group Decision and Negotiation, 15*, 389–406.

Tannenbaum, S. I., & Cerasoli, C. P. (2013). Do team and individual debriefs enhance performance? A meta-analysis. *Human Factors: The Journal of the Human Factors and Ergonomics Society, 55*(1), 231–245.

Von Glinow, M. A., Shapiro, D. L., & Brett, J. M. (2004). Can we talk, and should we? Managing emotional conflict in multicultural teams. *Academy of Management Review, 29*(4), 578–592.

Watson, W. E., Kumar, K., & Michaelsen, L. K. (1993). Cultural diversity's impact on interaction process and performance: Comparing homogeneous and diverse task groups. *Academy of Management Journal, 36*, 590–602.

Yammarino, F., Dionne, S., Chun, J., & Dansereau, F. (2005). Leadership and levels of analysis: A state-of-the-science review. *Leadership Quarterly, 16*, 879–919.

Zaccaro, S. J. (2007). Trait-based perspectives of leadership. *American Psychologist, 62*(1), 6–16.

Zaccaro, S. J., & DeChurch, L. A. (2011). Leadership forms and functions in multiteam systems. In S. J. Zaccaro, M. A. Marks, & L. A. DeChurch (Eds.), *Multiteam systems: An organizational form for dynamic and complex environments*. New York: Taylor & Francis.

Zaccaro, S. J., Heinen, B., & Shuffler, M. (2009). Team leadership and team effectiveness. In E. Salas, G. F. Goodwin, & C. S. Burke (Eds.), *Team effectiveness in complex organizations: Cross-disciplinary perspectives and approaches* (pp. 83–111). New York: Routledge.

Zaccaro, S.J., LaPort, K., & Jose, I. (2012). The attributes of successful leaders: A performance requirements approach. In M. Rumsey (Ed.), *Oxford Handbook of Leadership*.

Zaccaro, S. J., Rittman, A. L., & Marks, M. A. (2001). Team leadership. *Leadership Quarterly, 12*, 451–483.

Chapter 2
Globally Intelligent Leadership: Toward an Integration of Competencies

Julianna Fischer and Jessica L. Wildman

The business men and women of today are dealing with unique work contexts that a few decades ago were not prevalent. With advanced communication and transportation technologies facilitating global interconnectedness, globalization is altering today's working world. With these developments in the workplace, research fields such as Industrial-Organizational Psychology are needing to adapt to changing times. Research has greatly increased on culture and its effect in the workplace, "perhaps the result of globalization's emergence as the most significant change shaping today's work environment, forcing individuals, teams, organizations, and nations to adapt or become dinosaurs" (Erez 2011, p. 838).

The managers or leaders of this contemporary global workforce are facing novel issues due to cultural diversity. Naturally, some managers are able to handle these issues better than others. Much research has been conducted in an attempt to describe exactly what those abilities are—whether it is a form of intelligence, a style of leadership, a personality trait, or a combination of these factors. Thanks to the extensive Global Leadership and Organizational Behavior Effectiveness (GLOBE) project, we know that preferred styles of leadership vary across cultures (House et al. 2004).

To this point, most research on global leadership has dealt with a variety of competencies that would be beneficial for leaders. A literature review by Jokinen (2005) describes previous research on global leadership as "dispersed" and far from clear. The supported indicators of global leadership are typically looked at on an individual basis, and should be looked at in conjunction with one another. This chapter aims to bring different areas of research together theoretically in order to

J. Fischer (✉) · J.L. Wildman
School of Psychology and Institute for Cross-Cultural Management,
Florida Institute of Technology, 150 W. University Blvd, Melbourne, FL 32901, USA
e-mail: fischerj2015@my.fit.edu

J.L. Wildman
e-mail: jwildman@fit.edu

© Springer International Publishing Switzerland 2016
J.L. Wildman et al. (eds.), *Critical Issues in Cross Cultural Management*,
DOI 10.1007/978-3-319-42166-7_2

provide a more parsimonious and practical understanding of the most critical competencies for global leadership. A few researchers have developed frameworks that pinpoint competencies for global leadership, but many of them cite very specific factors that fall short of encompassing all of what it means to be an effective global leader. Although there have been a few integrative frameworks of global leadership competencies published (e.g., Jokinen 2005; Kim and McLean 2015), the framework put forth in this chapter goes beyond these works because it uses multiple well-established, conceptually solid predictors of global leadership, breaks them apart, and systematically recategorizes them in order to build a simplified model of the constructs that predict relevant effectiveness. In other words, the current model takes a step back to analyze the bigger picture of global leadership assessment to determine any overlap between a few existing global leadership predictors and continue to narrow the focus on what constitutes global leadership competency.

To begin, we provide an overview of the literature connecting global leadership effectiveness and several key antecedent constructs: cultural intelligence, emotional intelligence, and personality. Following this review, we introduce and build the case for a new theoretical framework in an attempt to target the competencies that distinguish an effective global leader. For the purposes of this chapter, a global leader will be defined as any individual working in a managerial position who is needed to make desirable changes and motivate employees to work together toward a common goal in an organization that operates in two or more countries.

The new framework, called Globally Intelligent Leadership (GIL), endeavors to tap into the underlying capabilities of effective global leadership by synthesizing several antecedents that have been found to be related to leadership effectiveness: cultural intelligence, emotional intelligence, and personality. Cultural intelligence allows an individual to deal effectively in settings of cultural diversity. We posit that a manager who is culturally competent and is working in cross-cultural settings would be able to lead more effectively than a manager who is less culturally competent. Emotional intelligence has been primarily supported as a predictor of domestic leadership effectiveness given it was not originally developed as a cross-cultural measure. However, given that accurate emotion recognition and management is critical to effective interpersonal interactions, it is expected that emotional intelligence will be beneficial for global leadership. It is possible this relationship has not been established because the existing measures of emotional intelligence are not designed to be used across cultures. However, the literature review by Jokinen (2005) found that emotional intelligence does appear to one of the major components of global leadership competency. Finally, various personality traits have been linked to effective leadership, and to global leadership in particular. For this reason, personality will be included in the development of GIL. The following sections will provide a more in-depth overview of the established literature regarding the predictors of global leadership effectiveness, with a particular emphasis on the three constructs integrated in the GIL model.

Predictors of Global Leadership Effectiveness

Before narrowing our discussion down to the three key competency-based predictors that make up our theoretical model, we first review the research on antecedents of global leadership effectiveness more generally. It is important to note that even the few well-supported predictors of global leadership effectiveness, such as cultural intelligence and personality, are not all-inclusive when it comes to assessing global leadership. Specifically, a lot of research has focused on how these factors predict cross-cultural adjustment (i.e., the extent to which an expatriate adjusts to the overall, interpersonal, and work contexts during an expatriate assignment), which in turn would provide a number of benefits in the workplace, including more effective leadership. Better adjustment will facilitate better work performance and leadership due to increased communication and decision-making among other enhancements.

Two of the relevant variables that have been shown to relate to global leadership effectiveness could be argued to be basic underlying enabling factors: general IQ and experience abroad. General IQ could be argued to predict essentially all types of performance, and is in no way unique to global leadership. Rockstuhl et al. (2011) reported that general IQ predicted both domestic and global leadership effectiveness. It is, however, a necessary enabling mechanism for global leadership, as it enables a person to develop global leadership competencies because having a higher IQ means having a higher capacity to develop those competencies. Similarly, experience abroad acts as an influential external factor, but because it is not something inherent to the individual, it is definitionally not a competency. Rather, experience abroad represents a learning opportunity that, when combined with high IQ, leads to the development of global leadership competencies. On examining cross-cultural adjustment of expatriates, Takeuchi et al. (2005) posited that previous international experience helps individuals behave appropriately in different cultures by providing a deeper understanding of global behavior and different ways of thinking. Essentially, people with high IQ and certain personality traits that have experience abroad will develop higher cultural and emotional intelligence over time. In sum, high IQ combined with experience abroad enable the development of global competencies.

Several other variables have been researched that could potentially impact global leadership effectiveness. Bhaskar-Shrinivas et al. (2005) promoted self-efficacy as a key factor in international adjustment, as well as support from leaders and coworkers and available resources. They defined self-efficacy as an individual's belief in their own ability to carry out any plan of action (Bandura 1977). Palthe (2004) found further evidence that self-efficacy can be an important factor in cross-cultural adjustment, along with: learning orientation, parent and host company socialization, family adjustment, work, and nonwork variables. Learning orientation could be argued as similar to the personality trait of openness to experience, which will be included as part of the proposed GIL framework. Most of these other variables are external or contextual factors, which fall outside of the scope of this chapter's focus on competencies. We argue that a focus on competencies has more utility for organizations because they represent assets that can be focused on during selection or training, whereas the external and contextual factors are often less controllable and, therefore, represent less of an opportunity for organizations to improve global leadership effectiveness.

Without a doubt, there exist a number of other factors that could potentially influence a leader's functionality across borders, but a thorough review is outside the scope of this chapter. Consequently, the theory presented in this chapter combines three particular competency-based predictors that we expect to be critically important: cultural intelligence, emotional intelligence, and personality. To see a more comprehensive list of variables that have been claimed as relevant to global leadership effectiveness, we refer you to the literature reviews of Jokinen (2005) and Kim and McLean (2015). Before providing a detailed description of the GIL framework, the existing research on each of the underlying competencies that were combined to create the framework is reviewed in order to illustrate the importance of these competencies to global leadership effectiveness.

Cultural Intelligence

Earley and Ang developed the concept of cultural intelligence (CQ) in 2003 and used it to describe an individual's capability to function effectively in cross-cultural settings (Ang 2011). The construct was broken down into four components: (1) metacognitive, "an individual's level of conscious cultural awareness during cross-cultural interactions," (p. 584) (2) cognitive, the knowledge of a culture, including social norms, values, and practices, (3) motivational, the ability to focus attention on functioning effectively in cross-cultural settings, and (4) behavioral, the capability to display appropriate actions during cross-cultural interactions (Ang 2011).

A book chapter written by Ng et al. (2012) provides a comprehensive review of cultural intelligence. The authors cite personality traits and international experience as antecedents of CQ. Additionally, Ng et al. (2012) provide a breakdown of the various outcomes of CQ: (1) cognitive, which includes cultural judgment and decision-making, (2) psychological, including general, work, and interaction adjustments, (3) behavioral, such as frequency of interactions and integrative and cooperative management behaviors, and (4) performance, which includes general job and adaptive performances, negotiation, and leadership. Of crucial significance here is the in-depth discussion of the empirical evidence, both quantitative and qualitative, found asserting effective global leadership as a well-supported outcome of CQ (Ng et al. 2012).

A number of studies have found CQ predicting effective global leadership. Rockstuhl et al. (2011) argued that cultural intelligence is "a critical leadership competency for those with cross-border responsibilities" (p. 825). They tested this hypothesis in a sample of Swiss military officers with both domestic and cross-border leadership responsibilities and found that EI was a stronger predictor of domestic leadership effectiveness, while CQ was a stronger predictor of cross-border leadership effectiveness (Rockstuhl et al. 2011). Dean (2007) and Deng and Gibson (2008) included qualitative interviews with global leaders that resulted in accounts of the significance of CQ when managing culturally diverse employees. Elenkov and Manev (2009) found CQ enhanced the effect of transformational leadership on organizational innovation. The literature supports the notion that an individual who is better able to function effectively in cross-cultural settings is naturally better able to lead effectively in cross-cultural work settings.

CQ is key in global leadership because it enables the leader to operate effectively across borders. As reviewed above, there is substantial evidence supporting the construct CQ as a whole, as well as its individual components of CQ, as valid predictors of effective global leadership. Various reasons behind this positive relationship include: setting culturally appropriate goals, achieving clarity in leadership, and implementing more innovations (Ang 2011). Ultimately, cultural intelligence gives leaders an advantage when working on a global platform.

Emotional Intelligence

Models for emotional intelligence (EI) are either based on various abilities regarding emotions or on a more "mixed" basis, including traits and competencies (Walter et al. 2011). The first is based on Mayer and Salovey (1997), which describes EI as a set of emotional abilities. These abilities include perceiving, using, understanding, and managing emotions in oneself and others. The second description was popularized by Goleman (1998) and Bar-On (2000) and is broader. This "mixed" model of EI includes dispositions, competencies, and perceptions that together make an individual more effective at managing emotions. Goleman (1998) included five components of EI for an effective leader: self-awareness, self-regulation, motivation, empathy, and social skill. Self-awareness refers to the perception or understanding of oneself, including emotions, strengths, and weaknesses, and then how those variables affect others. Self-regulation is an ability related to managing emotions in oneself and in one's relationships. Motivation describes qualities like commitment, positive outlook, and desire to achieve without money or status as the objects of the motivation. Empathy refers to an understanding of others' emotions and having the appropriate reactions to those emotions. Finally, social skill is a proficiency in building and maintaining relationships. Using either model, much research has examined EI as it relates to many organizational outcomes.

EI was not originally developed within the context of cross-cultural research, and consequently, there is more literature supporting EI as a domestic indicator. The relationship between EI and general leadership effectiveness shows positive association and "promising results" (Walter et al. 2011). A literature review by Khalili (2012) provides a summary of the significance and utility of EI. Khalili

(2012) found research on EI to indicate that individuals high in EI are seemingly more successful both in the workplace and outside of it for a number of reasons, including lower stress and higher job satisfaction, organizational commitment, and leadership, to name a few. Furthermore, EI predicted these outcomes beyond general IQ. Leaders high in EI are at an advantage because they can establish trust, respect, and close relationships with employees that lead to enhanced effectiveness (Khalili 2012). These developments can theoretically translate across cultures due to the benefits of interpersonal skill in management both domestic and abroad. Establishing trust, respect, and close relationships with employees could help a cross-cultural manager become an effective leader by gaining the support of employees. Additionally, leadership and EI logically correlate because a leader's effectiveness in part has to do with how well they can manage social interactions and conflicts in the workplace.

Numerous studies have supported the link between EI and leadership effectiveness (George 2000; Rosete and Ciarrochi 2005; Ramchunder and Martins 2014). Rosete and Ciarrochi (2005) discovered that higher EI was associated with higher leadership effectiveness, and more so than either personality or general IQ. When they examined the relationship between self-efficacy, EI, and leadership effectiveness, Ramchunder and Martins (2014) found a significant positive relationship. Furthermore, Humphrey (2002) described leadership as an intrinsically emotional process since leaders tend to recognize, evoke, and manage followers' emotions. EI has the potential to be a useful intelligence in leadership, both domestically and internationally, because this intrinsically emotional process occurs across leadership contexts. However, thus far, the literature has suggested limitations in applying EI to cross-cultural contexts despite the clear conceptual relevance. We argue that despite these mixed findings, EI is likely to be extremely critical for global leadership effectiveness, and that more research is needed to explore culturally embedded conceptualizations and measures of EI.

As an example of those limitations, Reilly and Karounos (2009) found that EI is valued cross-culturally more than other skills, including technical and cognitive skills, especially regarding social skill. However, their study could not support EI as a predictor of leadership effectiveness across four different cultural settings. Their results suggest that EI has potential to be a cross-cultural construct, but for reasons unstudied, falls short of being a dependable predictor of leadership effectiveness. Despite the negative findings from Reilly and Karounos (2009), other research has found EI to be valuable in global leadership. For example, Jassawalla et al. (2004) found EI to be an important consideration when selecting expatriate managers. A study of managers across the U.S., the U.K., and Malaysia by Shipper et al. (2003) found a positive relationship between manager effectiveness and EI, specifically the self-awareness component of EI. Furthermore, De Vries and Florent-Treacy (2002) mentioned that global leaders need a competency akin to "emotional global intelligence" but do not elaborate on what specifically that entails.

EI has faced further empirical examination on a cross-cultural basis uncovering some interesting relationships. Gabel-Shemueli and Dolan (2011) examined the link between EI and cross-cultural adjustment, finding a positive relationship. Specifically, EI was most strongly related to interactional adjustment. Building on that link, Lillis and Tian (2009) posited that individuals with higher EI are more likely to perceive 'context-driven emotion patterns' and this perception leads to better situational adaptation. Their main assertion is that in international business communications, EI would be an advantage due to increased comprehension of emotional dynamics while managing a culturally diverse workforce (Lillis and Tian 2009). The benefits of EI reach across borders due to its enlightenment of interpersonal interactions.

A book chapter on EI across cultures by Ekermans (2009) provides an in-depth review of cultural differences, such as values, when assessing EI and research needs. They caution that although EI measures are increasingly being used across the globe, future research needs to explore bias and equivalence across cultures in order to validate interpretations (Ekermans 2009). A further suggestion of the cultural potential of EI can be taken from Sharma et al. (2009) who, on exploring the future research needs surrounding EI, strongly recommended a measure of culture-specific EI. This recommendation was based on the idea that although EI does not have substantial validity yet for cross-cultural applicability, it could still be relevant and future research should explore this connection. Therefore, a separate measure should be developed that takes the construct of EI and globalizes it.

Given this research, certain components of EI may be more relevant regarding global leadership, specifically the social skill and self-awareness components. More research in this area would help clarify any relationships. Although the research linking EI to global leadership effectiveness could be stronger, EI has the potential to be a beneficial competency theoretically. Additionally, Forsyth (2015) explored the differences between EI and CQ in cultural situations, noting there are some cultural situations where emotions are not necessary. The aforementioned study by Shipper et al. (2003) also found that the relationship between EI and managerial effectiveness varied across cultures depending on what was valued in interactions (i.e., power distance). These discrepancies may be explained by the fact that cultures can differ significantly, and what may be valued in one country could be insignificant in the next. Therefore, it is important to keep in mind that although EI could be a predictor of effective global leadership, that prediction may vary significantly depending on the cultures involved.

Personality

The last predictor of global leadership effectiveness to be reviewed in depth is one that can be used as a predictor in a variety of work settings: personality. The Big Five personality model has been strongly correlated to leadership, with specific evidence that extraversion is the most consistent correlate (Judge et al. 2002). On a cross-cultural platform, Silverthorne (2001) conducted a study to examine the relationships between the Big 5 Personality traits and leadership effectiveness. His results demonstrated that there are some consistencies, but the Big 5 vary as it concerns leadership effectiveness across cultures. Specifically, he found that effective leaders were more extraverted, more agreeable, more conscientious, and less neurotic (Silverthorne 2001). Additionally, openness to experience has been supported as a predictor of cross-cultural adjustment (Huang et al. 2005). This is most likely because an individual who is open to new experiences is less judgmental, more curious, and ready to adapt to and appreciate a different environment.

Hogan and Benson (2009) wrote of review of personality as it predicts global organizational effectiveness via leadership. Their first assertion is that leadership is a function of personality. Hogan and Benson (2009) tie personality to leadership in the form of four competency domains that build upon in each other in a developmental sequence: (1) intrapersonal skills, (2) interpersonal skills, (3) technical skills, and (4) leadership skills. The logic here stems from Hogan and Kaiser (2005) in their article on leadership that posits "personality predicts leadership—who we are is how we lead" (Hogan and Kaiser 2005, p. 169).

Although lacking in consistency, there is sufficient evidence to say personality traits are related to global leadership effectiveness. More research in this area would greatly enhance our understanding of personality in this setting. However, personality predictors for a global leader will most likely vary depending on the specific cultures involved, which makes predictions regarding exactly which personality dimensions are most desirable difficult to make. Personality also relates to the constructs of EI and CQ, which our previous discussions clearly link to effective global leadership. Specific to cross-cultural settings, openness to experience has been found as highly correlated to CQ (Ang et al. 2006).

Integrative Research

As mentioned previously, CQ is defined as an individual's capability to function effectively in cross-cultural settings and EI is defined as perceiving, using, understanding, and managing emotions. In other words, these constructs show considerable definitional overlap. They both tap into similar competencies that are related to global leadership because the abilities in both constructs are useful in interpersonal relationships. The two intelligences form part of an individual's perspective and experience in the world—their awareness of both self and surroundings and their understanding and skill when interacting with others. EI and CQ could interact with each other, enhancing certain elements of each intelligence in turn. Parts of EI, such as social skill and self-awareness, could benefit an individual when connecting with others and maintaining relationships in settings of cultural diversity.

Looking at the sub-dimensions of each construct, there are clear theoretical connections. The self-regulation aspect of EI can be seen as similar to, or the same as, behavioral CQ because they both refer to the ability to self-regulate one's behavioral impulses in order to engage in a culturally appropriate behavior. The only difference is that self-regulation in EI is focused on emotional display behaviors only, whereas the behavioral CQ is broader and includes other nonemotional cultural behaviors as well. In other words, the underlying concept for both is behavioral self-regulation. Therefore, we argue that these constructs can be combined into one dimension that represents both emotional and other behaviors. Self-awareness and social awareness are both aspects of different models of EI which could relate to metacognitive CQ, a conscious cultural awareness. Being aware of one's self and perceptive of one's social surroundings could be expanded to a cross-cultural setting by picking up on cultural differences. Both CQ and EI include a motivation component. It follows logically that commitment, positive outlook, and desire to achieve would translate into the motivation to function effectively across cultures as well. Research has been conducted comparing the components of EI and CQ that affirm some of these logical connections.

Moon (2010) found that specific factors of EI are related to specific factors of CQ. He posited that "since EQ [EI] is the capacity for identifying one's and others' emotions, for motivating oneself, and for managing emotions effectively in oneself and others, this capability can have an influence when interacting with people from different cultural backgrounds" (Moon 2010, p. 882). His results show many relationships between components: (1) self-awareness (EI) and metacognitive CQ, (2) self-management (EI) and metacognitive, cognitive, and behavioral CQ, (3) social awareness (EI) and motivational and behavioral CQ, and (4) relationship management (EI) and metacognitive, behavioral, and motivational CQ. These links give us evidence that overlap does indeed exist between CQ and EI. Moreover, Lin et al. (2012) discovered that EI positively moderated the relationship between CQ and cross-cultural adjustment. In other words, an individual would be most prepared to work cross-culturally if they were both emotionally intelligent and culturally intelligent.

As a strong leadership predictor, personality has also been included in the development of this framework. Specific traits have been correlated with different components of both the EI and CQ constructs. Specifically, Ang et al. (2006) found links between: (1) conscientiousness and metacognitive CQ, (2) agreeableness and emotional stability with behavioral CQ, (3) extraversion with cognitive, motivational, and behavioral CQ, and (4) openness with all four factors of CQ. These findings suggest that "openness to experience is a crucial personality characteristic that is related to a person's capability to function effectively in diverse cultural settings" (Ang et al. 2006, p. 100).

At the same time, measures for EI and personality have been interpreted as overlapping empirically (Matthews et al. 2002). Van Rooy and Viswesvaran (2004) discovered that EI and personality "appear to be more highly correlated than many researchers would prefer" (Van Rooy and Viswesvaran 2004, p. 86). Given these correlations, personality traits were included in the foundation of GIL alongside EI and CQ. As reviewed earlier in this chapter, personality traits have proven pertinent when measuring leadership effectiveness, including global leadership. Given these conceptual connections and overlap, EI, CQ, and personality were integrated to reduce problematic construct proliferation and to theorize a new more parsimonious framework examining global leadership competency. Given the role of intelligences in the foundational theories, we call this framework "Globally Intelligent Leadership" (GIL).

Globally Intelligent Leadership

It is important to note this is not the first framework that has aimed to consolidate the literature surrounding global leadership, and it is likely to not be the last. We will briefly discuss other existing integrative frameworks for comparative purposes. The integrative framework developed by Jokinen (2005) includes three different types of competencies, similar to the structure of GIL. Those categories include: (1) self-awareness, engagement in personal transformation, and inquisitiveness, (2) optimism, self-regulation, social judgement skills, empathy, motivation to work in international environment, cognitive skills, and acceptance of complexity and its contradictions, and (3) social skills, networking skills, and knowledge (Jokinen 2005). These variables show considerable overlap with the components of CQ, EI, and Big 5 personality. Similarly, the framework created by Kim and McLean (2015) includes three levels: (1) core traits, (2) personal character, and (3) dimensions of ability. Again, these components can essentially be seen as subsumed within the GIL framework and essentially represent a different structure for modeling the same aspects global leadership competency. However, this framework does not seem to address the aspect of knowledge as it relates to global leadership effectiveness. The GIL framework is more systematic compared to existing frameworks because we explicitly started with conceptually well-established predictors of global leadership effectiveness, broke them down to their constituent components, analyzed definitional and conceptual overlap using a matrix approach, and then systematically recategorized them into overarching themes that ultimately reduced the complexity of a global leadership competency model while still representing the key overlapping constructs that impact global leadership effectiveness.

The Ang (2011) model of cultural intelligence was the particular approach included in the development of our GIL framework, but there are several other models of cultural intelligence which are composed of similar breakdowns. The model of Thomas and Inkson (2009) cites three components necessary for the development of cultural intelligence: knowledge, which is general knowledge of culture, how it can differ, and what it affects; mindfulness, which is an ability to reflect and pick up on cues in cross-cultural situations, including self-awareness, and; skills, which is knowledge and mindfulness put into action by displaying appropriate behavior. The resemblance of this model to the GIL framework reflects the applicability of categorizing CQ in such a way. Additionally, Plum (2008) broke cultural intelligence into three dimensions: emotional, or intercultural engagement; cognitive, or cultural understanding, and; action, or intercultural communication.

Because the approach of GIL is to start from all-inclusive constructs and then narrow those down into a more concentrated framework, Goleman's (1998) broader

Table 2.1 Sub-dimensions of GIL with EI, CQ, and personality constructs

Globally intelligent leadership			
	Mindset	Skill	Knowledge
EI	Motivation Empathy	Self-regulation Social skill	Self-awareness
CQ	Motivational	Metacognitive Behavioral	Cognitive
Personality	Openness to experience Conscientiousness Extraversion Agreeableness Neuroticism		

and more all-embracing "mixed" model of EI was chosen. This EI model has five components: empathy, motivation, self-awareness, self-regulation, and social skill (Walter et al. 2011). The CQ construct chosen is that described by Ang (2011), composed of four competencies: behavioral, cognitive, metacognitive, and motivational. Finally, in regards to personality, we opted to use the five factor model including openness to experience, conscientiousness, extraversion, agreeableness, and neuroticism. The 14 different subcomponents of EI, CQ, and personality are separated and recategorized into three sub-dimensions within GIL: mindset, skill, and knowledge. For a visual breakdown of EI, CQ, and the Big Five into the mindset, skill, and knowledge categories of GIL, see Table 2.1. The categorization of the components will now be explored in more detail.

Global Leadership Mindset

The first sub-dimension, mindset, refers to the underlying traits and attitudes that a person holds that act as the motivation or openness to behave in a manner that could be described as globally intelligent. Traits refer to a person's enduring characteristics or dispositions which become apparent in their behavior. The components of both EI and CQ constructs were spread across all three sub-dimensions while the personality traits, given they represent only underlying dispositional traits, were all categorized as mindset. We suggest that the EI component of motivation falls under the mindset sub-dimension because the internal desire to exert effort for reasons beyond either money or success is necessary for an individual to establish the appropriate attitudes toward becoming an effective global leader. Empathy is also placed in this category because understanding others' emotions prepares the individual to produce the appropriate behaviors and use any existing knowledge.

Given the aforementioned framework comparisons, the CQ construct is more feasibly sorted into the mindset, skill, and knowledge sub-dimensions even when using Ang's (2011) model. Motivational CQ is classified as a mindset component because, similarly to motivation in EI, the ability to focus one's attention on effective functioning gives an individual the appropriate attitude to act in the appropriate manner. On a similar note, all five personality traits of the Big Five construct are organized into the mindset sub-dimension because personality composes the underlying traits that a person holds. As mentioned earlier, Hogan and Kaiser (2005) promoted this link with "who we are is how we lead" (p. 169).

An individual's personality is directly linked to the other components of mindset: motivation (EI) and motivational (CQ). The trait most logically related to global leadership would be openness to experience. This trait is arguably similar to motivation in EI and motivational CQ because it captures the commitment and positive outlook that are part of the definition of the motivation component. As noted under the review of personality as a predictor, Silverthorne (2001) correlated the other four personality traits with global leadership effectiveness. Conscientiousness, similar to motivation, encompasses an achievement orientation and the desire to do one's work thoroughly. This mindset aspect with openness to experience is tied very closely to the motivation referred to in EI and CQ. As leaders, extraverted individuals are more at home interacting and managing people. Extraversion is a component of the mindset sub-dimension because it allows an individual to build off of that orientation toward engagement with others. More agreeable individuals working cross-culturally excel as leaders by valuing harmony and cooperation and being able to build trust with coworkers, an asset in leading employees with potentially diverse cultural backgrounds. Finally, low neuroticism would be an essential aspect of a global leader's mindset because any emotional instability would be detrimental to leadership effectiveness. Collectively, we suggest these five personality traits along with the motivational components of EI and CQ can be condensed into an overarching construct that we label mindset.

Global Leadership Skill

The second sub-dimension, skill, encompasses any proficiency developed with experience and training relevant to carrying out globally intelligent behavior. This is a distinct category because mindset reflects more of the underlying characteristics that form the foundation an individual's perspective and motivation, knowledge refers to the factual information one retains about culture and oneself, and skill reflects a behavioral dimension that can be seen as the mindset and knowledge components being put into action. Skills have the potential to develop from experience and training, but are also reflective of an individuals' natural capabilities.

The EI component of self-regulation is categorized as a skill because it is the behavioral ability to manage emotions which is reflected in displaying appropriate behavior. Similarly, the social skill component of EI is defined as proficiency in building and maintaining relationships. In other words, this component is essentially referring to a person's ability to behave in certain ways that are conducive to building and maintaining relationships, such as regulating emotions as necessary, and behaving in culturally appropriate ways so as not to offend and alienate others. Therefore, it is clear that social skill has considerable overlap with the other skill-based components of CQ, including metacognitive and behavioral CQ.

The placement of metacognitive CQ in the skill sub-dimension is supported by the development of strategies and rules for social interaction that are keys to the consciously aware interactions of metacognitive CQ and, in this perspective, could be comparable to a social skill. Metacognitive CQ is akin to cultural mindfulness. It implies control over one's own thoughts and learning. Having this mindfulness while interacting with others increases one's ability to control the interaction and behave in the desired manner. Mindfulness could be considered an aspect of mindset; however, the use of metacognitive CQ is in employing strategies during social interactions and, therefore, it falls closer to a social skill than a part of the individual's underlying mindset. Another argument for this distinction would be that metacognitive CQ is a conscious activity while the motivation and personality of an individual are less conscious. Behavioral CQ is more clearly categorized as part of skill because the capability to display appropriate actions is akin to a proficiency that produces the correct behavior. Like self-regulation, which enables an individual to control their own emotions, behavioral CQ is the control over one's actions. Therefore, these are categorized as skills that enhance social interaction and ultimately enhance leadership effectiveness.

Global Leadership Knowledge

The third and final sub-dimension, knowledge, refers to the theoretical and practical understanding of the self and of the relevant culture or cultures, which allow for a leader to use their skills to act upon the globally intelligent mindset. Knowledge can be gained by learning through personal experience, experiences of others, or in more formal educational settings. The EI component of self-awareness is placed in knowledge because it involves the knowledge or understanding of oneself through identifying one's own emotions. This awareness is most likely inherent in an individual or developed over time but nonetheless represents an individual retaining self-knowledge that would be useful when working cross-culturally and aiming to manage others in diverse settings. Cultural awareness would follow as an extension of self-awareness once an individual is aware of their own values, beliefs, and perceptions on a cultural level. This knowledge is crucial when working cross-culturally.

Knowing oneself prepares an individual to accept and partake in the culture of others. Building on knowledge of self, cognitive CQ, defined as the knowledge of a culture, also belongs in the knowledge sub-dimension, which includes in its definition the knowledge of culture. Without insight or comprehension of the relevant cultures being dealt with, an individual is left blind. Being aware of the values and beliefs of coworkers or subordinates is advantageous when trying to manage a place of work. Self-awareness and cognitive CQ are the only two components placed in this sub-dimension. Knowledge of both the self and the cultures involved is crucial to cross-cultural success. Without a strong knowledge background, an individual would have a limited reach of effectiveness. All three sub-dimensions of the GIL framework are essential to the overall development of effective global leadership. Without any one of them, a leader's success would be severely hampered.

Implications and Future Research

Assessing global leaders for the three underlying components of the GIL framework is a useful step toward getting a grasp of what it is that makes some leaders more effective than others in today's business world. This consolidated framework provides an integrated simplification of several of the multidimensional and abstract constructs from the scattered research on global leadership capabilities. It is an integration of several topics that are often discussed separately. Furthermore, the GIL framework could aid in the development of global leadership research that examines those capabilities and traits that set up some global leaders to be better able to handle their responsibilities than others.

To demonstrate how this new framework could aid in predicting global leadership success, we introduce a predictive example of related behaviors (Fig. 2.1). We posit that the mindset, skill, and knowledge competency sub-dimensions of GIL will predict both transformational leadership and cultural adaptability, which represent two critical behavioral outcomes that will ultimately lead to more effective global leadership. Transformational leadership is exemplified because there is indication for its universality as a leadership style (House et al. 2004; Reilly and Karounos 2009). Based on Bass (1985) construct, transformational leadership describes leaders who aim at increasing subordinates' awareness of valued outcomes by elevating their needs and motivating them to work beyond their self-interests (Bass 1985).

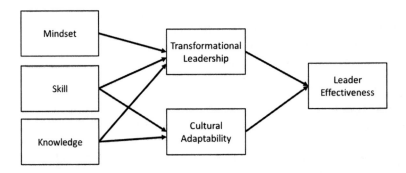

Fig. 2.1 Example predictive model of GIL competencies leading to effectiveness

The GIL sub-dimension of mindset would increase the likelihood that the leader would be motivated to inspire their diverse followers to work beyond their self-interests. Being proficient in the relevant skills in the GIL sub-dimension means the leader is more capable of enacting the culturally appropriate transformational leadership behaviors. For example, the individualized attention and consideration as a part of transformational leadership may be perceived differently across cultures and having the social skills, self-regulation, metacognitive CQ and behavioral CQ skills would make those transformational leadership behaviors more effective and culturally appropriate. Similarly, self-awareness and knowledge of the culture would enhance transformational leadership by enabling the leader to apply their inspirational talents in such a way to build off of local values and beliefs.

The second predicted variable, cultural adaptability, refers to the ability to alter behaviors in the appropriate manner that would lead the individual to function effectively in settings of cultural diversity. This behavior has been strongly linked to cultural intelligence in previous research (Ng et al. 2012) and it would follow that GIL would also be positively associated to cultural adaptability. Adapting to a new and unfamiliar setting would be facilitated by a personality that is open to experience, conscientious, agreeable, extraverted, and emotionally stable. Similarly, an individual would need the motivation to adapt in order to be successful. Having the skills of both EI and CQ would benefit an individual by aiding in all social interactions, making adjustment, and especially interpersonal adjustment, an easier process. Finally, knowledge of both oneself and the relevant cultures would be crucial to cultural adaptation because knowledge would help an individual get settled and be more receptive to the new environment. Practically speaking, knowledge of a new culture would come in handy in a variety of situations such as being aware of the social connotations of certain meals or coffee breaks. Both transformational leadership, as a universally preferred style of leadership, and cultural adaptability, would ultimately result in a more effective global leader. Given the potential predictive links between the framework and these behaviors, we argue that GIL would predict global leadership effectiveness.

The framework put forth in this chapter represents a conceptual starting point, and extensive further research is necessary to develop a consolidated measure for the three competencies of this framework. This process could begin with examining conceptual and statistical overlap between existing well-validated measures of CQ, EI, and personality. Following elimination of any redundant or repetitious items, these measures could be adapted into a consolidated scale and tested for reliability and validity. As mentioned throughout the chapter, future research would greatly benefit from the development of a more parsimonious measure that can assess global leadership competencies in a more concise and feasible manner. The research is quite scattered at the moment with a plethora of variables declared as having predictive value for global leadership effectiveness. Condensing the current theories and measures would help researchers uncover the core competencies. Therefore, research that compares current predictors to each other in search of any empirical or theoretical overlap would benefit that consolidation.

Because GIL takes broad constructs and attempts to narrow them to a smaller set of core underlying dimensions, this abridged theoretical framework is a step in the direction of figuring out what it is that truly makes some global leaders more effective than others. "Of crucial importance is our understanding of the leadership characteristics that contribute to global leadership success compared with leadership success in different cultural contexts" (Erez 2011, p. 841). We hope the parsimonious framework introduced in this chapter will spur new thinking and add a unique perspective to the assessment of global leadership while aiding in research development.

References

Ang, S. (2011) Cultural intelligence. *The cambridge handbook of intelligence*, 582–602.

Ang, S., Van Dyne, L., & Koh, C. (2006). Personality correlates of the four-factor model of cultural intelligence. *Group and Organization Management, 31*(1), 100–123. doi:10.1177/1059601105275267.

Bandura, A. (1977). Self-efficacy: Toward a unifying theory of behavior change. *Psychological Review, 84*, 191–215.

Bar-On, R. (2000). Emotions and social intelligence: Insights from the emotional quotient inventory. In R. Bar-On & J. D. A. Parker (Eds.), *The handbook of emotional intelligence: Theory, development, assessment, and application at home, school, and in the workplace* (pp. 363–388). San Francisco: Jossey-Bass.

Bass, B. M. (1985). *Leadership and performance beyond expectations*. New York: Free Press.

Bhaskar-Shrinivas, P., Harrison, D. A., Shaffer, M. A., & Luk, D. M. (2005). Input-based and time-based models of international adjustment: Meta-analytic evidence and theoretical extensions. *The Academy of Management Journal, 48*(2), 257–281.

De Vries, M. F. R. K., & Florent-Treacy, E. (2002). Global leadership from A to Z: Creating high commitment organizations. *Organizational Dynamics, 30*(4), 295–309. doi:10.1016/S0090-2616(02)00067-0.

Dean, B. P. (2007). *Cultural intelligence in global leadership: A model for developing culturally and nationally diverse teams* (Unpublished doctoral dissertation). Regent University.

Deng, L., & Gibson, P. (2008). A qualitative evaluation on the role of cultural intelligence in cross-cultural leadership effectiveness. *International Journal of Leadership Studies, 3*, 181–197.

Ekermans, G. (2009). Emotional intelligence across cultures: Theoretical and methodological considerations. In J. D. A. Parker, D. H. Saklofske, & C. Stough (Eds.), *Assessing emotional intelligence: Theory, research, and applications* (pp. 259–290). Dordrecht: Springer.

Elenkov, D. S., & Manev, I. M. (2009). Senior expatriate leadership's effects on innovation and the role of cultural intelligence. *Journal of World Business, 44*, 357–369.

Erez, M. (2011). Cross-cultural and global issues in organizational psychology. *APA handbook of industrial and organizational psychology, 3*.

Forsyth, B. (2015). Cultural intelligence and global leadership. *Journal of Leadership, Accountability and Ethics, 12*(2), 130–135. Retrieved from http://search.proquest.com/docview/1726791075?accountid=27313

Gabel-Shemueli, R., & Dolan, S. (2011). Do emotions matter? The role of emotional intelligence competences in cross-cultural adjustment for international assignment. *Management Research, 9*(3), 207–229. doi:10.1108/1536-541111181912.

George, J. M. (2000). Emotions and leadership: The role of EI. *Human Relations, 53*(12), 1027–1041. doi:10.1177/0018726700538001.

Goleman, D. (1998). What makes a leader? *Harvard Business Review, 76*(6), 93–102.

Hogan, R., & Benson, M. J. (2009). Personality, leadership, and globalization: linking personality to global organizational effectiveness. *Advances in Global Leadership.* 11–34 (Published online: 09 March 2015).

Hogan, R., & Kaiser, R. B. (2005). What we know about leadership. *Review of General Psychology, 9,* 169–180.

House, Robert J., Hanges, Paul J., Javidan, Mansour, Dorfman, Peter W., & Gupta, Vipin (Eds.). (2004). *Culture, leadership, and organizations: The GLOBE study of 62 societies.* Thousand Oaks, CA: Sage.

Huang, T. J., Chi, S. C., & Lawler, J. J. (2005). The relationship between expatriates' personality traits and their adjustment to international assignments. *International Journal of Human Resource Management, 16*(9), 1656–1670.

Humphrey, R. H. (2002). The many faces of emotional leadership. *The Leadership Quaterly, 13* (5), 493–504. doi:10.1016/S1048-9843(02)00140-6.

Jassawalla, Avan, Truglia, Ciara, & Garvey, Jennifer. (2004). Cross-cultural conflict and expatriate manager adjustment. *Management Decision, 42*(7), 837–849.

Jokinen, T. (2005). Global leadership competencies: A review and discussion. *Journal of European Industrial Training, 29*(3), 199–216.

Judge, T. A., Bono, J. E., Ilies, R., & Gerhardt, M. W. (2002). Personality and leadership: A qualitative and quantitative review. *Journal of Applied Psychology, 87*(4), 765–780. doi:10. 1037/0021-9010.87.4.765.

Khalili, Ashkan. (2012). The role of emotional intelligence in the workplace: A literature review. *International Journal of Management, 29*(3), 355.

Kim, Junhee, & McLean, Gary N. (2015). An integrative framework for global leadership competency: Levels and dimensions. *Human Resource Development International, 18*(3), 235–258. doi:10.1080/13678868.2014.1003721.

Lillis, M. P., & Tian, R. G. (2009). Cross-cultural communication and emotional intelligence. *Marketing Intelligence & Planning, 27*(3), 428–438. doi:10.1108/02634500910955272.

Lin, Yi-Chun, Chen, Angela Shin-Yih, & Song, Yi-Chen. (2012). Does your intelligence help to survive in a foreign jungle? The effects of cultural intelligence and emotional intelligence on cross-cultural adjustment. *International Journal of Intercultural Relations, 36*(4), 541–552. doi:10.1016/j.ijintrel.2012.03.001.

Matthews, G., Zeidner, M., & Roberts, R. D. (2002). *Emotional intelligence: Science and myth.* Cambridge, Mass: A Bradford Book.

Mayer, J. D., & Salovey, P. (1997). What is emotional intelligence? In P. Salovey & D. J. Sluyter (Eds.), *Emotional development and emotional intelligence: Educational implications* (pp. 3–31). New York: Basic Books.

Moon, T. (2010). Emotional intelligence correlates of the four-factor model of cultural intelligence. *Journal of Managerial Psychology, 25*(8), 876–898.

Ng, K. Y., Van Dyne, L., & Ang, S. (2012). Cultural intelligence: A review, reflections, and recommendations for future research. In A. M. Ryn, F. T. L. Leong & F. L. Oswald (Eds.), *Conducting multinational research: Applying organizational psychology in the workplace* (pp. 29–58). Washington, DC: American Psychological Association.

Palthe, J. (2004). The relative importance of antecedents to cross-cultural adjustment: Implications for managing a global workforce. *International Journal of Intercultural Relations, 28*(1), 37–59. doi:10.1016/j.ijintrel.2003.12.004.

Plum, E. (2008). *Cultural intelligence: The art of leading cultural complexity.* London: Middlesex University Press.

Ramchunder, Y., & Martins, N. (2014). The role of self-efficacy, emotional intelligence and leadership style as attributes of leadership effectiveness. *SA Journal of Industrial Psychology, 40*(1), 1. doi:10.4102/sajip.v40i1.1100.

Reilly, Anne H., & Karounos, Tony J. (2009). Exploring the link between emotional intelligence and cross-cultural leadership effectiveness. *Journal of International Business and Cultural Studies, 1,* 1.

Rockstuhl, T., Seiler, S., Ang, S., Van Dyne, L., & Annen, H. (2011). Beyond general intelligence (IQ) and emotional intelligence (EQ): The role of cultural intelligence (CQ) on cross-border leadership effectiveness in a globalized world. *Journal of Social IIssues, 67*(4), 825–840.

Rosete, D., & Ciarrochi, J. (2005). Emotional intelligence and its relationship to workplace performance outcomes of leadership effectiveness. *Leadership & Organization Development Journal, 26*(5), 388–399. doi:10.1108/01437730510607871.

Sharma, S., Deller, J., Biswal, R., & Mandal, M. K. (2009). Emotional intelligence: Factorial structure and construct validity across cultures. *International Journal of Cross Cultural Management, 9*(2), 217–236.

Shipper, Frank, Kincaid, Joel, Rotondo, Denise M., Hoffman, I. V., & Richard, C. (2003). A cross-cultural exploratory study of the linkage between emotional intelligence and managerial effectiveness. *International Journal of Organizational Analysis, 11*(3), 171–191.

Silverthorne, C. (2001). Leadership effectiveness and personality: A cross cultural evaluation. *Personality and Individual Differences, 30*(2), 303–309. doi:10.1016/S0191-8869(00)00047-7.

Takeuchi, R., Tesluk, P. E., Yun, S., & Lepak, D. P. (2005). An integrative view of international experience. *The Academy of Management Journal, 48*(1), 85–100.

Thomas, David C., & Inkson, Kerr. (2009). *Cultural intelligence: Living and working globally.* US: Berrett-Koehler Publishers.

Van Rooy, D. L., & Viswesvaran, C. (2004). Emotional intelligence: A meta-analytic investigation of predictive validity and nomological net. *Journal of Vocational Behavior, 65*(1), 71–95. doi:10.1016/S0001-8791(03)00076-9.

Walter, F., Cole, M. S., & Humphrey, R. H. (2011). Emotional intelligence: Sine qua non if leadership or folderol? *The Academy of Management Perspectives, 25*(1), 45.

Chapter 3
Considerations and Best Practices for Developing Cultural Competency Models in Applied Work Domains

Winston R. Sieck, Louise J. Rasmussen and Jasmine L. Duran

John has been preparing for his upcoming assignment in Thailand for months. He has a good grasp of the Thai language, customs, people, and political landscape. Ready as he's going to be. Then he get the news. The bottom falls out of his stomach. Leadership has changed direction. John is suddenly assigned to an office in Ouadda. "Where precisely is that again?"

How can we help professionals like John be less worried when their international assignments change? Or, when they inevitably end up working in places and with people they never expected? The first step is to identify the culture-general competencies that allow professionals to go anywhere in the world at a moment's notice and work effectively with members of diverse populations.

A large number and variety of abilities relevant to competence of this sort have been identified over the years. For example, in a review of intercultural competence models, Spitzberg and Chagnon (2009) identified approximately 300 potential constructs that might be included in models of general competence. These items, which Spitzberg extracted from the broad literature related to intercultural competence, range from characteristics such as openness and creativity, to cross-cultural difference dimensions such as power distance, and to admonitions such as "be friendly." The constructs vary a great deal in their degree of specificity. They include a mixture of personality traits and malleable knowledge and skills. Culture-specific concepts (e.g. "face") are listed alongside culture-general skills and processes. A possible reason for this diversity is that the items are drawn from models developed with very different problems in mind, such as people with different backgrounds getting along with one another in general, students having

W.R. Sieck (✉) · L.J. Rasmussen · J.L. Duran
Global Cognition, 1771 Southview Dr, Yellow Springs, OH 45387, USA
e-mail: sieck@globalcognition.org

L.J. Rasmussen
e-mail: louise@globalcognition.org

J.L. Duran
e-mail: duran@globalcognition.org

© Springer International Publishing Switzerland 2016
J.L. Wildman et al. (eds.), *Critical Issues in Cross Cultural Management*,
DOI 10.1007/978-3-319-42166-7_3

positive overseas enrichment experiences, and professionals needing to perform effectively in jobs that involve intercultural interactions.

The Spitzberg and Chagnon (2009) review was an important theoretical exercise. It gives a clear sense of a wide array of researcher's insights and results. Yet, how can we move from this wealth of big ideas to a competence model that supports professionals who have to work in a variety of cultures?

These lists distilled from the literature may loosely inform hypotheses about competencies that could be important to professionals working in different job sectors. However, although there is a temptation to stick closely to past literature, doing so is problematic for this purpose. Direct culling of ideas from the wider literature is unlikely to fare well for several reasons.

One problem with such an approach is that, in attempting to provide "foundational" solutions, academic studies often tend to ignore job context or demands. Another caveat is that the language used to define competencies includes academic jargon. This means that even if the competencies are useful, they are not presented in a format that professionals can readily comprehend and incorporate in their routines. A last limitation of direct translation from the literature is that research is rarely conducted with an eye towards practical implementation. For example, it would not be clear how to incorporate many of the concepts reviewed by Spitzberg and Chagnon in professional development programs.

An alternative to culling competencies directly from the literature is to undertake a field study of accomplished professionals who have experience working in a wide variety of cultures. Examining the competencies these professionals use in practice allows the researcher to identify and refine cultural knowledge and skills to include in an actionable model of culture-general competence for the associated work domain. We use the term "culture-general," to refer to the skills and knowledge that allow adaptation and interaction in any culture (Rasmussen and Sieck 2015). This sense of the term culture-general broadens Cushner and Brislin's use of the term to describe cultural training that covers recurring themes of cultural difference (Cushner and Brislin 1996).

A premise of the field-study approach is that a model of culture-general competence for professionals ought to be grounded in study of what personnel actually do when they apply cultural skills and knowledge on the job. And in order to guide future practice, a model of culture-general competence should reflect current best practices. These principles are not arbitrary, but rather stem from the broader literature on competency model development.

A fundamental principle underlying the development and use of competency models as human resource management tools is that competency models describe behaviors that are associated with desired job performance. The ability of a competency model to successfully guide practice hinges on the faithfulness with which it describes actual behaviors that job holders can meaningfully engage to meet or exceed their organization's objectives. From this view, the goal of analysis aimed at developing competency models is to identify a realistic set of norms for behavior based on what superior performers do rather than to promote a romanticized vision fashioned from what someone thinks they should be doing in an idealized setting (McClelland 1973).

An established method for developing competency models in any work domain involves interviewing current skilled and experienced job holders about how they handled challenging incidents they encountered on their jobs (Campion et al. 2011; Spencer and Spencer 1993). Collecting and analyzing the thoughts and actions of people who are successful in their jobs as they cope with challenging situations enables researchers to more objectively examine the tacit characteristics that influence behavior and that result in excellent performance. This approach makes it possible to formulate competency requirements from an examination of job experience instead of relying on idealized attributes, characteristics, or activities that may or may not be effective.

There are two primary benefits for an organization to using a competency model that is based on an analysis of current best practices of experienced job holders. First, it ensures that the model identifies specific behaviors and strategies that make sense within the job domain. This enables the organization to provide guidelines for practice that can feasibly be carried out within the constraints of the job. This also makes it a useful foundation for developing or identifying content that can be used to train and educate novice personnel. It makes it easier to incorporate into instruction demonstrations of the ways competencies are practiced within the context of the job. This, in turn, ensures that instruction clearly communicates the relevance of the competencies to job objectives which in turn increases the chances of adoption.

Second, basing a competency model on analysis of what job holders already do makes it possible to express competencies in the language of the job holder, as opposed to in the language of the researcher. This has several implications for the ways the competency model can be used. For one, this means that personnel who are already engaging in desirable and productive behaviors will be able to recognize they are doing the right things. This in turn will serve as motivation for them to continue to engage in these behaviors. It can also serve as an external reference that can help experienced professionals influence others to engage in them too, as it provides an accessible vocabulary for communicating expectations for behavior. Finally, a competency model that is grounded in practice and expressed in the language of job holders makes it easier for supervisors to determine members of their staff who are doing well, and ones who need training or refreshers.

In the remainder of this chapter, we prescribe a general approach for developing practical competency models that describe the skills and knowledge needed to be successful on a last minute assignment to, for instance, Ouadda. A first step is to establish the specific purpose of the model. We focus here on developing a model to support training and education of culture-general competence. Next, criteria need to be specified for the inclusion of Subject Matter Experts (SMEs) in the study. Finally, suitable procedures for data collection and analysis are needed that allow the researchers to extract applications of cultural skills and knowledge in the job context. We discuss each of these activities in turn.

The Purpose of the Model Is to Set Standards for Training Culture-General Competence

There are many interesting questions cultural researchers might ask related to competence, such as, "What is necessary for people from different cultural backgrounds to get along with each other?" and how can we, "define intercultural competence from a variety of cultural perspectives." (Deardorff 2009, p. 264).

When developing a competence model in service of working professionals, the purpose needs to be more clearly focused on aiding them. In the case of our efforts to support professionals in the military, the purpose of the model is to set standards for training that supports the ability of personnel to interact effectively with members of foreign populations no matter where they might be assigned. The purpose of the model is not to provide guidance for working in specific cultures. Although culture-specific information is not included, competencies in the model foster the ongoing development of regional knowledge to further enhance comprehensive cultural competence across a person's career.

Two crucial aspects of the model are thus the focus on culture-general competence, in contrast to region-specific knowledge, and on training and education, as opposed to personnel selection for instance.

Not all definitions related to intercultural competence sharply discriminate the concept of culture-general competence, as complementary to regional expertise. For example, Spitzberg defines intercultural competence as, "the appropriate and effective management of interaction between people who, to some degree or another, represent different or divergent affective, cognitive, and behavioral orientations to the world." (Spitzberg and Chagnon 2009). Cultural intelligence presents another interesting example. Although the concept itself appears to promise culture-general, standard definitions are not completely obvious in this regard: "... an individual's capability to function and manage effectively in culturally diverse settings, CQ is a multidimensional construct targeted at situations involving cross-cultural interactions arising from differences in race, ethnicity and nationality." (Ang et al. 2007, p. 336). In both of these definitions, the culture-general and culture-specific aspects of the proposed ability are ambiguous. Either would seem to include enhanced functioning with members of particular cultural groups due to increased knowledge of the ways of those groups.

On the other hand, a few descriptions that hone in on aspects of culture-general competence include:

The skill that allows individuals to learn about new and different cultures, to analyze the cultural underpinnings of context, and to understand intentions and behaviors from different cultural perspectives. Important aspects of this ability, include being free of an over attachment to previous ways of thinking that have worked in the past, the generation of rival hypotheses that explain conflict other than those from their own cultural framework, and the creation of a new set of ideas about social interaction. (Matsumoto et al. 2001, p. 505).

Metacognitive CQ refers to the processes individuals use to acquire and understand cultural knowledge. (Ang et al. 2007, p. 338).

For instance, some general skills might be to avoid stereotyped thinking about a problem, to be willing to seek out more information, and to be unsatisfied with an obvious explanation based on the most colorful or vivid (not necessarily the most important) part of a problem. (Cushner and Brislin 1996, p. 28).

The value of a model of culture-general competence stems from the vast amount of cultural content that could be provided to professionals who are required to work with people from all over the world. Candidate topics for any region might include such diverse topics as demographics and political divisions, religion, local clothing, food, or distinctive customs and communication preferences.

In attempt to arrive at the essentials, on could draw on the abundance of frameworks for thinking about similarities and differences between national cultures, such as value differences identified by cross-cultural psychologists (e.g., Schwartz 1992), or on cultural anthropology topics, such as kinship systems, social organization, and subsistence patterns. Some culture-general instruction appears to consist of content knowledge primarily grounded in theoretical frameworks that describe cultural differences (e.g., Bhawuk 1998; Cushner and Brislin 1996).

Cultural frameworks provide a systematic starting point for analyzing and understanding national cultures. However, the frameworks were primarily developed to provide theoretical support to investigations of cultural comparisons, and not for the purpose of making sense of specific behaviors of members of other cultures in particular situations. These distinct purposes call the value of applying such frameworks for preparing professionals for intercultural interaction into question (Earley and Peterson 2004). The employment of such dimensions for the latter purpose may additionally encourage a sophisticated form of stereotyping by suggesting that differences are more regular and systematic than as indicated in research results (Osland and Bird 2000; Schwartz 2014).

These considerations suggest that the starting point for a practical model of culture-general competence should not be research frameworks of cultural differences. Instead, the behaviors and strategies that enable personnel to learn, think, and interact effectively in new cultures ought to be the main ingredient. This requires that we delineate as clearly as possible the knowledge and skills that are useful in any region, as distinct from content knowledge pertaining to specific cultures.

The challenge in distinguishing culture-general competence and regional proficiency is that although they can be distinguished theoretically, they tend to work together in practice. To think about situations in which culture-general competence is clearly exhibited, it's useful to consider instances when regional proficiency is lacking. For regional experts, culture-general competence is most obviously at play when they are operating in an area that is outside their regional focus. Even so, a subject matter expert (SME) whose experiences fall primarily within a specific region may not exhibit the same skills as another who has spent significant time in multiple diverse locations.

Given that the focus of the model is on culture-general competence, there remains the question of how it will be used. Overall, the main purpose of competency model development in our own work has been to set standards for training and education. In particular, the model defines the skills and knowledge that should be targeted by culture-general instruction.

A potential confusion that sometimes arises about this general approach is to think that the resulting model would only apply to people who have the same level of cross-cultural experience as the members of the study sample. The key consideration to resolve the confusion is the definition of "model applicability" in this context. Specifically, a distinction that needs to be made is between models that have a prescriptive, rather than purely descriptive purpose (e.g., Yates 1990). Prescriptive (or normative) models attempt to specify how things should be done, whereas descriptive models aim to explain human behavior as is. Competency models, such as a model of culture-general competence, have prescriptive purposes, such as application to developing training and education programs, or to support performance management more generally.

Hence, for our application, the research aim is to describe the competence of an experienced, proficient sample of relevant SMEs in order to develop a model that then prescribes the knowledge and skills the broader professional community needs in order to be effective.

This overall purpose further suggests a need to specify competencies in a way that enables them to be readily translated into culture-general learning objectives for specific courses or other training applications. And to do so in a way that aids instructors to straightforwardly communicate these learning objectives to their students. Adult learners want to know why they need to learn something before they engage in educational activities (Knowles et al. 2014). This means that instruction must make it a priority to identify the connection between course content and job relevance.

In addition to defining culture-general objectives, the model should be specified so as to enable instructors to identify culture-general learning objectives they may already be covering in their courses, as well as to distinguish culture-general learning objectives from region or culture-specific learning objectives within courses that have dual objectives.

Finally, the model should be specified in a way that helps instructors recognize how culture-general competence not only relates to, but enhances the primary job or task personnel are accomplishing overseas and will thus enable them to help their students appreciate this relationship. Perhaps the most direct way of accomplishing this is to provide behavioral examples elicited directly from relevant SMEs as a component of the model.

Similarly, when education is the primary objective, it is advantageous if the effort to build a culture-general competence model also yields content that could be used to develop scenarios and related instructional materials. Scenarios from and information about particular foreign cultures are usefully incorporated when teaching general skills. A caveat is that it is important that educators are able to distinguish the learning objectives that relate to culture-general skills and knowledge from culture-specific knowledge.

This latter point is also relevant to assessment. The goal of instruction stemming from a culture-general competence model along the lines described should not be that students are able to select the "right answers" to questions about culture-specific facts, customs, or patterns of behavior. Such is often the case in culture-specific training and research, for example, when respondents are asked to pick the best behavioral interpretations (i.e., attributions) in cultural assimilator training (e.g., Cushner and Brislin 1996). Instead, they should have acquired a way of thinking about and responding to the world that is consistent with the competencies outlined in the competence model.

The Best Sources Are Culture-General SMEs Who Work in the Profession

As noted above, researchers could draw on a variety of sources to develop a model of culture-general competence. The roles, functions, and other characteristics of study participants can vary considerably, including students engaging in study abroad, scholars' personal experiences, and professionals working overseas. This presents a potential issue, in that the particular skills identified in one population may not apply to other populations or settings. In addition, similar skills may be enacted differently depending on the sojourner's role or function overseas.

The nature of the participants' experience-based may also differ in important ways. In many existing studies, participant experience is either not controlled, or limited to a single, significant sojourn. To identify the culture-general competencies that support professionals in a particular work domain, the opposite sample criteria are needed: SMEs from a specific work domain who have experiences operating in a variety of regions.

We have followed this principle to establish criteria for participant inclusion in our studies to identify culture-general competencies for the U.S. military. Specifically, the criteria for inclusion in our studies were at least two tours of duty overseas to different regions, extensive interaction with local populaces, civilians or partnered forces during those assignments, and some form of peer-nomination (Rasmussen and Sieck 2015). These minimum criteria resulted in participant samples that represented repeated and varied intercultural experiences from all over the world. In one study, participant SMEs had worked overseas in at least two different locations in their careers at minimum. Three quarters of the sample had three or more distinct sojourns, with the overall sample averaging 3.7 overseas assignments (Rasmussen and Sieck 2015). Participants in a more recent study worked in 7.8 distinct countries on average, ranging between 2 and 40 countries overall. In addition, many of these participants completed a number of additional shorter assignments, completed longer sojourns for study or nongovernment related work, or interacted extensively with foreign military partners as part of joint training programs in the U.S. (Rasmussen et al. 2015).

With respect to theoretical development, why might it be important to systematically study a population that has had repeated and varied intercultural experiences for the purposes of developing a model of culture-general competence?

From a cognitive perspective, key differences can be expected to exist between individuals who have spent significant time in a single culture and individuals who have spent time in a variety of cultures. For example, Endicott and colleagues suggest that as people increase their intercultural expertise their schemas for intercultural problem solving grow in breadth and depth. However, the way in which their schemas grow may depend on the types of intercultural experiences they have had. Specifically, a person who spends significant time in a single culture tends to develop a complex, highly interconnected schema for that culture. Someone who visits many cultures for shorter periods of time develops several, shallower schemas (Endicott et al. 2003).

Given the cognitive differences between generalists and specialists, there is a possibility that the performance of these two types of cultural SMEs is supported by different competencies. Specifically, the SME with extensive experience in a particular region likely matches patterns of behavior directly and maps to appropriate responses, whereas the culture-general SME is more typically operating in a deliberative mode, applying generalized methods (Anderson 1983).

A potential issue with selecting cultural generalists has to do with whether individuals who do not have a specific regional occupational specialty can reasonably be considered cultural SMEs. That is, can the "SME" designation really be considered appropriate, given the general nature of the competence? After all, participants may well be novices in the specific regional cultures in which they are operating. On the other hand, not having an in-depth knowledge of the culture is an important condition under which culture-general competence is expressed. From this view, it is simply part of what is meant by a culture-general SME.

These considerations of generalists and specialists are closely related to the issues of transfer and generalization in cognitive science and education (Perkins and Salomon 1989). When people face the same kinds of problems in a variety of contexts the likelihood of successful transfer of learning to novel situations is increased. With respect to culture, this implies transferring skills that are called on and used in each culture visited, across a wide variety of cultures. And it's these transferrable skills that belong in a model of culture-general competence.

General, transferrable cultural skills constitute an especially important core set of competencies for military professionals. In the U.S. military, it is perhaps all too common to have a strong regional background for a particular area, and then wind up serving elsewhere. For example:

> How did you come to be assigned to Norway? By the US military logic. I was a fully trained French Foreign Area Officer (FAO). Instead of being assigned to my first choice of a French speaking location, I was sent to Norway, where I didn't know the language. My friend who had a Scandinavian background was assigned to his second choice of France.

> I had studied German and Spanish in high school and college; I was an International Studies major. I lived in the Netherlands for a year and a half to go to graduate school before I came into the military...I was asked to do a two year job as a junior level military

attaché…in Saudi Arabia. And that position was outside my area of expertise; didn't have any language or culture background on it… I had to apply what I did in Germany and the Netherlands to the Saudi Arabia and the Middle Eastern environment.

In addition to breadth of experience, another essential criterion of inclusion in our studies is that SMEs have recent and relevant experience in the content area. For the purpose of identifying culture-general competencies that support a class of professionals, it is particularly important that interviewees demonstrate specific skills in the context of relevant job demands.

An alternative here is to rely on the input of scholars, such as anthropologists or cultural psychologists, who may have considerable experience sojourning across cultures, in addition to knowledge of theories and studies from their respective literatures about culture-general skills and abilities. Indeed, intercultural experts are sometimes defined as individuals who have considerable tenure studying culture or intercultural interaction (Deardorff 2006).

Yet, cultural experiences by themselves are not sufficient for informing a culture-general competence model that can aid professionals in a specific domain, such as the military. Appropriate SMEs must have specific experience working within the setting and constraints of military operations. For example monitoring, establishing, and maintaining the security is an important, pervasive component of military work. An important related skill relates to the ability to use cultural information to adjust assessments of risk in potentially physically threatening or confrontational settings.

> When you're first meeting your interpreters, you have to figure out where they're coming from, what they believe. My feeling is I don't want to get blown up… so what is it going to take and can I trust him? Is he a suicide bomber? I have to figure these things out. And, you can't just ask that question, 'are you Taliban?' You have to weasel your way into it somehow, and maybe throw some hints out there… I know some nuggets of information that I think would kind of call your bluff-type of information. Like "what do you think of Massoud?" I'll just throw it out there and see what happens. Then I look for indicators, looking for any reason to doubt, and I guess that is the bottom line. …So the more I know, the more I can roll in certain situations and test the water.

Given these considerations, cultural scholars are not themselves reasonable SMEs for developing a culture-general competence model that is intended to serve a particular professional population, such as military personnel. They do not have the necessary domain knowledge of the profession, and they lack the necessary credibility among practitioners to serve in that role:

> Academia will always have someone "smarter" or more informed on regional issues and more adept in linguistics skills, but they aren't Marines, and they won't be culturally and linguistically adept in our way of life—the application of military power, the planning associated with it, and the readiness to forward deploy to distant and austere locales. (LtCol Bolden (2012), Marine Corps Gazette)

Studies of cultural adaptability that draw on study-abroad students or other nonmilitary populations should likewise be treated carefully for the purpose of making recommendations for military personnel. Conversely, it does not make sense to evaluate military culture-general SMEs according to the standards held in other professions, e.g., that of an anthropologist or cross-cultural psychologist. The particular objectives and demands associated with these different jobs call for somewhat distinct knowledge, skills, attitudes, and abilities. For example, a cultural scholar may have exceedingly well developed ethnorelative communication patterns (cf. Bennet 1986). Among other things, these patterns serve to indicate expertise among their scholarly peers. Yet, communicating at the highest ethnorelative stages is not necessarily better in work situations demanding intercultural competence (Hammer et al. 2003). Culture-general expertise within a job domain must be evaluated according to its own standards, constraints, and pressures (and those alone). These considerations would hold for developing models to support medical, business, legal, military and other professions.

This stance on the appropriate background for SMEs is for practical, as well as theoretical reasons. At the end of the day, the professionals themselves have final say as to the utility and value of the model of culture-general competence. They will accept or reject models depending on perceived usefulness to their work. An ideal outcome for models of culture-general competence is that they help to motivate and entice personnel with nonculture occupational specialties to view "culture" as both relevant and doable.

In order to accomplish this outcome, researchers need to emphasize pragmatic over ideological concerns. For example, the language of the model should use the professionals' words, as much as possible, rather than trying to find the definitive expression of concepts in academic jargon. Models of culture-general competence also need to offer clear value for job functions and tasks. Concepts that may be theoretically interesting but do not have clear applied value should be sidelined as they will be filed away as 'good to know' (a euphemism for useless) by a practitioner audience and thus lessen perceived utility of the endeavor as a whole.

How to Uncover Culture-General Competence from Interviews

Cultural scholars may sometimes find themselves falling into the same pattern as management consultants. Campion et al. (2011) described credible, rigorous methods for competency model development, including literature reviews, critical incident interviews, and questionnaires, among others. He contrasted these methods with earlier practices of having management consultants, who did not work on the job, offer their opinions as to the competencies personnel should possess.

A more useful role for scholars in the development of cultural competency models is to employ their research methods to tease out the knowledge and skills actually used by culture-general SMEs in a work domain. Which research methods should investigators use?

We have found critical incident interviews to provide an excellent starting point for identifying competencies. Although generally recognized as a sound method for competency modeling, critical incident interviews are sometimes bypassed in the development process in favor of questionnaire-based surveys. This is likely due to the relative disadvantages of interview and other verbal protocol methods, as compared with closed-form questionnaires. And perhaps to overlooked advantages of interview methods and disadvantages of questionnaires.

First among the disadvantages of interviews is that such studies are difficult to complete. The data collection and analysis process associated with open-ended verbal reports is time consuming and labor intensive. Because of this, interview studies tend to rely on smaller samples of SMEs than do questionnaires. Big sample sizes feel good. Yet, qualitative methods that enable the collection of in-depth data from each of a selected set of SMEs have proven useful in many domains (e.g. Schraagen et al. 2000; Spencer and Spencer 1993). Although large sample study designs clearly have their place in the researcher's repertoire, treating sample size as the single overriding consideration is overly restrictive, especially early in research efforts.

One of the benefits of conducting in-depth interviews with a relatively small sample of participants, as compared with large-scale questionnaire studies, is that the interview approach enables researchers to set highly stringent criteria for SME inclusion, as we described earlier. In addition, the interview approach allows the competency developer to build rapport with the SMEs, who are stakeholders in the process. Interviewees often indicate that they find the personal aspects of sharing their critical incidents enjoyable and thought-provoking, all of which helps to build stakeholder support for competency model results. Another important benefit of leading early with interviews is that they enable the acquisition of information from culture-general SMEs in their own words, with elicited knowledge and skills woven into work experiences. And on the other side, since participating SMEs are answering questions within their own work context, the researcher can be more certain that SMEs are interpreting the questions appropriately.

There are also disadvantages in the approach of moving directly from literature review to self-report questionnaire, as compared with conducting interview studies as the starting point. For example, an interesting and important line of research has been on the investigation of relations between personality characteristics and intercultural adaptability (e.g., Van Oudenhoven and Van der Zee 2002). Following results of studies along these lines, trait-like personality characteristics such as "open-mindedness" and "flexibility" might be considered as good things to have in a model of culture-general competence. Hence, the researcher could include self-report items such as "I work according to a strict scheme" to measure flexibility (or "I avoid surprises"—indicating lack of flexibility) in a questionnaire distributed to thousands of respondents working in the job domain.[1] However, even if the

---

[1] We should acknowledge that attaining a sample of thousands that meets the stringent criteria for inclusion we described is unlikely to be feasible.

results supported the constructs, a model developed along such lines would not readily support instructional design processes for building training applications or education programs. Characteristics of this sort are framed in terms of outcomes. It would thus be more useful to determine malleable knowledge and skills associated with these outcomes. For instance, we might attempt to identify the strategies that SMEs use to manage surprises that crop up in their critical incidents (Sieck et al. 2013). Such strategies can then be usefully incorporated into a model of culture-general competence.

A separate but related issue with questionnaire methods as used in studies of culture-general competence is that they rely primarily on self-report. Self-report is a reasonable approach if the aim of a study is to understand how certain personality factors relate to cultural adaptability among international students. When conducting competence studies to inform the design of instruction and related assessments, then it's more useful to measure demonstrated competence of SMEs. As Ward and Fischer (2008) commented about cultural intelligence questionnaires, "A more valid test of intelligence would not ask respondents if they have the knowledge or ability to solve a problem, it would require respondents to engage in problem solving!" (p. 169).

Within critical incident interviews, culture-general SMEs describe in great detail how they handled some of their most challenging intercultural interactions on the job. Frequent indications of demonstrated knowledge and skills found in the verbal reports provide evidence of relevant competencies. Hence, this approach requires that study participants spontaneously generate and apply competencies in the context of their own lived intercultural problems.

An alternative way to use questionnaires in competency modeling is to have respondents report on the frequency and importance they assign to different tasks. This may work reasonably well when job incumbents are asked to report on very concrete, readily recognizable tasks, such as: "Uses a computer or word processor to create, edit, print, retrieve, or manipulate files" (Rodriquez et al. 2002). While judgments of frequency are acceptable for tasks, especially concrete tasks, they are less well suited to identify competencies, especially ones that involve abstract cognitive processes, such as those that are used when SMEs take another's perspective, are confronted with moral dilemmas, and deal with uncertainty.

A current challenge with developing a model of culture-general competence that deserves greater recognition is to identify and discriminate tasks and competencies. These often appear to be conflated in extant models. One approach towards solving this problem would discriminate different types of engagements, such as "social interaction" and "negotiation." These intercultural tasks could then be meaningfully aligned with the competencies that influence performance on those tasks, such as perspective taking and managing attitudes. In any case, it's reasonable to expect that considerable conceptual development would be required before reasonable questionnaires could be constructed that enable respondents to provide accurate self-reports regarding the frequency and importance of cross-cultural and intercultural tasks. Critical incident interviews with SMEs provide an important source of information to support the necessary conceptual development.

The interviews we have conducted to inform the development of a model of cultural-general competence for military personnel have employed critical incident-based elicitation (Flanagan 1954; Rasmussen and Sieck 2015). Critical incident-based interviews are considered to belong among best research practices in disciplines such as human factors and personnel psychology (Hoffman et al. 1998; Campion et al. 2011).

Critical incident elicitation can be contrasted with other interview approaches that ask respondents to speculate on their competence or infer their own mental processes (cf. Ericsson and Simon 1993). A different set of responses are encouraged when SMEs are asked to report their beliefs and opinions about culture-general competencies, are asked to speculate about the component skills and knowledge that support culture-general competence, or are asked to assess their own competence levels. Critical incident approaches avoid those kinds of interview questions in favor of direct reporting of lived experiences.

The focus of our interviews with professionals in the military was on critical incidents in which the participants personally experienced challenging intercultural interactions during their most recent overseas assignment (Rasmussen and Sieck 2015). The participants' own examples of recent interactions were used as a point of departure for asking more focused questions designed to elicit information about ways specific competencies allowed participants to cope with intercultural challenges.

Each culture-general SME was interviewed individually by a pair of interviewers. One led the interview and the other took notes and listened for additional opportunities to ask follow-up questions. The interviews went into considerable depth, with each lasting about 2 h. The interviewers first asked participants to describe their background and professional history, focusing on their overseas assignments. Interviewers then asked the lead question to elicit an initial account of a critical incident. Subsequently they made additional passes through the account to elicit more detailed descriptions of the event, including the cultural others' behaviors, and the participant's in the moment assessments, actions, thoughts and reactions during the event.

We elicited the participants' personal experiences during overseas assignments in which cultural differences played a critical role or presented an obstacle. The lead question used to elicit such experiences was:

> Please tell me about a time, during your most recent overseas assignment, when you interacted with members of the local populace (civilians, tribal leaders, local officials, partnered forces, etc.), coalition partners, or third country nationals and found the interaction particularly challenging? (Rasmussen and Sieck 2015, p. 6)

If participants indicated they could recall more than one such experience, the interviewer would ask them to provide high level descriptions of two or three experiences and then picked one for further examination.

In this investigation, we incorporated past literature by using it to specify hypothesized competencies with clear behavioral indications. We identified a set of nine competency areas from a review of the literature related to intercultural competence (Rasmussen and Sieck 2015). The nine competency areas were: Cultural sense making, perspective taking, cultural knowledge, self-presentation, language proficiency, emotional self-regulation, managing affect and attitude toward difference, withholding and suspending judgment, and self-efficacy and confidence.

Again, each of these constructs was defined in terms of specific behaviors. These hypothesized competencies were translated into a set of open-ended questions that were designed to obtain detailed information about associated knowledge and skills. A semi-structured interview format was adopted in order to prevent biasing the SMEs towards these particular competencies. Specifically, the follow-up questions were only asked when the associated behaviors were mentioned by participants in the context of their reported incidents.

For example, if the participant made references to confusions or surprises in the context of an intercultural interaction, explicitly saying things like "I was puzzled", or "I didn't get it" the interviewer would come back to that specific part of the critical incident and ask detailed questions designed to elicit more information about the nature of the surprise and the participant's response to it, such as:

How was it different than what you expected?
What aspects of the situation/their behavior were you paying attention to?
What was it about the situation that let you determine what was happening?
How were you interpreting the situation/their behavior at that time?

Analysis of Verbal Protocols for Competency Model Development

It is common to take into account frequency information in competency model development. However, the frequencies are often limited to concrete tasks that can be readily self-assessed. With interview and other verbal protocol studies, a different, more comprehensive count of frequencies of competency use can be obtained. In interview studies, SMEs are not asked to report directly on their competence. Instead, they describe, in significant detail, their experience handling challenging situations. The researchers are able to extract tacit knowledge and skills from the transcripts using standard approaches for quantifying text-based data (Chi 1997). The basic process starts with the development of a scheme for coding the verbal protocol data by determining behavioral indicators of each of the competency categories. Analysts apply the scheme to determine instances where particular competencies occur in the transcripts. Then, the number of times a competency code appears is calculated for each participant. This provides the basis for computing frequency measures that are amenable to statistical analyses.

An important part of the process is to have two independent raters code the data, or at least a portion of the data, to establish reliability of the coding scheme. This helps to ensure that the competency categories are sufficiently well defined to be distinguishable. The process of developing a reliable coding scheme is iterative. In early phases, categories that tend to be confused are clarified, revised, or combined. The independent rating process serves a similar function with verbal protocol data as that of a factor analysis applied to questionnaire data.

Researchers use the final data to make comparisons between the competency categories, such as which competencies are indicated more often, relative to others. The data can also be used to identify potential supporting relationships between competencies. This is accomplished with an analysis of the cooccurrence relationships between competencies that arise in close proximity to one another in the incidents.

In addition to conducting a quantitative analysis to determine the frequencies of competency use, qualitative analyses can be used to obtain further insights from the data. For example, researchers can use thematic analysis to look for previously unidentified competencies. In addition, qualitative analyses can provide specific details related to competency use that help further define or redefine them. They also yield behavioral examples of ways the competencies are used, and aid in the determination of the precise knowledge and skills that comprise the competency category.

Although coding practices exist for extracting several kinds of information from text (see Saldaña 2012), we focus on the identification and explicit inclusion of knowledge and skills as compared with other potential aspects of competence that are sometimes discussed, such as abilities, traits, and attitudes, among others. We do this for both practical and theoretical reasons. First, knowledge and skills can be acquired, and so are the essential ingredients of a competency model intended to guide the development of education and training. Motivation and attitudes are also important, yet their direct inclusion is somewhat of a sensitive issue for informing instructional design. For example, learning objectives based on the model that imply students must hold certain attitudes regarding culture or cultural practices before they are considered to have mastered the content would be controversial. They are also not needed, as any attitude statement can be rewritten as a cause-effect type of knowledge element that specifies costs or benefits. As a simple example, consider the attitude statement, "I like culture." This statement can be instead expressed as a knowledge statement, such as, "Culture leads to mission success." In the latter case, learning objectives might be written along the lines of students being able to list the benefits of cultural information.

As an example of qualitative analysis helping to redefine a competency, consider the "cultural knowledge" code reported in the quantitative results of Rasmussen and Sieck (2015). As mentioned previously, this was one of the categories that was established from the literature review prior to data collection. And it was found to occur quite frequently within the data. Our original thinking was that the code might reveal different frameworks or dimensions of culture that were referred to repeatedly by the SMEs, thereby suggesting recurring items or categories of cultural knowledge that were commonly found to be useful within this professional community. Instead, by examining the interview excerpts tagged with that code, we found that the SMEs' cultural knowledge was richer and more idiosyncratic than would be expected by any of the common cultural frameworks. Furthermore, the items of cultural knowledge were often related to a SMEs' own personnel preferences and interests, or to the perceived preferences and interests of their conversation partners. For instance:

> I was really interested in their crossbows. So I went to a village with my interpreter and we were in a village museum, and the museum had a bunch of crossbows up on the wall. And I was asking one of the guys in the village museum, hey, does anybody still make these crossbows. He said, yes, yes we do. We have a crossbow maker, and it's sort of the village crossbow maker. That is what he does. So they brought this guy up there […] And I am asking him, we are talking about how he makes these things and technically how to do it; and I am really soaking this up. […] And I am out there for work, so I am really happy.

> I travel with gifts, no matter where I go. So when I show up, there's a gift to give. [I don't give it to them] the first time I meet them, it'll be the fourth or fifth time, because I don't want to look like I'm buying the way in. But, the fourth or fifth time I'll bring in a gift in and say, "Hey, I really enjoyed our interactions with each other." And that also gives me a chance to figure out their personality and what they might be…are they interested in food, alcohol, or knives. […] Then we'll talk about the things they're interested in. I learn more about it.

We additionally uncovered further information regarding SME views on the purpose of the cultural knowledge, such as why they wanted it and how they were using it. In addition to use of cultural knowledge to explain local behavior, SMEs also employed it the process of establishing rapport, deepening relationships, or developing or assessing trust as in the following example:

> When you're first meeting your interpreters, you have to figure out where they're coming from, what they believe…You have to weasel your way into it somehow, and maybe throw some hints out there… I know some nuggets of information that I think would kind of call your bluff-type of information. Like "what do you think of Massoud?" I'll just throw it out there and see what happens. Then I look for indicators, looking for any reason to doubt, and I guess that is the bottom line …So the more I know, the more I can roll in certain situations and test the water (from Rasmussen and Sieck 2015)

We thus revised competencies to include skills of selecting topics in a self-directed way as well as to reflect domain relevant applications of local cultural knowledge:

- Identifies key topics for study that enhance ability to operate in host country
- Uses cultural knowledge to assess risk within social and operational environment.

As these excerpts illustrate, our model is supported by behavioral evidence that goes beyond traditional self-report of opinions that one may have regarding what competencies are important to function effectively overseas. To take another example, many researchers have recognized that perspective taking is an important component of culture-general competence, and we have found that to be the case, as well. Beyond the high level statement, "perspective taking," critical incident interview data demonstrates the use of perspective taking in action. For example an Air Force Captain had accompanied his work team on a river rafting trip to get a sense of a certain mountain region in Turkey. Along the trip one of his colleagues was thrown from the raft and was possibly injured. The Turkish guide appeared to be more concerned with the schedule than with safety:

> I tried to put myself in his shoes…Maybe he is not intentionally trying to be a jerk, maybe sometimes or maybe he might care about my friend, but maybe he cares about feeding his family more. Maybe he is under some sort of financial pressure, because he might lose his job or something to that effect. Or maybe he is just upset; I have no idea. Maybe he went on 1,000 whitewater rafting trips in a row without having a flip over, and these bunch of stupid Americans broke his record. I don't know. But it seemed that he was very concerned about his schedule…I am trying to be as diplomatic as I can right now. Because someone is hurt, no matter who they are, we need to get that individual medical attention. [I have] to make sure that this guy doesn't get out of hand, because I don't know this guy from Adam.

Another example of perspective taking in action involves a U.S. major who is meeting the Columbian Marine unit whose military capabilities he has been assigned to assess. It illustrates the use of perspective taking to make sense of how foreign partners are viewing him and to adapt his strategy for interaction.

> My first exposure to the unit was very standoffish in regards to, not only do we see you from the military, or from the embassy, but now you are bringing us someone else that we have no clue who it is. And so immediately I caught on to that standoffish perspective and tried to build a rapport, you know, with, first of all, we are not there telling them, hey, we are here to analyze you and see what your capability is.

We have mentioned the importance of expressing a competency model in a language that is easily digestible by the population it supports. There is often a translation issue between scientific jargon and the ability to implement the ideas expressed by these technical terms into real world domains. Culture-general SMEs who are serving in a professional domain of interest naturally express aspects of culture-general competence in ways that fit within their community.

In our modeling efforts, we were careful to incorporate the expression of culture-general competencies by military personnel, and to restrain ourselves from introducing unnecessary scientific jargon. In addition, we wrote the knowledge and skills that form each competency as action-oriented statements, and included behavioral examples to further clarify the competency and its descriptive characteristics (Rasmussen et al. 2015). For example

- *Competency label*: Maintains a Mission Orientation
- *Competency definition*: Builds rapport and intercultural relationships to achieve mission objectives, using cultural knowledge and skills to develop, monitor, and maintain them.
- *Specific skill item*: Defines mission-relevant social objectives
- *Behavioral example of skill item*: Setting an objective to talk to the young Afghan soldiers who are still on guard on a religious day, so they will be more willing to help when needed.

As can be seen, the format of our model supports easy comprehension by military professionals, which is part of what makes it actionable for this community.

The latest version of the model, which we have termed Adaptive Readiness for Culture, describes 12 culture-general competencies. Each competency is further defined by several knowledge and skill items, along with corresponding behavioral examples for each (Rasmussen et al. 2015). We tested the generality of the model across key military specialties, as well as across services. The competencies were found throughout the sample, though skills appeared to be applied differently by distinct specialist groups.

This series of research studies make a unique contribution both to military leaders and trainers who are seeking pertinent, actionable guidance on how to prepare their personnel, as well as, to researchers who are intent on uncovering culture-general aspects of intercultural competence. For professionals in the military, the model emphasizes pragmatic skills that are vetted for relevance to the nature of their work. Because it was designed with a clear focus on informing instructional design, each element of the model represents a malleable knowledge or skill that is defined in behavioral terms. In addition, carefully defined criteria for selecting SMEs, such as experience living and working among multiple cultures, ensure that the model includes foundational knowledge and skills that generalize across cultures. For researchers interested in the cultural-general competence, the considerations, approach, and execution of our studies provide a template for the development of similar models in other professional domains.

References

Anderson, J. R. (1983). *The architecture of cognition*. Cambridge, MA: Harvard University Press.

Ang, S., Van Dyne, L., Koh, C., Ng, K. Y., Templer, K. J., Tay, C., & Chandrasekar, N. A. (2007). Cultural intelligence: Its measurement and effects on cultural judgment and decision making, cultural adaptation and task performance. *Management and Organization Review, 3*(3), 335–371.

Bennett, M. J. (1986). A developmental approach to training for intercultural sensitivity. *International Journal of Intercultural Relations, 10*, 179–196.

Bhawuk, D. P. (1998). The role of culture theory in cross-cultural training a multimethod study of culture-specific, culture-general, and culture theory-based assimilators. *Journal of Cross-Cultural Psychology, 29*(5), 630–655.

Bolden, C. A. (2012). The marine FAO program. *Marine Corps Gazette, 96*(6), 71–74.

Campion, M. A., Fink, A. A., Ruggeberg, B. J., Carr, L., Phillips, G. M., & Odman, R. B. (2011). Doing competencies well: Best practices in competency modeling. *Personnel Psychology, 64*, 225–262.

Chi, M. T. (1997). Quantifying qualitative analyses of verbal data: A practical guide. *The Journal of the Learning Sciences, 6*(3), 271–315.

Cushner, K., & Brislin, R. W. (1996). *Intercultural interactions: A practical guide* (2nd ed.). Thousand Oaks, CA: Sage.

Deardorff, D. K. (2006). Identification and assessment of intercultural competence as a student outcome of internationalization. *Journal of Studies in International Education, 10*(3), 241–266.

Deardorff, D. K. (2009). Synthesizing conceptualizations of intercultural competence. In D. K. Deardorff (Ed.), *The SAGE handbook of intercultural competence* (pp. 264–269). Thousand Oaks, CA: Sage.

Earley, P. C., & Peterson, R. S. (2004). The elusive cultural chameleon: Cultural intelligence as a new approach to intercultural training for the global manager. *Academy of Management Learning & Education, 3*(1), 100–115.

Endicott, L., Bock, T., & Narvaez, D. (2003). Moral reasoning, intercultural development, and multicultural experiences: Relations and cognitive underpinnings. *International Journal of Intercultural Relations, 27*(4), 403–419.

Ericsson, K. A., & Simon, H. A. (1993). *Protocol analysis: Verbal reports as data* (2nd ed.). Cambridge, MA: MIT Press.

Flanagan, J. C. (1954). The critical incident technique. *Psychological Bulletin, 51*(4), 327–358.

Hammer, M. R., Bennett, M. J., & Wiseman, R. L. (2003). Measuring intercultural sensitivity: The intercultural development inventory. *International Journal of Intercultural Relations, 27*, 421–443.

Hoffman, R. R., Crandall, B., & Shadbolt, N. (1998). Use of the critical decision method to elicit expert knowledge: A case study in the methodology of cognitive task analysis. *Human Factors: The Journal of the Human Factors and Ergonomics Society, 40*(2), 254–276.

Knowles, M. S., Holton, E. F, I. I. I., & Swanson, R. A. (2014). *The adult learner: The definitive classic in adult education and human resource development* (8th ed.). New York, NY: Routledge.

Matsumoto, D., LeRoux, J., Ratzlaff, C., Tatani, H., Uchida, H., Kim, C., & Araki, S. (2001). Development and validation of a measure of intercultural adjustment potential in Japanese sojourners: The Intercultural Adjustment Potential Scale (ICAPS). *International Journal of Intercultural Relations, 25*, 483–510.

McClelland, D. C. (1973). Testing for competence rather than for "intelligence". *American Psychologist, 28*, 1–14.

Osland, J. S., & Bird, A. (2000). Beyond sophisticated stereotyping: Cultural sensemaking in context. *Academy of Management Executive, 14*, 65–79.

Perkins, D. N., & Salomon, G. (1989). Are cognitive skills context bound? *Educational Researcher, 18*, 16–25.

Rasmussen, L. J., & Sieck, W. R. (2015). Culture-general competence: Evidence from a cognitive field study of professionals who work in many cultures. *International Journal of Intercultural Relations.48*, 75–90.

Rasmussen, L. J., Sieck, W. R., & Duran, J. L. (2015). *A model of culture-general competence for education and training: Validation across services and key specialties*. Yellow Springs, OH: Global Cognition.

Rodriguez, D., Patel, R., Bright, A., Gregory, D., & Gowing, M. K. (2002). Developing competency models to promote integrated human resource practices. *Human Resource Management, 41*(3), 309–324.

Saldaña, J. (2012). *The coding manual for qualitative researchers* (No. 14). New York: Sage Publications.

Schraagen, J. M., Chipman, S. F., & Shalin, V. L. (2000). *Cognitive task analysis*. Mahwah, NJ: Lawrence Erlbaum Associates.

Schwartz, S. H. (1992). Universals in the content and structure of values: Theoretical advances and empirical tests in 20 countries. *Advances in Experimental Social Psychology, 25*(1), 1–65.

Schwartz, S. H. (2014). Rethinking the concept and measurement of societal culture in light of empirical findings. *Journal of Cross-Cultural Psychology, 45*(1), 5–13.

Sieck, W. R., Smith, J. L., & Rasmussen, L. J. (2013). Metacognitive strategies for making sense of cross-cultural encounters. *Journal of Cross-Cultural Psychology, 44*(6), 1007–1023.

Spencer, L. M., & Spencer, S. M. (1993). *Competence at work: Models for superior performance*. Hoboken, NJ: Wiley.

Spitzberg, B. H., & Chagnon, G. (2009). Conceptualizing intercultural communication competence. In D. K. Deardorff (Ed.), *The SAGE handbook of intercultural competence* (pp. 2–52). Thousand Oaks, CA: Sage.

Van Oudenhoven, J. P., & Van der Zee, K. I. (2002). Predicting multicultural effectiveness of international students: The multicultural personality questionnaire. *International Journal of Intercultural Relations, 26*, 679–694.

Ward, C., & Fischer, R. (2008). Personality, cultural intelligence and cross-cultural adaptation: A test of the mediation hypothesis. In S. Ang & L. Van Dyne (Eds.), *Handbook of cultural intelligence: Theory, measurement, and applications* (pp. 159–173). Armonk, NY: M. E. Sharpe.

Yates, J. F. (1990). *Judgment and decision making*. Englewood Cliffs, NJ: Prentice-Hall Inc.

Chapter 4
Cultural Dilemmas and Sociocultural Encounters: An Approach for Understanding, Assessing, and Analyzing Culture

Jerry Glover, Harris Friedman and Marinus van Driel

The study of culture is almost as varied as the human experience. Originally the domain of anthropologists and sociologists, culture has emerged as a topic of interest and application in many disciplines, including the social sciences, management, and other areas in which people and their behaviors are important. Associated with the broader interest in culture by researchers from a variety of disciplines is a variation in how culture is conceived, explained, and assessed. Unfortunately, many professionals from those disciplines with newly found interest in culture have limited depth and breadth in their understanding of the concept. Ethnocentric theories and methods have sometimes emerged, while the 150 years of cultural research in anthropology and sociology has been mostly overlooked. We believe that culture must be studied with theories congruent with it as a subject, based on culturally relative research methods appropriate for the collection and analysis of cultural data. It is our concern that the "cultures of people who study culture" needs to be an important consideration to avoid limited disciplinary perspectives (Glover and Friedman 2015).

This chapter is based on Glover and Friedman (2015).

J. Glover
Institute for Culturally Adaptive Leadership, 1270 Tom Coker Road, LaBelle,
FL 33935, USA
e-mail: jerryglover75@gmail.com

H. Friedman (✉)
Goddard College, 1270 Tom Coker Road, LaBelle, FL 33935, USA
e-mail: harrisfriedman@hotmail.com

M. van Driel
cut-e USA Inc., 1345 Park Avenue, 17th Floor, c/o Enterprise Ireland,
New York, NY 10154-0037, USA
e-mail: marinus.van.driel@cut-e.com

© Springer International Publishing Switzerland 2016   53
J.L. Wildman et al. (eds.), *Critical Issues in Cross Cultural Management*,
DOI 10.1007/978-3-319-42166-7_4

We propose a three-part approach to the study and application of culture. Those three parts are (1) prerequisites for understanding culture, (2) frameworks designed for making culture operational, and (3) methods that permit the collection and analysis of data with minimal biases from national, disciplinary, institutional, and other limiting paradigms. We propose our approach as the basis for the scientific study of culture that is fundamentally necessary for developing transcultural competence through appropriate perspectives (theories) and approaches (methods).

Prerequisites for Transcultural Competence

All human interactions occur in cultural contexts and require different types of competence to be effective. Transcultural competence refers to being able to adaptively operate within diverse cultural contexts without knowing in advance the specifics of any culture but, rather, through being able to have a more general understanding as to how culture works within any context. The following are what we consider prerequisites for this type of competence.

Cultural Relativity

Cultural dilemmas do not lead to judgments with right answers. Rather they reflect profound cultural differences that first have to be recognized and respected. A prerequisite for transcultural competence involves embracing cultural relativity, which means not privileging any cultural difference as being inherently better or worse. Privileging one way as being best when that singular way happens to be that of one's own culture constitutes ethnocentrism.

Ethnocentrism is often the reason for professional and disciplinary biases in the way culture is defined and operationalized. One of the best ways to grow beyond ethnocentrism is by gaining experiences in different cultures, which can lead to recognizing one's own culture more clearly as a culture, as well as respecting the cultures of others (Glover and Friedman 2015).

Achieving Synchronic and Diachronic Perspectives

Synchronic perspectives look at people in the present broadly across space (e.g., cross-culturally), whereas diachronic perspectives look at people throughout time (e.g., through tradition and history). As an example, understanding how humans make decisions requires looking across different cultures (using a synchronic perspective), which includes decision-making used by all humans, not just those taken from one culture. When decision-making is observed across the continuum of human culture that exists in the contemporary global community, a wide range of cultural perspectives and practices for making decisions are found. An American who wants to negotiate a contract in locations such as Japan, China, and the Middle East may become very frustrated because the American contractual models for negotiations and decision-making are not practiced in those different cultural settings.

In addition, cultures do not arise in a vacuum, but always have a historical context. Another prerequisite to transcultural competency is developing a sense of how things became what they are, not just what they are in the present. A diachronic perspective allows looking across time. In cultures that privilege the present and future at the expense of the past, such as in much of the U.S.A., this view presents temporal limitations for deep understanding.

Holistic Vantage

Having a view in which all aspects of a culture are taken into consideration is another prerequisite to transcultural competency. A culture's economic, political, religious, and other institutions are all crucial to consider. Focusing only on just one-dimensional variables, such as currently observed behavior, lack holism. Without holistic perspectives, professional researchers and practitioners may not realize the obvious, that the "whole is greater than the sum of its parts." In cultures, it is especially important to recognize that components are always interrelated. In fact, relationships may hold more importance than any specific cultural components in understanding culture and cultural differences. A failure to see the "bigger picture" in a cultural context may lead to unanticipated consequences, faculty theoretical perspectives, and flawed methods for understanding culture and how it works.

Understanding Values

Cross-cultural studies have revealed many important cultural values dimensions, and understanding these is another prerequisite for transcultural competence. Although there are many value dimensions that can be explored, we illustrate the *universal-particular* and *specific-diffuse* dimensions. Universal values involves wanting everything to be uniform, without exceptions. For example, a discipline's focus on finding "laws" that account for all cultural differences illustrates universalism, while particularism would involve respecting variations by not attempting to find invariances across all settings. Specific values refers to setting clear boundaries, such as separating business from social roles, while diffuse values refers to allowing more permeable boundaries, as in treating business associates as family.

Appropriate Frameworks for Understanding and Analyzing Culture

The fields of anthropology and, to a lesser extent, sociology have focused on understanding culture from the perspective of value dimensions for over a century, as well as have emphasized the prerequisites we have discussed: cultural relativity, both synchronic and diachronic perspectives, holism, and value dimensions. Further, we rely on cultural values dimensions to provide a framework that meets the prerequisites we expect.

Cultural Dimensions

Cultural dimensions are based on cultural values (Trompenaars and Hampden-Turner 2002; Hofstede 2005). Cultural values are essentially what is important to people. Values are embedded in the worldviews, beliefs, and paradigms held by people from different societies, organizations, ethnic groups, and other social groups. We use Trompenaars and Hampden Turner's "7D" model to provide a framework for cultural values dimensions. This model includes the values of individual-collective, universal-particular, achievement-ascription, neutral-affective, specific-diffuse, internal–external, and time (sequential-synchronic and past–present–future). These values dimensions can be used to observe, understand, and analyze human behavior in any setting, regardless of the location and sociocultural context.

Sociocultural Encounters (SCE)

A SCE occurs in any situation in which there are social actors meeting with other social actors. Each SCE has a context, stakeholders with cultural values orientations that may differ, as well as various other dynamics, such as power differentials. These hold the potential for generating cultural dilemmas, situations in which values may seem in opposition. Cultural dilemmas never simply have a right or wrong answer, as values are subject to cultural relativity, but rather they involve a nuanced response to differing worldviews. We consider the SCE concept as a means for providing a culturally relative conceptual framework, for there are no absolute right or wrong answers in dealing with SCEs, but there is only what does or does not work within a given cultural context. During SCEs in which cultural dilemmas need to be handled, certain performances of actors may be more or less adaptive, but these are not based on any rote application of simple rules. In brief, SCEs provide an entrée to better conceptually frame culture without either losing relevance or imposing one's own culture in understanding others' culture.

All human interactions, including mono-, multi-, cross-, and transcultural ones, take place within a SCE. For example, early humans began to develop cultural knowledge as a means for adapting to a variety of ecological and social contexts. SCEs were the location and means by which early language, social relations, and cooperative activities among band and tribal members developed. SCEs were the settings for human knowledge acquisition and transfer within and across societies. SCEs became the platform for subsistence acquisition and sharing, economic exchanges, kinship, socialization, conflicts, and all the human activities recognized as human culture. Further, worldviews, beliefs, and values formed the basis for actors' behaviors within SCEs. Last, SCEs provide opportunities for observation and replication, allowing a scientific approach not dependent only on self-report methods.

Making Culture Operational

The methodological approach we present derives from these long-standing traditions, meets the prerequisites identified as necessary for culturally valid scientific work, and is grounded in the cultural values dimensions. We use SCEs to scientifically operationalize our approach through mixed methods, employing both qualitative and quantitative, as well as other (e.g., graphical) approaches to gathering and analyzing data in what we call *cultural metrics*. Theories and methods for transcultural competence must be appropriate for any local situation, yet have relevance across all of humanity to be valid.

Cultural metrics meet the prerequisites for validity in researching and working with culture. Our scientific approach is culturally relative, both synchronic and diachronic, holistic, and involves value dimensions. SCEs provide opportunities for gathering data that meet the standards of science (e.g., observability, minimizing biases, replication, etc.), while cultural value dimensions provide the framework from which we interpret SCEs.

Cultural dilemmas occur, and can be observed, during SCEs in which there are actors with different and often competing and even conflicting worldviews, beliefs, and values. These dilemmas involve differences that are often not well understood by the actors involved, who may approach the dilemma from their ethnocentric vantage, while being relatively blind to the vantage point of the other. SCEs are fundamental to our approach to culture, but it is the concept of cultural dilemmas that holds the real power during SCEs. The outcome of SCEs in which cultural dilemmas need to be handled provides our way to approach transcultural competence operationally. When cultural dilemmas are handled successfully, this reflects high transcultural competence in that context. This approach is culturally relative in that what might work well within one cultural context might fail abysmally in another, so there are literally no right or wrong ways to demonstrate transcultural competence. Instead, there are adaptive behaviors (Glover et al. 2002) that work within the SCE and involve interactional, not just individual, attributes.

Transcultural competence in reconciling and realizing cultural dilemmas within SCEs is fundamental for creating adaptive responses.

Cultural dilemmas are found in all sociocultural contexts, and are particularly relevant in culturally diverse situations (SCEs). We focus on illustrating how to resolve conflicts in two culturally diverse situations using this approach. The following two cases are examples of dilemmas we have used in our work. Each illustrates a different value dimension.

Aligning Vision and Values

Commonly corporate, government, and community leaders develop vision statements in the belief that it will result in improving performance of employees. That may or may not be the case in specific organizations. However, for these vision statements to be effective, they need to be experienced as real by the employees and consumers, not just as empty rhetoric.

Two of us (Glover and Friedman) conducted an organizational culture project involving the merger of a financial services company with a government-owned bank in the South Pacific. The cultural dilemmas method had been used to assess the cultural values among stakeholders and functional areas in both organizations. Our goal was to use the data from the assessment to anticipate potential merger problems and to create appropriate change initiatives to smooth the transformation. In other words, we conducted a "cultural due diligence" assessment for the merger.

The content of the assessment had been based on cultural dilemmas elicited in focus groups and interviews in both the financial services company and the bank. After constructing and administering a cultural dilemmas instrument, we met with the executives of the newly merged organization to present the results.

As we arrived in the venue for the meeting, we noticed a large banner draped on the wall. It stated the newly formed company's vision, which the executives had developed in a consultant-led retreat the previous weekend. The CEO told us that the new vision statement would be the guiding influence on the merger as it progressed. The vision was simple and well-stated: "We will be the leader in our region in providing quality financial solutions which exceed our customers' expectations." The executives appeared to be quite happy with the statement until we raised the issue of a dilemma identified in the cultural merger assessment.

One of the cultural assessment items we had asked staff from both companies to address posed this dilemma: "A long standing and important customer walks into a sales office and requests an exception to the loan limit on his existing insurance policy. What action should be taken with the customer's request?" When we reviewed the responses given, we found some interesting differences between functional areas in the company. Accountants in both companies had chosen the response "do not approve the exception," while sales and marketing staff had chosen the response "give the exception."

The problem presented to the executives of both merging organizations was not just the different responses, but matching the reality of this dilemma to the new vision statement. It became obvious to the executives that they would need to do more than just post an aspirational banner in their meeting room. They needed to find ways to make the vision operational in the workplace and with the company's interactions with its customers. If they met the customers' needs, many of the fiscal policies developed to manage the company might have to be changed. On the other hand, if they held the line and denied the customer's request for an exception, they would be disingenuous to their vision.

This cultural dilemma primarily involves tension within a universal-particular value continuum. The universal pole of the continuum involves a one-size fits all approach to every situation, whereas the particularistic pole involves a recognition of the uniqueness of each situation. This dilemma illustrates a common problem faced by many leaders, and has no clear solutions. It involves the universal value that the "rules are the rules" without exception, as opposed to a particular value that catering to a specific customer evidences good customer services. It is no surprise that accounting preferred the former position, while sales and marketing preferred the latter. By working with such conflicts, organizational culture can be accurately assessed and appropriate interventions, such as working to align vision statements to the reality of the day-to day operations of an organization, can be used to reconcile and realize such dilemmas. Clarifying techniques include identifying values, stakeholders, and other important aspects of the dilemma without imposing any right answer.

Hookah Pipe Dilemma

We (all three authors) harvested a perplexing dilemma from actual experiences of U.S. warfighters who had missions to build rapport with the elders of a traditional rural village in Afghanistan (Friedman et al. 2013). The village was located in an important area of a region occupied by so-called insurgents. Winning the support and cooperation of the village elders was critical to the security of the region.

When entering this village to search for hidden weapons, the warfighters were offered a hookah pipe by the Afghan elders. The interpreters explained that the elders would be insulted if the warfighters refused to participate in this ritual, but the pipe probably contained hashish, which is against military law. If warfighters did not smoke, then lives could be lost through not finding the hidden weapons, but to smoke could result in dire consequences for the warfighters.

When presented with this dilemma, warfighters varied greatly in their responses, suggesting it is a valid dilemma without a clear right or wrong answer. This dilemma involves the cultural value dimension of specific-diffuse, namely the warfighter might tend to hold specific U.S. values to get down to business (as in finding the weapons), while the values of the elders might be more diffuse, demanding time to first build a trusting relationship through the hookah ceremony before revealing where the weapons are hidden. Examining this dilemma helped assess underlying dynamics important for transcultural competence in this population, as well as frame appropriate training and other goals.

Using cultural dilemmas provides a practical avenue toward developing and employing transcultural competence, as well as researching it. Dilemmas can be used to both assess and intervene. Although using dilemmas requiring interaction within SCEs may be less convenient and more expensive than performing individual-based assessments and interventions, they offer great potential for dealing with the complexity of culture.

Conclusion

We have presented an approach for understanding, assessing, and developing transcultural competence based on a scientifically rigorous approach to culture. We have identified prerequisites necessary for minimizing conceptual flaws and methodological biases, including cultural relativity, synchronic and diachronic perspectives, holism, and understanding values dimensions. Our approach also includes a framework for using cultural values dimensions. SCEs and cultural dilemmas are used to make culture operational and replicable for furthering understanding and applications. Two cultural dilemmas are shown, illustrating how we have engaged relevant processes related to transcultural competence. We recommend this cultural metric approach for assessing and developing transcultural competence in a scientifically based manner.

References

Friedman, H., Glover, G., Sims, E., Culhane, E., Guest, M., & Van Driel, M. (2013). Cross-cultural competence: Performance-based assessment and training. *Organizational Development Journal, 31*(2), 18–30.

Glover, J., & Friedman, H. (2015). *Transcultural competence: Navigating cultural differences in the global community.* Washington, DC: American Psychological Association.

Glover, G., Friedman, H., & Jones, G. (2002). Adaptive leadership: When change is not enough—Part One. *Organizational Development Journal, 20*, 15–31.

Hofstede, G. (2005). *Culture's consequences. Comparing values, behaviors, institutions, and organizations across nations.* Thousand Oaks, CA: Sage Publications.

Trompenaars, F., & Hampden-Turner, C. (2002). *Riding the waves of culture: Understanding cultural diversity in business.* New York: McGraw Hill.

Chapter 5
Conflict Competence in a Multicultural World

Craig Runde and Brigitte K. Armon

When people are asked if conflict is inevitable in the workplace environment, most respond in the affirmative. This is equally true in Shanghai, Berlin, and New York. So, it is not really a question of whether we will experience conflict, but more importantly, what will come from it.

As a training exercise, we frequently have people share words that come to mind when they think about conflict. Common responses include terms like *stress*, *frustration*, and *tension*. When groups are asked to characterize the words they use to describe conflict, they categorize a majority of the words as negative in nature time and time again.

In a follow-up question, we ask people how they usually deal with organizational conflicts. The overwhelming majority of responses suggest that they usually avoid addressing these conflicts. A much smaller percentage describe angry confrontations. Together the descriptions mirror the survival instinct of *fight* or *flight*. Although people typically use these types of approaches, they also readily admit that neither is particularly effective.

So people in organizational contexts are faced inevitably with conflicts—that they perceive as negative—over the course of which they typically default to fight or flight responses that do not work. When asked why this is so, most people say that they have never learned how to deal with conflict and become anxious when it arises. These ineffectual conflict strategies to which individuals default may well be

C. Runde
Center for Conflict Dynamics and Mediation Training Institute at Eckerd College, 4200 54th Avenue South, St. Petersburg, FL 33711, USA
e-mail: rundece@eckerd.edu

B.K. Armon (✉)
Organizational Effectiveness, Cox Communications, 6205-B Peachtree Dunwoody Road NE, Atlanta, GA 30328, USA
e-mail: brigitte.armon@cox.com

© Springer International Publishing Switzerland 2016
J.L. Wildman et al. (eds.), *Critical Issues in Cross Cultural Management*,
DOI 10.1007/978-3-319-42166-7_5

behind research results that suggest that workplace conflict is very difficult to manage productively (DeDreu and Weingardt 2003).

The common responses to the types of questions mentioned above suggest that some elements of our experience of conflict are related to our human nature. Our evolutionary heritage has equipped us as a species to be able to recognize and respond to certain kinds of threats. For example, humans and other primates are hardwired to be able to recognize snakes as possible threats (Van Le et al. 2013). Moreover, our limbic system produces similar responses to social stimuli. Thus, beyond responding to purely physical and environmental dangers, our limbic system can be activated by workplace situations that we perceive as threats to our interests. When others behave in ways that threaten our position or well-being, they can activate a neural auto-appraisal system, resulting in emotional to response to social threats that mirror reactions to environmental dangers (Ekman 2003). In other words, even though these threats are not life threatening, they provoke primal responses common to most people.

While humans share a number of common elements of conflict, culture contributes to our considerable variety of responses to it (Ting-Toomey and Oetzel 2001). We may all get anxious or upset when faced with threats to our well-being at work, but people from various cultural backgrounds may behave quite differently in these situations. Thus, in global society in which intercultural interactions are common, it is essential to explore the impact of culture on conflict and conflict resolution. The first step to optimizing conflict outcomes in intercultural settings is to consider the ways in which culture contributes to individuals' understanding of and response to conflict.

Culture can be thought of as imperfectly shared system of meaning (Rohner 1984). While there are multiple approaches to understanding culture, the constructivist approach offers a clear lens for understanding how culture shapes conflict across and between cultures (Paletz et al. 2014). Culture influences individuals' mental models—their explanations of the world around them—that guide their attention, evidence search, interpretation, and inference (e.g., Weber and Morris 2010). Through its sway on individuals' mental models, culture influence the sources of conflict by directing attention to different cues and behaviors as well as by coding those cues and behaviors as harmless or threatening. It further impacts the prevalence, appropriateness, and effectiveness of different conflict management styles.

For example, in honor cultures, typically found in the Southern Unites States, Middle East, Latin America, and around the Mediterranean (Cohen et al. 1996; Leung and Cohen 2011; Rodriguez Mosquera et al. 2000), individuals base their judgments of self-worth on their ability to live up to a set of culturally determined behavioral guidelines and their reputation within their communities. Their value is, then, partially external to the individual. Good people in these cultures are those people known by the community to act properly. This definition of self-worth contrasts the one commonly held by individuals in dignity cultures, mostly in the

Northern United States and Northern Europe, who believe that individual worth is inherent, residing within individuals and, therefore, more resilient to the judgments of others. One's reputation as a good person not related to one's own evaluation of self-worth in a dignity culture.

With regard to conflict, the strict behavioral guidelines and the focus on reputation of honor cultures impact both sources and management of conflict. While insults may spur conflict world over, individuals from honor cultures are more likely than those from dignity cultures to respond aggressively or to escalate conflict (Beersma et al. 2003; Cohen et al. 1996; IJzerman et al. 2007; Rodriguez Mosquera et al. 2008). Northern American children learn "I am rubber and you are glue, whatever you say bounces off of me and sticks to you." In contrast, Southern American children learn that more aggressive responses to insults may be justifiable, rather than censurable. However, more recent research highlights a contrasting effect resulting from the strict norms of hospitality and politeness common to many honor cultures (Harinck et al. 2013). This research suggests that in the absence of insult, individuals from honor cultures react more constructively to conflict than individuals from dignity cultures, because deviations from polite behavior are heavily frowned upon. Consider the case of a tedious coworker whose insistence on his own less than insightful plan might be holding up the progress of a meeting. Following the logic of this new research suggests that individuals from honor cultures, bound more strictly to norms regarding appropriate meeting conduct, may be more likely than individuals from dignity cultures to hold back the sigh, face, or comment that would devolve this hypothetical task conflict into relationship conflict.

Other cultural variables, such as collectivism and concern for face, play a part in determining the prevalence and appropriateness of conflict management styles. Membership in face cultures, which are characterized by an increased concern for maintaining social standing and reputation, increases the likelihood of individuals choosing avoiding and accommodating styles of conflict resolution, as they are concerned with causing others to lose face (e.g., Oetzel et al. 2001; Oetzel and Ting-Toomey 2003; Sadri 2013). Individuals from collectivistic cultures may choose the same strategies, fearing that direct conflict may damage relationships, though their choice may be influenced by the other person's status as in-group or out-group. Providing more evidence of the essential influence of culture on conflict, researchers have discovered two types of avoidance in Chinese conflict management styles: disintegration and harmony-enhancing avoidance. These two styles allow for the distinction between the adaptive and useful form of avoidance that promotes relationship well-being and the more maladaptive form that leads to the destruction of relationships (Leung and Brew 2009).

Conflict is inevitable and most people respond in ways that lead to ineffective outcomes. These individual failings also contribute to organizational problems. When conflict is not managed well, tensions can mount, relationships can be damaged, and productivity can be eroded. On the other hand, effective management of conflicts can contribute to enhanced creativity and decision-making, and improved organizational effectiveness. As a consequence, it is important for leaders to improve their personal competence in managing conflict and to enhance their organizations' responses to it.

On an individual level, leaders need to better understand conflict dynamics, enhance their self-awareness of how they personally respond to conflict, improve their ability to manage their conflict emotions, clarify their understanding of what is happening in conflict situations, and engage others in a constructive manner. From an organizational perspective, leaders need to foster a climate where conflicts can be addressed effectively and promote systems to help individuals explore options for resolving issues constructively.

This chapter provides an overview of the cognitive, emotional, and behavioral skills individuals need to be conflict competent leaders and teammates. Specifically, this chapter addresses the need for self-awareness, reflection, emotion and behavior regulation, as well as differences in conflict resolution styles. It also explores the importance of developing normative approaches to conflict that enable teams and larger groups to interact more effectively in conflicts. In each case, it considers the unique adjustments required to address conflicts with people from different cultural backgrounds in order to further elevate individual's ability to navigate intercultural conflict.

In the following sections the specific elements of conflict competence will be discussed from in practical context. These include cognitive aspects related to understanding conflict dynamics and improving personal self-awareness of one's own responses to conflict. Emotional regulation and related reflective processes will be explored to help illustrate how "cooling down" and "slowing down" can help prepare people to engage with others. Constructive behavioral responses will be examined because these can influence how conflict conversations unfold. Finally, the importance of creating norms for how teams and groups respond to conflict will be reviewed. These norms can provide legitimacy for using the cognitive, emotional, and behavioral techniques described in the other sections.

Understanding Conflict Dynamics

As mentioned earlier, most people tend to avoid dealing with conflict because of the anxiety it creates and their lack of skills and strategies to manage it. Understanding more about the dynamics of conflict situations can help leaders and others improve their own self-confidence. Part of this process involves exploring individuals' attitudes towards conflict and how those attitudes affect their approaches in managing it (Runde and Flanagan 2010). This aspect of improving conflict competence also involves studying cultural differences in conflict management (Ting-Toomey and Oetzel 2001). Improved understanding of cultural differences can help explain why these differences can contribute to the initiation of conflict as well as how they complicate the resolution of conflict.

For example, in some cultures people prefer to tell others how they are feeling about a conflict and view this type of interaction as honest sharing, helpful to improving understanding. Other cultures view emotional expressiveness as too direct and likely escalate the situation. Appreciating how others view these matters enables a person to be able to consciously choose how to adjust their behaviors to best adapt to the situation and the others involved in it.

Enhancing Self-awareness

Conflict competent leaders take time to explore the ways in which they respond to conflict. When they know more about what upsets them, their preferred approach to conflict, and the behavior patterns they typically use to resolve conflicts, leaders are able to leverage areas of strength and work on improving the aspects that do not serve them and their organizations well. Thus, a degree of self-awareness is necessary to effectively manage conflict. Assessment instruments can be very effective in improving conflict self-awareness. The Conflict Dynamics Profile can be used to measure conflict triggers (i.e., behaviors in others that upset an individual) and an individual's typical patterns of behavioral responses when triggered. The Thomas-Kilmann Conflict Mode Instrument works to measure more general conflict styles (i.e., preferred approaches to addressing conflict; Runde and Flanagan 2010).

Some assessments also help illustrate personal styles related to intercultural conflict. One instrument, the Intercultural Conflict Style Inventory, measures two domains. The first domain is the degree of emotional expressiveness versus emotional reserve individuals demonstrate in conflict. The second domain captured is the degree to which people utilize direct versus indirect styles to communicate the substantive aspects of the conflict (Hammer 2005). Knowing one's own style helps clarify difficulties that could arise when interacting with someone of a different style in conflict contexts.

Consider a small intercultural team in which two of the team members disagree about content of an important presentation. From the perspective of the team member whose conflict style is expressive and direct, the group discussion seems strangely circular—they keep returning to the same "settled" sections of the presentation, and she has to keep repeating her point of view before they can, without actually changing anything, move on again. Does her Norwegian colleague not understand the point she is making? Not realizing the extent of disagreement experienced by her non-expressive and indirect colleague as he continues to return to "settled" topics, she blithely risks relationship damage and a disenfranchised teammate. Counterfactually, awareness of these differences would have given her insight into the potential discontent of her colleague and promoted a more fruitful (and shorter) discussion.

Regulating Emotions

Conflict and emotions are closely intertwined. When people are asked why conflict can be difficult to manage, emotional stress is mentioned usually. While there are cultural differences in the way people handle the emotions surrounding conflict, it is almost always present and challenging.

Emotions arise during conflict from individual perceptions regarding the situation. Our interpretations of the things we have seen and heard either align or misalign with our values or expectations. In cases where they do not align well, people typically become upset, angry or anxious. When this happens, their ability to maintain an open mind is compromised (Frederickson 2001). If, for example, a situation in which, running late, one employee jumps the queue for the communal printer in order to make it on time to an important meeting. Another employee individual becomes angry, because a coworker has violated a norm. They may interpret the behavior as evidence of untrustworthiness, a demonstration of a deficit in benevolence, even if the norm violation occurred only due to cultural differences regarding "normal" behavior. Future interactions between the two employees may be colored by increased suspicion on the part of the second employee, to the bafflement of the first, who has not even registered a conscious wrongdoing.

Conflict competent leaders learn how to manage their emotions so they can regain composure and think more clearly about matters. In one instance, a surgeon was challenged by a nurse during an operation. Traditionally, the doctor would have exploded at the nurse, but he had recently taken a conflict management course, during which he first learned tot control his initial emotional response and then calmly inquire after the other person's point of view. In this case, the nurse, upon inquiry, raised an overlooked, yet key issue. If he had not stopped to listen, it is likely that he would have made a life threatening error. There are a number of research-based strategies that can be utilized to calm emotional knee-jerks. Some involve attentional deployment processes to refocus an individual away from issues that have been causing the upset. These processes are supported by various techniques including various centering and breathing methods and mindfulness practices (Runde and Flanagan 2012; Siegel 2010). Other approaches use a process called cognitive reappraisal, which has individuals search for alternative, nonhostile interpretations of the conflict (Ochsner and Gross 2005).

Leaders can also build their resilience to negative conflict emotions by cultivating and fostering the experience of positive emotions. These positive emotions can help serve as an antidote to negative emotions when they arise, acting as a sort of buffer for negative emotional experiences. They improve emotional resilience, making it easier to regain balance and bounce back in times of stress (Frederickson 2011).

Slowing Down and Reflecting on Conflict

When a person is upset, it can be difficult to manage emotions. In the heat of the moment, one may do or say something one regrettable or outside of one's typical behavior. As a consequence, it is suggested to have an arsenal of strategies at hand that effectively slow the escalation of conflict and create additional time in order to regain composure. For instance, one can request a short break. As a conflict picks of steam, it is possible to tell the other person that the issue is an important one and you would like some additional time to reflect on it. Buying time to calm down is particularly important for people from high emotionally expressive cultures when dealing with others from more emotionally reserved ones. An emotionally expressive individual is at a higher risk for saying something the more reserved individual will find incredibly inappropriate or offense. A key component of these strategies is practice or at least mental rehearsal. These techniques are the most helpful when they can be employed without having to think them through in the moment, because thinking is more difficult when people are under the grip of negative emotions (Frederickson 2001).

Conflict can be very chaotic and confusing. Before taking steps to address the conflict, it is important to gain a better understanding of what is happening and clarify how you want the issue at hand to be resolved. Once a person has regained balance of their emotions, with less of the constraint strong negative emotions can place on constructive thought, they can then explore potential disconnections in perceptions, values, and preferences that might be the root of the conflict. Considering who is involved, understanding their respective interests, and reflecting on one's own experience of the conflict can help clarify matters before taking further steps (Runde 2014).

When reflecting on the experience of conflict, it is useful to consider multiple viewpoints. This includes one's own perceptions, thoughts, and feelings about a situation as well as those of others involved in the conflict. Thinking about parties' interests in advance of discussions provides a basis for developing solutions designed to address what each one wants to achieve. Creating win-win solutions rests on addressing these needs and builds the framework for more sustainable outcomes. Before reentering a potentially contentious discussion consider the priorities and goals of the other person—what they might want from the situation—and how their desired outcomes can be achieved in conjunction with your own. Step into their shoes, too. Take what you know about their values and preferences and reflect on how their mindset influences their interpretation of the situation. Conflict competent leaders enter into conflict situations forearmed with their reflections.

Engaging Constructively

Having managed emotions and reflected on the nature of the conflict, an individual may then engage tactics to help resolve the situation. It is in this phase of conflict that we see the largest differences among cultures. For example, some emphasize the resolution of the substantive differences (e.g., many North American and Northern European cultures), while others focus on supporting the ongoing relationship of the parties (e.g., many Asian cultures) (Hammer 2005). The specific behaviors enacted to address conflicts will differ to match each culture's preferred focus for resolution. Individualist cultures such as those found in much of North America and Western Europe tend to favor active behaviors like perspective taking, listening for understanding, expressing thoughts and feelings, and creating solutions. They are seen as more likely to contribute to the constructive resolution of the substantive issues associated with the conflict (Runde and Flanagan 2012). In collectivist cultures, more indirect approaches, such as withholding emotional expression, sharing messages through third parties, or mediation, are seen as more constructive in that they preserve the relationship threatened by the conflict.

Both approaches have their merits and work within their respective cultural contexts when all of the parties abide by similar cultural norms, though emotional strain permeates conflict even when parties share resolution styles. Yet, when the disputants come from cultural backgrounds whose norms present distinctly different approaches about conflict resolution, the challenges and potential for suboptimal solutions and relationship damage increase. In these cases, an already challenging situation is complicated by not understanding how to interact with someone whose behavioral approaches may differ from one's own. Negotiations between American and Chinese managers provide a frequently cited example of this struggle. American managers often have a shorter term focus and want to address substantive issues in a very direct manner. Their Chinese counterparts may show more concern about the relationships and prefer a longer term approach. In such cases the Americans may make specific suggestions which are met with nods from the Chinese. The Americans may take the nods as agreement, whereas the Chinese may have only meant "I am listening" and actually disagree with their suggestions.

Fortunately, research is emerging that suggests that improving one's intercultural competency may help resolve conflicts involving people with different cultural backgrounds. Intercultural competency may be defined as a "person's capability to function effectively in situations characterized by cultural diversity" (Van Dyne and Nielsen 2007). While the exact nature of intercultural competency remains hotly debated (for a recent review see: Leung et al. 2014), work with one particular conceptualization of the construct demonstrates the promise of these competencies for individuals facing cross-cultural conflict: Cultural Intelligence (CQ; Earley and Ang 2003). This construct partitions intercultural competence into four intercultural capabilities: metacognitive CQ (i.e., one's ability to gain and understand cultural knowledge), cognitive CQ (i.e., one's mental library of cultural information), motivational CQ (i.e., one's ability to devote and sustain energy towards intercultural dealings), and behavioral CQ (i.e., one's ability to behave flexibly in intercultural dealings). CQ has been shown to be important for leadership development in general (Kim and Van Dyne 2012) and, more specifically, related to the ability to generate more effective outcomes in negotiations (Umai and Gelfand 2010). It has also been found to promote sharing of ideas with culturally different others (Chua et al. 2012) and intercultural cooperation (Mor et al. 2013). Additionally, CQ has also been found to help promote the use of more constructive forms of conflict responses (Reguieg 2014). It appears to promote and enhance curiosity about what is happening in a multicultural conflict context. This curiosity can help open people to try to understand the viewpoints of others in the conflict. Improved understanding can help illuminate the parties' respective interests and make it more possible to find solutions that both preserve relationships and address differences.

Cross-cultural training, language training, and cultural immersion experiences have all been found be help improve CQ as it pertains to enhancing cross-cultural conflict resolution processes (Reguieg 2014). Leaders dealing with cross-cultural contexts should look into these types of learning experiences to help them appreciate other cultures more fully and to help them deal more effectively with conflicts which will arise in these settings.

Creating Effective Team and Organizational Norms

Conflict is stressful for individuals. While they know it is inevitable, they rarely prepare for ways to handle it in advance. Yet, developing norms and an organizational culture for how to address the inevitable differences that arise is crucial for supporting effective conflict management processes (Runde and Flanagan 2008). As highlighted above, however, the specific approaches must take into account culture-bound variance preferences. Often the norms will need to be adjusted to acknowledge the multicultural reality of today's organizations.

Leaders seeking to build productive conflict resolution processes into their cultures will want to get involved in promoting the acknowledgement of conflict as something that happens universally. Leaders may consider extra vigilance during the launch of new intercultural teams, as this time is a key window of opportunity for productive norm development, as well as overseeing the creation of a team charter that includes a conflict resolution plan (Burke et al. 2010). Individuals should be encouraged to work out their differences in ways that respect each others' cultures and find creative solutions that provide positive outcomes for those involved and for the organization. Such a conflict competent organization can foster positive interpersonal relationships and high performance.

Conclusion

Conflict is inevitable in intercultural organizations. Thus, it is not a question of whether conflict will happen, but rather what will result from it. Conflict can be challenging enough between people of the same culture. When it involves individuals from different cultures, the processes become more complex due to variances in the ways cultures address conflict.

In order to manage conflicts more effectively, individuals need to:

- Better understand the basic dynamics of conflict and their own responses to it,
- Improve their own emotional intelligence including the ability to regulate their emotions while under pressure, and
- Use constructive communications techniques to discover how various parties view the conflict and work to develop mutually productive solutions.

To address conflicts in multicultural contexts, people must also:

- Work to recognize the different ways that parties prefer to address conflicts in their cultures and
- Develop norms or agreements for how to manage conflicts when they involve people from different cultures.

When people become more confident in their ability to address conflicts, they begin to see it as a natural process. They learn to look for ways to create mutually beneficial outcomes from it. They also recognize that working through conflict can help bring people closer, particularly when the individuals involved have shown respect for each other and for their respective cultures.

Acknowledgments Craig Runde is the Director of the Center for Conflict Dynamics and Mediation Training Institute at Eckerd College in St. Petersburg, FL. Email: rundece@eckerd.edu.

Brigitte Armon is a product development manager with the Institute for Cross-Cultural Management at Florida Institute of Technology, where she is currently completing her Ph.D.

References

Beersma, B., Harinck, F., & Gerts, M. J. J. (2003). Bound in honor: How values and insults affect the experience and management of conflicts. *The International Journal of Conflict Management, 14,* 75–94.

Burke, C. S., Shuffler, M. L., Salas, E., & Gelfand, M. (2010). Multicultural teams: Critical team processes and guidelines. *Going global: Practical applications and recommendations for HR and OD professionals in the global workplace, 27,* 46–71.

Chua, R. Y., Morris, M. W., & Mor, S. (2012). Collaborating across cultures: Cultural metacognition and affect-based trust in creative collaboration. *Organizational Behavior and Human Decision Processes, 118,* 116–131.

Cohen, D., Nisbett, R. E., Bowdle, B. F., & Schwarz, N. (1996). Insult, aggression, and the southern culture of honor: An "experimental ethnography". *Journal of Personality and Social Psychology, 20,* 943–960.

DeDreu, C., & Weingardt, L. (2003). Task versus relationship conflict, team performance and team member satisfaction: A meta-analysis. *Journal of Applied Psychology, 88*(4), 741–749.

Earley, P. C., & Ang, S. (2003). *Cultural intelligence: Individual interactions across cultures.* Stanford, CA: Stanford University.

Ekman, P. (2003). *Emotions revealed.* New York: Holt.

Frederickson, B. (2001). The role of positive emotion in positive psychology: The broaden-and-build theory or positive emotions. *American Psychologist, 56*, 218–226.

Frederickson, B. (2011). *Positivity.* New York, NY: Harmony.

Hammer, M. R. (2005). The intercultural conflict style inventory: A conceptual framework and measure of intercultural conflict resolution approaches. *International Journal of Intercultural Relations, 29*, 675–695.

Harinck, F., Shafa, S., Ellemers, N., & Beersma, B. (2013). The good news about honor culture: The preference for cooperative conflict management in the absence of insults. *Negotiation and Conflict Management Research, 6*, 67–78.

IJzerman, H., van Dijk, W. W., & Gallucci, M. (2007). A bumpy train ride: A field experiment on insult, honor, and emotional reactions. *Emotion, 7*, 869–875.

Kim, Y. J., & Van Dyne, L. (2012). Cultural intelligence and international leadership potential: The importance of contact for members of the majority. *Applied Psychology: An International Review, 61*(2), 272–294.

Leung, A. K. Y., & Cohen, D. (2011). Within- and between-culture variation: Individual differences and the cultural logics of honor, face, and dignity cultures. *Journal of Personality and Social Psychology, 100*, 507–526.

Leung, K., Ang, S., & Tan, M. L. (2014). Intercultural competence. *Annual Review of Organizational Psychology and Organizational Behavior, 1*, 489–519.

Leung, K., & Brew, F. P. (2009). *A cultural analysis of harmony and conflict: Towards an integrated model of conflict styles* (pp. 411–428). Understanding culture: Theory, research and application.

Mor, S., Morris, M., & Joh, J. (2013). Identifying and training adaptive cross-cultural management skills: the crucial role of cultural metacognition. *Academy of Management Learning & Education, 12*, 453–475.

Ochsner, K., & Gross, J. (2005). The cognitive control of emotion. *Trends in Cognitive Sciences, 9*(5), 242–249.

Oetzel, J. G., & Ting-Toomey, S. (2003). Face concerns in interpersonal conflict a cross-cultural empirical test of the face negotiation theory. *Communication research, 30*, 599–624.

Oetzel, J., Ting-Toomey, S., Masumoto, T., Yokochi, Y., Pan, X., Takai, J., & Wilcox, R. (2001). Face and facework in conflict: A cross-cultural comparison of China, Germany, Japan, and the United States. *Communication Monographs, 68*, 235–258.

Paletz, S. B., Miron-Spektor, E., & Lin, C. C. (2014). A cultural lens on interpersonal conflict and creativity in multicultural environments. *Psychology of Aesthetics, Creativity, and the Arts, 8*, 237–252.

Reguieg, S. (2014). Conflict resolution skills and cultural intelligence: Exploring relationships and antecedents. Doctoral dissertation. To be available from ProQuest Dissertations & Theses Database.

Rodriguez Mosquera, P. M., Fischer, A. H., Manstead, A. S. R., & Zaalberg, R. (2008). Attack, disapproval, or withdrawal? The role of honour in anger and shame responses to being insulted. *Cognition and Emotion, 22*, 1471–1498.

Rodriguez Mosquera, P. M., Manstead, A. S. R., & Fischer, A. H. (2000). The role of honour-related values in the elicitation, experience, and communication of pride, shame, and anger: Spain and the Netherlands compared. *Personality and Social Psychology Bulletin, 26*, 833–844.

Rohner, R. P. (1984). Toward a conception of culture for cross-cultural psychology. *Journal of Cross-Cultural Psychology, 15*, 111–138.

Runde, C. (2014). Conflict competence in the workplace. *Employment Relations Today, 40*(4), 25–31.

Runde, C., & Flanagan, T. (2008). *Building conflict competent teams*. San Francisco, CA: Jossey-Bass.

Runde, C., & Flanagan, T. (2010). *Developing your conflict competence*. San Francisco, CA: Jossey-Bass.

Runde, C., & Flanagan, T. (2012). *Becoming a conflict competent leader* (2nd ed.) San Francisco, CA: Jossey-Bass.

Sadri, G. (2013). Choosing conflict resolution by culture. *Industrial Management, September,* 10–15.

Siegel, D. (2010). *The mindful brain*. New York, NY: Bantam.

Ting-Toomey, S., & Oetzel, J. (2001). *Managing Intercultural conflict effectively*. Thousand Oaks, CA: Sage.

Umai, L., & Gelfand, M. J. (2010). The culturally intelligent negotiator: The impact of cultural intelligence (CQ) on negotiation sequences and outcomes. *Organizational Behavior and Human Decision Processes,*. doi:10.1016/j.obhdp.2010.02.001.

Van Dyne, L., & Nielsen, T. (2007). Cultural intelligence. In S. Clegg & J. Bailey (Eds.), *International encyclopedia of organization studies* (pp. 345–350). Thousand Oaks, CA: Sage.

Van Le, Q., Isbell, L., Masomoto, J., Nguyen, M., Hori, E., Maior, R., & Tomaz, C., et al. (2013). Pulvinar neurons reveal neurobiological evidence of past selection for rapid detection of snakes. *PNAS, 2013, 110*(47), 19000–19005.

Weber, E. U., & Morris, M. W. (2010). Culture and judgment and decision-making: The constructivist turn. *Perspectives on Psychological Science, 5,* 410–419.

Chapter 6
One Finger Pointing Toward the Other, Three Are Back at You

Sharon Glazer

Conflict is inevitably at least a two-way street. Engaging in conflict has numerous benefits, such as stimulating creativity, commitment and growth, but along the journey to the positive sides of conflict are its downsides. Unless people recognize their contributions to conflict, it can be difficult to overcome the challenges posed by it. A person's contribution to conflict might not only be in how a person responds to a situation, but also the situation in which the person finds him or herself. This chapter focuses on different types of conflict, contributing factors to conflict, namely the different factors that influence a person's work role(s) and thus serve as explanations for conflict, and the influence of culture on resolving conflict situations.

The overarching goal of this chapter is to identify aspects of a person's role that might be fueling conflict in order to help the person in the role better cope with the conflict. Understanding one's own role that might be fueling conflict is important because as conflict increases, it is often easy to project one's frustrations toward others and forget about one's own contributions to the conflict. As goes the idiom, *when you point a finger at someone else, three are pointing back at you.* This basically means that focal individuals are as culpable for conflict situations as others are and in order to remedy the conflict it behooves focal individuals to think about their own responsibility in the conflict.

The objectives of this paper are to (1) categorize types of conflicts that might emerge as a result of role demands, (2) understand types of role conflicts people may face when crossing cultural boundaries, and (3) address culturally influenced constraints and culture's influence on fulfillment of roles. This chapter addresses each of these three objectives, but first establishes a foundational understanding of

S. Glazer (✉)
Division of Applied Behavioral Sciences, University of Baltimore, 1420 N. Charles St., Baltimore, MD 21201, USA
e-mail: sglazer@ubalt.edu

© Springer International Publishing Switzerland 2016   73
J.L. Wildman et al. (eds.), *Critical Issues in Cross Cultural Management*,
DOI 10.1007/978-3-319-42166-7_6

roles and situates role conflict as one of several types of role stressors, as well as a thematic category that encapsulates different kinds of role conflict. The chapter concludes with recommendations for navigating through intercultural challenges that might yield role conflict and areas ripe for further study and inquiry.

Understanding Roles

As a starting point, on the basis of multiple organizational development consulting projects, the author has come to learn that most impediments to effective interactions are a result of unclear goals and poorly defined and/or understood roles. It is not surprising then that when people traverse national boundaries or interact with others who have different cultural backgrounds, they face similar threats or challenges (i.e., role stressors; Glazer and Beehr 2005). These role stressors, bolstered by idiosyncratic cultural differences, require organizational interventions, starting with clarifying the goals toward which people are working. Assuming people are clear about the goals that need to be fulfilled, the next step is to know the role or roles one is expected to assume, which includes the responsibilities, tasks, and job activities associated with a position.

A role is neither a position nor a set of responsibilities, but the expected or understood behaviors a person portrays as his or her "character part(s)" in a domain (e.g., work, family, friends, and other social spheres) and includes responsibilities within a given position (Ivanitskaya et al. 2009). Roles are formal or informal, implicitly inferred or explicitly directed (Beehr and Glazer 2005). A person may have the position of a supervisor, but the function that position is expected, understood, or inferred to serve makes up a person's role. The person in a role is referred to here within as "focal person." A focal person's expectations are influenced by cultural norms, rules, and values (Smith et al. 2011). Thus, a role evolves as a focal person learns about or interprets influential others' explicit (stated or written) and implicit (unwritten and unstated) expectations of a role. Roles, therefore, inherently involve at least two individuals.

Role Theory. According to role theory, in any given interaction amongst people who have a stake at fulfilling some goal, there are role senders and role receivers. 'Role senders' is the term used to refer to individuals who influence what a person does to fulfill his or her role. Consequently, they are socializing agents, as their communications help to shape a focal person's role. All role senders of a focal person's role belong to the focal person's role set and each has a stake in a focal person's role. Role senders could include subordinates, supervisors, administrators, coworkers, clients, vendors, partners, etc. In order for role senders to transmit messages of their understandings, desires, expectations, or preferences for a focal person's role, they must encode the messages in a way that makes sense to themselves and (typically) think makes sense to the focal person who is to receive

Fig. 6.1 Basic flow of communication

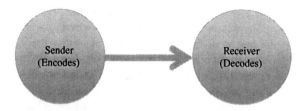

the messages. The focal person is often also the role receiver.[1] The role receiver decodes and interprets messages (see Fig. 6.1).

Any focal person receives messages from various role senders. Some role senders are more influential than others, but all have a stake in influencing the role a focal person fulfills. Through various connections with relevant stakeholders, roles take shape and definition (McGrath 1976). Over time people learn what is expected of them in their roles through various modes and channels of communications. However, it is imperative to point out that the intended message is a derivation of what is sent and received. People's own past experiences (either in the workplace or home life), first-hand observations, and stories passed down from others influence how people encode and send messages.

Common Ground Theory. As an extension of role theory, common ground theory frames communication as a process by which communicators work together to arrive at a shared meaning of expectations (Leung et al. 2013). This process of encoding and decoding is often referred to as "filtering." When role senders encode and transmit messages and role receivers decode and interpret the expectations, they are often filtered through the communicators' meta-knowledge. Much like a coffee machine works by water filtering through coffee grinds to produce drinkable coffee, so do people filter messages through a complex system of prior experiences and knowledge.

To find common ground (no pun intended), role senders and role receivers will pick up on information that is common between them and then formulate messages in a way that others should understand it. Thus, a role receiver takes information from his or her environment, perhaps assuming that it was encoded with elements that are mutually understood, and tries to make sense of it. This sensemaking process refers to a person's cognitive efforts to give meaning to experiences and to understand and explain information (or data points) received in order to create a sense of coherence (Antonovsky 1979; Korotkov 1998). More specifically, sensemaking is a process by which an individual identifies situational cues, tries to explain the situation on the basis of past experiences, as well as his or her identification with the event, and enacts a way of responding that is influenced by cultural values and history (Osland and Bird 2000). Meta-knowledge of culture, therefore,

---

[1]The role receiver, while often the focal person, is not always the focal person. There might be layers of role receivers before a focal person receives intended messages of expectations (e.g., from upper level managers, to mid-level managers, to individual contributors, who are the focal persons).

also influences sensemaking. In reality, the perception of sharing common ground with others is not always accurate. However, the onus of sensemaking is not only on the role receiver. All parties in a role set are responsible for the way an intended message is encoded and decoded (Ivanitskaya et al. 2009). The more accurate communicators' meta-knowledge the more capable they will be at encoding and decoding messages as intended (Leung et al. 2013).

Various factors influence how a focal person makes sense of his or her role and thus these factors shape the person's role. These factors include: (1) organizational goals, position, tenure, education, experience, (2) expectations that others have about how a focal person (i.e., the incumbent of a role) ought to behave, (3) the focal person's interpretation of those expectations, and (4) meta-knowledge of culture. Furthermore, a focal person filters observations of (a) past communications, (b) messages sent to other people, or (c) ways people of similar roles behave (McGrath 1976). Role receivers also derive implicit meaning on that which is *not stated*. Thus, interpretation of a lack of communication, as well as interpretation of that which is stated can lead the focal person to perceive demands, constraints, or opportunities.

Role Stressors

Communications perceived as imposing demands, constraints, or opportunities are also referred to as *role stressors* (see Table 6.1 for a list of various role stressors and examples). Role stressors develop when roles are poorly or insufficiently communicated, or the focal person has been presented ambiguous or conflicting messages, such that the focal person is unable to or believes he or she is unable to fulfill his or her role. In other words, role stressors often develop when the intended message, which is a derivation of what is sent and what is received, goes through both encoding and decoding filters. The resulting meaning a focal person imposes on the message serves as the basis for the focal person's perception of role ambiguity, role overload, or role conflict.

For nearly 60 years, researchers have been studying role stressors (e.g., Kahn et al. 1964). Role stressors refer to aspects of a person's role that may or may not become a source of strain. They represent real or perceived problems within a person's social system or role set (Jex and Beehr 1991). Sometimes role stressors do not lead to strains because they are not appraised as a problem requiring remediation. Other times, the stressors are perceived as a threat or challenge that needs to be overcome and individuals successfully employ strategies to cope with the stressors. Still, there are also times when the role stressor is not (adequately) dealt with and strain ensues.

Strains might develop as a result of the focal person feeling that established expectations are unclear. This is known as *role ambiguity*. When people are inadequately informed, information is insufficient, misleading, or restricted, then a

Table 6.1 Types of role stressors and examples

Role stressor	International/cultural example
Role ambiguity	A person (from USA) understands his/her role as supervisor to include individually praising subordinates for a job well-done, but in a different cultural environment (e.g., Japan) the supervisor erroneously causes recipients of the praise to feel inadequate (the exact opposite intention)
Role misconception	A person clearly understands the expectation of involving others in a decision-making capacity, but the functional meaning of "involve" culturally differs (e.g., ranging from informing of decisions rendered to asking for others' perspectives for resolving problems)
Role overload	A focal person in one country feels burdened by too much work and not enough time to do the work, but this same amount of work is perceived as manageable, because the amount of time allotted in a work week differs across cultures
Role conflict	
Intersender	The focal person receives instructions from his or her home supervisor on how to complete an assignment, but instructions from local host superiors differ. The focal person then has to determine to which of the competing expectations he or she should adhere
Interrole	An international assignee has to serve as a leader and supporter of the host country's workers who are reluctant to voice their opinions, while also fulfilling the expectations from headquarters of improving organizational processes through consensus decision-making
Intrarole	An international assignee might feel s/he must accept a gift that may be seen as a bribe
Intrasender	A supervisor advises a negotiating team to use aggressive negotiating tactics, but at the same shows compliance and saving face actions such that the negotiators are conflicted with how to behave with their counterparts
Role discretion	A focal person in a new cultural environment decides to hold team meetings in which extensive minute taking is imposed, when it had never been done before
Role novelty	A focal person (e.g., from Spain) moves to a new country (e.g., USA) and must learn how to incorporate sports terms into PowerPoint presentation slides and include few words or phases per slide
Role innovation	An international assignee has to learn to contend with informing and educating a spokesperson responsible for negotiating on behalf of the company instead of having the international assignee engage in direct negotiations

sense of ambiguity develops about their duties, objectives, and responsibilities. Role ambiguity can develop when one has to learn or adapt to new technology, social/organizational structures, new personnel, job changes, or new workplace. Part of the problem with inadequate or insufficient information is that the role receiver might completely understand what is expected within the boundaries of information presented, but that interpretation is incorrect due to unaligned understanding of cultural factors along with the information.

Floyd and Lane (2000) note "expectations for a given role do not arise in a vacuum but, rather, develop in the context of other interdependent behaviors and expectations that make up a social system" (p. 157). By extension, role expectations are also encoded within the role sender's perception of the cultural context, and the receiver interprets the expectation with cultural lenses that may or may not align. For example, if someone is asked to carry out a job task and responds "maybe," the role receiver might be meaning "no," but the role sender interprets the 'maybe' as a real possibility and a very likely "yes." Similarly, if a manager says "I expect the project to be done by close of business," the role receiver might interpret "close of business" as having until the next business morning (e.g., 8 a.m.), because the work day is ending and the boss surely is not working. However, the role sender, when stating "end of business" might have planned on working on the project from 5 p. m. through the night. These examples of cultural misunderstandings, as a function of role ambiguity, might better be termed as *"role misconception."* Although related to ambiguity, it is a special kind of ambiguity in which a person clearly understands the expectation as interpreted from the receiver's lens, but there was a fallacy and misunderstanding of the cultural premise or culturally nuanced meaning of the expectation. The role receiver does not even know that a mistake was made and the strain does not develop until the person realizes that a cultural misunderstanding of an expectation had occurred.

Role conflict occurs when a focal person has to contend with two or more sets of incompatible demands. Role misconception could lead to role conflict too. A person experiencing role conflict is often pulled by differing expectations and feels pressured into having to choose between different demands or expectations. *Role overload* also occurs when one faces incompatible demands. These demands may be time-based demands or limitations (i.e., quantitative role overload) or resource-based demands or limitations due to insufficient qualifications, knowledge, or skills to fulfill duties, commitments, and responsibilities (i.e., qualitative role overload). Role overload is often folded into role conflict, because it also has to do with navigating role expectations, however, in this case it is a need to cope with incompatible role expectations and time or capabilities vs. incompatible demands. For the sake of parsimony, and on the basis of prior studies (e.g. Glazer and Beehr 2005), these two concepts are treated distinctly and role conflict is conceptualized as a function of two or more incompatible demands.

The remainder of this paper is framed around the assumption that while not all role conflict leads to strains (and could even be a growth opportunity; e.g., Ghorpade et al. 2011), in cross-cultural or intercultural interactions, some of the greatest strains people experience are due to poorly understood, incompatible role demands. Thus, role conflict is a potentially deleterious stimulus against which the focal role player could apply coping resources, such as increased self-awareness of his or her own role limitations, in order to temper possible consequences. Below different types of role conflict are presented.

Types of Role Conflict

Ivanitskaya et al. (2009) summarize four types of role conflict. These are inter-sender, interrole, intrarole, and intrasender role conflict. These types of conflict are distinguished by the centrality of the focal person in the conflict situation. Is the focal person perceiving the incongruence with his or her own standards or values (intra-) or does the focal person recognize the conflict arising due to incompatibilities amongst others and/or policies (inter-)? The four types of role conflict are defined below.

1. *Intersender role conflict*: This type of role conflict is most prevalent when two or more people or groups expect or demand different kinds of behaviors from the focal person. In other words, a person is faced with at least two competing requests or incompatible processes. For example, the focal person receives instructions from his or her home supervisor on how to complete an assignment, but instructions from local host superiors differ. The focal person then has to determine to which of the competing expectations he or she should adhere.
2. *Interrole conflict*: This type of role conflict transpires when a single focal person has to cope with two or more competing roles, such as that of a superior and that of a subordinate. Another example is when an international assignee has to serve as a leader and supporter of the host country's workers who are reluctant to voice their opinions, while also fulfilling the expectations from headquarters of improving organizational processes through consensus decision-making. When a focal person is confronted with too many discordant roles, conflict can arise.
3. *Intrarole conflict*: This type of conflict is also referred to as person–role conflict, because it involves one's own need to wrestle with his or her own personal values and an organization's requirements and the organization's expectations of fulfilling obligations to others. When a focal person faces intrarole conflict, he or she contends with having to do things in different ways than what he or she would find appropriate. The challenge the person faces is whether to violate his or her own values and standards of how to do things or heeding to the organization's demands. In other words, the person and the organization's values do not match. An example of intrarole conflict might be when an international assignee has to cope with a behavior that might be perceived as immoral in his or her parent country, but perfectly acceptable and desirable in the host country. Specifically, an international assignee from the USA might find the idea of giving gifts to the host country managers as unethical and creating a situation labeled in the USA as "conflict of interest." However, in the host country, gift-giving might be perceived as a way of acknowledging the already established gift of time to meet with the counterparts or as a way of establishing an understanding of the international assignees intentions to support workers in the host country. Similarly, an international assignee might experience intrarole conflict when s/he feels s/he must accept a gift that may be seen as a bribe.
4. *Intrasender role conflict*: This type of role conflict occurs when two or more opposing demands are sent from same role sender. In this type of role conflict,

the focal person is faced with fulfilling one set of expectations, but then is required to deviate from performing according to the same role sender's other expectations. This is a situation in which one might say "damned if I do and damned if I don't." Conflict develops when the focal person perceives that a role sender's expectations are unrealistic and it would be impossible to fulfill given the other set of expectations. For example, the focal person might be tasked with preparing a report on a topic he or she has no background on and to get it done within a couple of days. Another example is when a focal person is told to be a risk-taker and communicate departmental needs to appropriate others, but is then told to refrain from communicating needs to others as it comes across as condescending and unappreciative. In an intercultural interaction, an example of intrasender role conflict may be observed when a supervisor advises a negotiating team to use aggressive negotiating tactics, but at the same shows compliance and saving face actions such that the negotiators are conflicted with how to behave with their counterparts (Gelfand et al. 2013).

Reflection

Think about a time when you said something that someone has misinterpreted.
1. What was the message and how do you think the person misinterpreted the message?
2. What about your filters shaped the way you molded your message?
3. What might have been the filters acting on the other person's interpretation of the message?

International Assignee Role Conflict

A special case of role conflict arises when a focal person who is quite experienced and perceived as skilled in his or her work position is then required to engage in intercultural interactions via an assignment abroad. In addition to changing cultural venue, an international assignee has to work with people who are not normally in his or her role set. In this new capacity the focal person might have increased or decreased *role discretion*. Role discretion refers to the extent to which employees can decide how they perform their jobs and adapt the setting to themselves (Aryee and Stone 1996; Black and Gregersen 1991). One of the major challenges is going into the social context of an international organization and assuming that one has the authority to impose his or her own work style. If one does not exercise caution with the extent to which role discretion is employed in the new work environment, role conflict is likely to develop. Still, there is evidence that having role discretion helps an international assignee adjust to the host country and work situation, as well as increases job satisfaction and quality of life (Aryee and Stone 1996; Black and Gregersen 1991).

Another factor that might affect role conflict for international assignees is *role novelty*. Role novelty refers to the new tasks, skills, and work processes a person must learn when coming into a new cultural context (Aryee and Stone 1996). If one is not adaptable and flexible to learn these new competencies, he or she might have to cope with intrarole conflict, as the person comes to terms with what is required and his or her own understandings of how things get done. Finally, in a new organizational context, an international assignee has to adjust to new role expectations and requirements. This is referred to as *role innovation* (Black 1992). If the focal person pays attention to his or her new role set and experiences relevant work events with members of the new role set, role innovation will be a positive experience, but if the focal person fails to immerse with the collective and does not socialize into the new social system on the basis of local role senders' expectations, the focal person will likely face intersender and intrarole conflict.

Navigating Through Role Conflict Across Cultures

In order to competently and easily work with people from different cultural backgrounds, particularly when the focal person is a sojourner overseas, the individual must have both a depth of knowledge regarding best practices in a host culture and, for competent communication, meta-knowledge of culture. Meta-knowledge of culture refers to declarative knowledge regarding the knowledge held by people of a certain culture (Leung et al. 2013). Knowing what others in a culture know influences how people formulate communication with people of that culture. For example, Leung et al. (2013) showed that people of the same cultural background were less likely to provide explicit instructions regarding navigation directions and more likely to name generally known landmarks. However, with people from a different cultural background, the landmarks that are unlikely to be known to a people from a different culture would not even be mentioned for navigation purposes. In other words, by knowing what people in a certain culture know, it is possible to modify communication approaches. Taking for granted what people know or do not know are often root causes for conflict. For example, giving someone instructions to write a grant proposal budgeting for X amount of money when the person clearly knows that only Y amount of money is acceptable could lead to intrarole conflict.

The sources of role conflict are many and varied and often people have the resources to clarify expectations, however sometimes the problems are not in clearly identifying and adapting to new role expectations, but in incomplete meta-knowledge of the other culture (Leung et al. 2013). Given the challenges presented by meta-knowledge of culture, how can one resolve role conflict?

Resolving Role Conflict by Mastering One's Role

Although a person might have a general understanding of his or her role, it is not sufficient for keeping conflict at bay. As culture influences how people interpret messages, it is entirely possible that a person might be made aware of role misconception and once aware, the person will need to cope with any conflict that developed as a result of it. Thus, to ensure ongoing effective intercultural communication, and thus role clarity, a person must have a genuine interest in getting to know others, demonstrate flexibility in communication style, maintain sociability, and engage in self-monitoring (i.e., personal characteristics). Second, one ought to be able to overcome adversity caused by cultural misunderstandings (i.e., resilience). Third, a person needs to be open to making mistakes and learning from mistakes, take advantage in learning from others, seek new knowledge and experiences, and have an ability to analyze situational cues (i.e., learning orientation). Finally, a person needs to prevent conflict by having an adaptable and social integrated style of communication (i.e., communication competence). Each of these four general guidelines is discussed below.

Guideline 1: Personal Characteristics. A genuine interest in getting to know others is a personality trait that cannot be rhetorically and insincerely managed. Political skill refers to a focal person's ability to use information obtained about others to influence the others' work behaviors in a way that enhance the focal person's personal agenda (Shi et al. 2012). This ability is not considered genuine, because there is an underlying current of manipulation. The focal person observes interpersonal work relationships, develops social networks, and puts on a show of sincerity (to make others believe in the focal person's integrity) in order to get what one desires. Thus, while some people might know how to play the game, disingenuous care for others in intercultural interactions will backfire. Genuine interest in others is likely an important trait and one that cannot be taught. In addition to genuine interest in others, one can learn to develop flexibility in communication style. To be flexible, one must learn to actively listen and observe others' styles of communication, and to pursue alternative plausible (and possibly implausible from one's own cultural perspective) explanations for communication exchanges.

Maintaining sociability is also a personal characteristic that one can develop over time and with practice. Sociability might not be natural for everyone, but there are ways that one can learn how to ask culturally appropriate questions. For example, in Hungary, it is unusual to ask a new acquaintance about the kind of work he/she does nor about his/her family. Instead, it is acceptable to have conversations on news events, being careful to stay away from political events. Finally, self-monitoring refers to getting to know oneself, let alone others.

While the need to understand oneself is vitally important in any interaction, it is all the more important in intercultural interactions due to the cultural biases one has that might interfere with effective communication. It is important to question what it is that one is observing in others and ask why the perceived behavior was noticed or mattered. Was the behavior different or similar to what one normally expects to find in a given situation? What about the observation was particularly interesting or why was it uninteresting if someone else took note of it, but "you" did not?

Guideline 2: Resilience. Resilience, sometimes referred to as hardiness (Eschleman et al. 2010), refers to a person's ability to cope with stressors by perceiving them as challenges that can be overcome. Resilient people can overcome and recover from difficult situations by interpreting those situations as having purpose. Finally, they take responsibility for resolving the stressors and maintaining a positive, energetic attitude. These attributes of resilience are akin to those of hardiness, which comprises perceiving stressors as "challenges," having a sense of "commitment" to overcome the challenges, and having a sense of "control" over the strain-producing event. In intercultural experiences a hardy personality or a resilient disposition is vital for cognitively reframing situations in order to maintain healthy relationships with others. International assignees would benefit from a hardy personality. With a hardy personality, international assignees are more likely able to (1) develop and draw upon communication resources that would improve their sense of control, (2) reorient how they perceive situations as challenges to learn from and opportunities to further develop oneself in a new environment, and (3) persevere through the difficult, ambiguous situations.

When international sojourns become difficult, it may be easy for international assignees to give up and return home. In order to prevent early return home and to prepare the international assignee for the international experience, the international assignee must be encouraged to or self-reinforce the importance of staying the course, exploring alternative explanations for observed or experienced behaviors, and employing newly formed skills or identifying resources that could help resolve ambiguities and conflict. An example of this kind of demonstrated resilience is depicted well in the television show "Outsourced." The main character from the USA, who was sent to manage a call center in India, is seen struggling with keeping his employees in the office on a special Indian holiday. To overcome the struggle, he learned about the holiday and its symbolic meaning. Despite his initial resistance to the employees' need to take time off to observe the holiday, he eventually took the opportunity to partake in the festivities too.

Guideline 3: Learning Orientation. When a person travels abroad, role misconceptions and ambiguities are inevitable. Often these misunderstandings and lack of clarity serve as the catalysts for conflict and work overload. When one maintains a learning orientation, one is apt to employ proactive strategies that include talking with others to learn not only what mistakes were made, but also why they were mistakes in the first place and how to prevent them in the future. Further, as one develops a deeper understanding of cultural norms, values, beliefs, and practices in a host country, one can begin to see situational cues that were otherwise ignored or misunderstood before. Much like an organization that has a climate for learning (London and Mone 1999; Mohr 2002; Rothwell 2002), eventually, a person will develop practices and personal policies to learn about others and situations. The person will develop procedures for exploring situations and events, and even find those procedures for exploring and learning to be rewarding. As with the above example for Guideline 2, when one seeks to learn about another's culture one grows to appreciate and acclimate to the differences (even if one does not like them).

Guideline 4: Communication Competence. The starting point for many people who are beginning to develop cross-cultural communication skills is at a level of unconscious incompetence (Bhawuk 1998). This is where the person does not even know (i.e., completely unaware) that s/he lacks an understanding of culture's influence on a given situation, interaction, or event. As a person begins to learn about culture and culture's influence on people's behaviors, feelings, and thinking, the person becomes attuned to realizing how much knowledge, skills, abilities, and personal characteristics s/he might be lacking. This is referred to as conscious incompetence. A big leap is then made into the area of conscious competence, whereby the learner begins not only to recognize cultural differences, but even how to navigate and interact with people of different cultural backgrounds. Unfortunately, this type of conscious competence comes with a drawback that if one is seemingly proficient, one might actually cause some cultural errors that could lead to undesirable consequences. For example, two consciously competent individuals from different cultural backgrounds who are interacting might each be trying to accommodate to the other, which could lead to a "Shakespearean comedy of errors." It is at this level that a person must continue to be resilient and demonstrate a willingness to adapt and consider plausible alternative explanations for intercultural role misconceptions. Finally, an individual who becomes native with respect to a culture's practices, traditions, language, rituals, values, beliefs, norms, perceptions, etc.—a person who has a deep meta-knowledge of others will have achieved a level of unconscious competence. This person will be so comfortable and fluid in an intercultural situation that s/he does not even recognize that s/he is in it. The person will have become the "fish in the sea" as s/he does not even realize how naturally the intercultural interactions are flowing.

When Role Stressors Lead to Strains: Job Demands Control Model

The above recommendations for buffering against role conflict notwithstanding, it is not always preventable. According to the Job Demands Control Model (Karasek 1979), people who perceive high demands and little control to temper the demands will likely develop strains. Specifically, when facing high role stressors in an intercultural context, feelings of not having control over one's intercultural competencies would yield strain.

In order to remedy this situation, it might be helpful to employ strategies that increase perceived control. Indeed, confidence in one's cross-cultural competence would serve as a resource to gain control over role stressors could buffer the effects of role stressors on strains. Communication topics that would benefit those who have intercultural interactions more comfortably cope with culturally influenced role conflict include temporal perspective (Glazer and Palekar 2013) and social support (Beehr and Glazer 2001; Glazer 2006).

Temporal perspective refers to a nonconscious process in which personal and social experiences are assigned to time frames (past, present, or future) in order to give order, coherence, and meaning to the events (Hall 1983; Zimbardo and Boyd 1999). Each of these perspectives could either help one cope with role conflict or intensify the implications of role conflict on strain. For example, a person who tends to think of experiences from a nostalgic (past positive) time perspective, draws upon those positive experiences to explain events, thereby reinforcing resiliency and a belief that conflict situation, with time and effort, will resolve, thereby mitigating feelings of frustration (Karniol and Ross 1996). Likewise, a person who tends to hold a future time perspective is driven by goals and might interpret role conflict as an opportunity to overcome challenges toward achievement of the goals; these individuals are likely to be engaged toward goal fulfillment (Horstmanshof and Zimitat 2007). However, a negative past time perspective could intensify conflict and undermine social relationships (Holman and Zimbardo 2009). According to Glazer and Palekar (2013), the cultural context in which people work influences temporal perspective; people who had been socialized in one cultural context will tend to maintain a preference for that temporal perspective. This might be evident in a research finding that the relationship between role conflict and strains (low affective organizational commitment and high anxiety) was stronger for Indians in the USA who were high (vs. low) on negative past time perspective, but the slopes were congruent for Indians in India. Thus, competence in temporal perspectives could help a person who engages in many intercultural interactions to take on a different temporal lens when also managing role conflict.

In another study, Staffanson and Glazer (2008) presented results of a 25-country study of HR professionals grouped into nine clusters of cultural regions, showing that social support, while often imagined to be helpful, in fact, can have deleterious effects depending on whether the source of support is the supervisor, coworker, organization and the regional cultural context in which the support is given. For example, for North Americans, as role stressors increased favorable attitudes toward the organization increased when organizational support was high, but decreased when organizational support was low. Similarly, for Nordic Europeans, when role stressors increased, favorable attitudes increased with increased supervisor support, but the stressor–attitude relationship was less positive with low supervisor support. Finally, in Latin Europe, the role stressor–favorable attitude relationship decreased more sharply when coworker support was high, but was tempered a bit when coworker support was low. These findings suggest that international managers learn about locals' preferences for and conditions for eliciting positive responses to different sources and types of social support. For example, for North Americans, companies might want to reinforce the availability of resources that would help someone get work done efficiently, but for Nordic Europeans knowing and trusting that their supervisors are available to support them helps to prevent deleterious consequences of stressors. In fact, for Nordic Europeans, conflict is seen as a way of developing and progressing (Sippola 2009) and thus a supervisor who provides support might be engaging in a conflict approach manner to help a subordinate overcome the stressor. However, it is important that international assignees working in Latin Europe not provide observable support to coworkers as that type of support would have a detrimental impact on a person's perceptions of their workplace by reducing the recipient's sense of autonomy (a highly valued principle for Latin Europeans (Schwartz 1999). The importance of machismo may be so important (Cliffe 2005; Newman et al. 2012) that any signs of support from a person of equal rank might lead to feelings of inadequacies. Instead, it might be beneficial to step back and give the person (who seems to need support) the time to process and explore alternative avenues for working on and through the challenges (Schramm-Nielsen 2001).

The above results and implications clearly show that culture matters not only in trying to untangle etiology of conflict and work through role conflict, but it also matters when resources to "cope" with the role conflict, such as support systems, are implemented or encouraged. In other words, it's not only a matter of unraveling sources of conflict, but also of understanding the utility of various erroneous global management practices (typically supported in the USA) in other national cultures.

Directions for Future Research

This chapter integrated literature on culture and role stressors, particularly role conflict, to argue that culture plays a pivotal role in the development of role conflict. However, there is little empirical research that would support the positions taken here. For this reason, each and every one of the points raised that links culture to role stressors needs to be researched. As an example, it is still unknown to what extent culture influences role stressors. One way to research this question would be to identify an occupation that requires similar levels of education across the globe and through an emic approach identify factors in their work roles that are a source of strain. Glazer and Gyurak (2008) had conducted a study along those method- ological lines and found that the nurses' stressors in Hungary, UK, Italy, Israel, and USA were quite different and in a related study the same role stressors had different implications on strains (Glazer and Beehr 2005). Another study ripe for investi- gation is how do people in different cultures cope with various kinds of role conflict and what are the implications of those coping strategies on management practices? Finally, is there a point in which favorable (for intercultural interactions) personal characteristics, resilience, learning orientation, and communication competence simply do not help? The answer to this question is important, as organizations must be prepared to pull their international assignees off of assignments that are simply futile.

Practical Tips

To summarize, despite little empirical evidence of culture's influence on role conflict, there are anecdotal examples coupled with empirical studies on culture and role conflict (separately) that, conceptually integrated, form the below guidelines for minimizing intercultural role conflict. These guidelines are:

1. *Know thyself*: Conflict arises when a person is unaware of his/her own contributions to the messaging barriers. Know your own values and general beliefs about the nature of human relationships. Understand why those values and beliefs would *not* be acceptable to people from other cultures. Then can you begin to develop and understanding of others' values and beliefs.
2. *Summon your internal strength*: Conflict brews when one feels defeated and incapable. An intercultural experience can be interpreted as something scary or as something adventurous that can reveal one's own inner strengths. Remember that your counterpart is also experiencing an intercultural interaction.
3. *Develop a passion for learning*: There is no reason for conflict to escalate when one chooses to learn of others' habits, customs, values, beliefs, practices, norms, etc. Assume you do not know, observe and, if culturally acceptable, ask questions (at least to a confidant).
4. *Communicate*: Avoiding conflict in important intercultural assignments only breeds more conflict. As cliché and redundant as it may be, communication through listening, studying (from others and from one's own mistakes), repeating, and doing will lead to greater cultural competence.

Take-Home Message

The overarching goal for this chapter was to help individuals realize the extent to which they are responsible for understanding their roles, particularly in an intercultural situation, and, by extension, potential sources of conflict, as only through this initial step of understanding can conflict resolution interventions work. In other words, what aspects of a focal person's role might be a source of conflict in the culture within which the person is working and what aspects of cultural clarifications could help resolve some of those aspects. More specifically, this chapter's objectives were achieved by paving a common understanding of communication processes and then digging deeper into the complexities of various kinds of conflicts that might arise as a result of the role(s) one has in an organization. Another objective was met by stimulating thoughts about how culture both incites role conflict and shapes the resources to cope with role conflict. As presented in this chapter, in order to understand others' roles, people have to first understand their own roles and what they contribute to shaping their own and others' roles. It is important to consider culture's influence on communication structures, as well as the cultural implications of framing expectations and decoding expectations in order to interpret role conflict as a growth opportunity, rather than a hindrance and strain-producing event. Finally, it is important to develop a cognitive understanding of what people in other cultures know, as a way of shaping focal persons' intercultural communications. However, meta-knowledge of culture needs to be considered cautiously; if the meta-knowledge is wrong, perspective-taking will derail any authentic, good attempts at encoding and/or decoding messages with as much accuracy as possible (Leung et al. 2013). Thus, with accurate meta-knowledge of culture and perspective-taking abilities a person will be equipped with the skills and abilities to engage in quality intercultural interactions and adjust swiftly if the cultural assumptions or expressions are misconceived.

References

Antonovsky, A. (1979). *Health, stress and coping*. San Francisco: Jossey-Bass.
Aryee, S., & Stone, R. J. (1996). Work experiences, work adjustment, and psychological well-being of expatriate employees in Hong Kong. *The International Journal of Human Resource Management, 7*, 150–164.
Beehr, T. A., & Glazer, S. (2001). A cultural perspective of social support in relation to occupational stress. In P. Perrewé, D. C. Ganster, & J. Moran (Eds.), *Research in occupational stress and well-being* (pp. 97–142). Greenwich, CO: JAI Press.
Beehr, T. A., & Glazer, S. (2005). Organizational role stress. In J. Barling, K. Kelloway, & M. Frone (Eds.), *Handbook of work stress* (pp. 7–33). Thousand Oaks, CA: Sage.
Bhawuk, D. P. S. (1998). The role of culture theory in cross-cultural training: A multimethod study of culture specific, culture-general, and culture theory-based assimilators. *Journal of Cross-Cultural Psychology, 29*, 630–655.
Black, J. S. (1992). Socializing American expatriate managers overseas. *Group and Organization Management, 17*, 171–192.
Black, J. S., & Gregersen, H. B. (1991). Antecedents to cross-cultural adjustment for expatriates in Pacific Rim assignments. *Human Relations, 44*(5), 497–515.
Cliffe, J. (2005, Aug. 1). From macho Italians to progressive Swedes. Published in Café Babel. http://www.cafebabel.co.uk/article/from-macho-italians-to-progressive-swedes.html. Retrieved 17 June 2014.
Eschleman, K. J., Bowling, N. A., & Alarcon, G. M. (2010). A meta-analytic examination of hardiness. *International Journal of Stress Management, 17*, 277–307.
Floyd, S. W., & Lane, P. J. (2000). Strategizing throughout the organization: Managing role conflict in strategic renewal. *Academy of Management Review, 25*, 154–177.
Gelfand, M. J., Brett, J., Gunia, B. C., Imai, L., Huang, T., & Hsu, B. (2013). Toward a culture-by-context perspective on negotiation: Negotiating teams in the United States and Taiwan. *Journal of Applied Psychology, 98*(3), 504–513.
Ghorpade, J., Lackritz, J., & Singh, G. (2011). Personality as a moderator of the relationships between role conflict, role ambiguity, and burnout. *Journal of Applied Social Psychology, 41*, 1275–1298.
Glazer, S. (2006). Social support across cultures. *International Journal of Intercultural Relations, 30*(5), 605–622.
Glazer, S., & Beehr, T. A. (2005). Consistency of the implications of three role stressors across four countries. *Journal of Organizational Behavior, 26*, 467–487.
Glazer, S., & Gyurak, A. (2008). Sources of occupational stress among nurses in five countries. *International Journal of Intercultural Relations, 32*, 49–66.

Glazer, S., & Palekar, A. A. (2013). Indian perspective of time and management. In H. Helfrich, E. Hölter, & I. V. Arzhenowskij (Eds.), *Time and management from the perspective of different cultures* (pp. 41–63). Cambridge, MA: Hogrefe & Huber.

Hall, E. T. (1983). *The dance of life: The other dimensions of time.* New York: Anchor.

Holman, E. A., & Zimbardo, P. G. (2009). The social language of time: The time perspective-social network connection. *Basic and Applied Social Psychology, 31*, 136–147.

Horstmanshof, L., & Zimitat, C. (2007). Future time orientation predicts academic engagement among first-year university students. *British Journal of Educational Psychology, 77*, 703–718.

Ivanitskaya, L. V., Glazer, S., & Erofeev, D. A. (2009). Group dynamics. In J. A. Johnson (Ed.), *Health organizations: Theory, behavior, and development* (pp. 109–136). Boston: Jones & Bartlett.

Jex, S. M., & Beehr, T. A. (1991). Emerging theoretical and methodological issues in the study of work-related stress. In G. R. Ferris & K. W. Rowland (Eds.), *Research in personnel and human resources management* (pp. 311–365). Greenwich, CT: JAI Press.

Kahn, R. L., Wolfe, D. M., Quinn, R. P., Snoek, J. D., & Rosenthal, R. A. (1964). *Organizational stress: Studies in role conflict and ambiguity.* New York: Wiley.

Karasek, R. A. (1979). Job demands, job decision latitude, and mental strain: Implications for job redesign. *Administrative Science Quarterly, 24*, 285–308.

Karniol, R., & Ross, M. (1996). The motivational impact of temporal focus: Thinking about the future and the past. *Annual Review of Psychology, 47*, 593–620.

Korotkov, D. L. (1998). The sense of coherence: Making sense out of chaos. In P. T. P. Wong & P. S. Fry (Eds.), *The human quest for meaning: A handbook of psychological research and clinical applications* (pp. 51–70). Mahwah, NJ: Erlbaum.

Leung, A. K-y, Lee, S., & Chiu, C-y. (2013). Meta-knowledge of culture promotes cultural competence. *Journal of Cross-Cultural Psychology, 44*, 992–1006.

London, M., & Mone, E. M. (1999). Continuous learning. In D. R. Ilgen & E. D. Pulakos (Eds.), *The changing nature of performance* (pp. 1–18). San Francisco: Jossey Bass.

McGrath, J. E. (1976). Stress and behavior in organizations. In M. D. Dunnette (Ed.), *Handbook of Industrial and organizational psychology* (pp. 1351–1395). Chicago: Rand McNally College Publishing.

Mohr, D. C. (2002). *Continuous learning climate and individual continuous learning orientation: Assessing constructs and implications.* (Doctoral Dissertation).

Newman, M. A., Carabí, A., & Armengol, J. M. (2012). Beyond Don Juan: Rethinking Iberian masculinities. *Men and Masculinities, 15*, 343–345.

Osland, J. S., & Bird, A. (2000). Beyond sophisticated stereotyping: Cultural sensemaking in context. *Academy of Management Executive, 14*, 65–77.

Rothwell, W. (2002). *The workplace learner: How to align training initiatives with individual learning competencies.* New York: AMACOM Books.

Schramm-Nielsen, J. (2001). Cultural dimensions of decision-making: Denmark and France compared. *Journal of Managerial Psychology, 16*, 404–423.

Schwartz, S. H. (1999). A theory of cultural values and some implications for work. *Applied Psychology: An International Review, 48*, 23–47.

Shi, J., Johnson, R. E., Liu, Y., & Wang, M. (2012). Linking subordinate political skill to supervisor dependence and reward recommendations: A moderated mediation model. *Journal of Applied Psychology, 98*, 374–384.

Sippola, M. (2009). The two faces of Nordic management? Nordic firms and their employee relations in the Baltic States. *The International Journal of Human Resource Management, 20*, 1929–1944.

Smith, P. B., Peterson, M. F., & Thomason, S. J. (2011). National culture as a moderator of the relationship between managers' use of guidance sources and how well work events are handled. *Journal of Cross-Cultural Psychology, 42*(6), 1101–1121.

Staffanson, M., & Glazer, S. (2008, July). *Implications of social support and culture in the context of work-related stress.* Paper presented at the XIX International Congress of the International Association for Cross-Cultural Psychology, Bremen, Germany.

Zimbardo, P. G., & Boyd, J. N. (1999). Putting time in perspective: A valid, reliable individual-differences metric (personality processes and individual differences). *Journal of Personality and Social Psychology, 77,* 1271–1288.

Chapter 7
Culture and Peacemaking

Borislava Manojlovic

Peacemaking is an exceptionally complex practice in terms of its social, political, and humanitarian impacts and potential. The mixture of ideological, pragmatic, and emotional considerations that drive the parties' decision-making makes it very difficult for the peacemaker to predict their moves and objectives in the first place. Peacemakers cannot be certain that they will respond positively to their actions and proposals. However, understanding various cultural contexts and practices in which the parties are embedded is a key precondition for anticipating and implementing successful peacemaking processes. This study offers insights into the cultural challenges of peacemaking work from the point of view of third-party negotiators. While there is some literature about specific cases, in-depth analysis of peacemaking performances in various cultural contexts from the point of view of practitioners is still lacking. In this study, culture is seen as a powerful system of beliefs, traditions, scripts, identities, and symbols through which people make sense of the world and relationships. However, cultures are constantly in flux and as they change, cultural groups have to find a way to adapt in dynamic and sometimes unpredictable ways. Abrupt changes of cultural conditions and dynamics often lead to conflicts, and understanding the cultural dynamics of conflict as well as developing strategies for its resolution is some of the primary tasks of peacemakers.

Conflict-prone environments exist at various levels, from international to organizational, and they require leaders and managers to have different conflict management skills and strategies. In addition, work conflicts often have cultural and gender aspects, which are often neglected. However, whether we talk about international or organizational conflicts, we cannot ignore cultural impacts. Through

B. Manojlovic (✉)
School of Diplomacy and International Relations, Seton Hall University,
South Orange, NJ, USA
e-mail: borislavam@gmail.com

© Springer International Publishing Switzerland 2016
J.L. Wildman et al. (eds.), *Critical Issues in Cross Cultural Management*,
DOI 10.1007/978-3-319-42166-7_7

interviews with actual practitioners[1] who performed official and unofficial negotiations at organizational, communal, and international levels, the author has identified key themes, lessons learned, and challenges that provide insights into the role of culture in peacemaking processes. The following sections focus on the peacemaking processes in general and what they entail, the powerful role of culture in conflict and peacemaking, and finally the lessons learned and challenges from the peacemakers' points of view.

Peacemaking Processes

Peacemaking processes can be broadly placed into "writ small" and "writ large" categories. In a narrow "writ small" sense, peacemaking can be done through negotiation, mediation, conciliation, and arbitration. Peacemaking "writ large" entails a variety of practices done by different actors, from interfaith dialogues to program development and diplomacy, that contribute to peaceful resolution of conflict. Peacemaking, according to the UN, is "action to bring hostile parties to agreement, essentially through such peaceful means as those foreseen in Chapter VI of the Charter of the United Nations" (Boutros-Ghali 1992). However, due to the volatility and complexity of conflict, peacemaking activities are often closely intertwined with other peace efforts, such as preventive diplomacy, peacekeeping, peacebuilding, and post-conflict reconstruction. Peacemaking processes provide a platform for a dialogue between two or more parties, facilitated by a third party, with the intention of

---

[1]The author conducted interviews with the following peacemaking practitioners: Dr. Andrea Bartoli, Dr. Susan Allen Nan, Dr. Miriam Anderson and Dr. Joyce Neu.

Dr. Andrea Bartoli is an international conflict resolution expert who has served in key academic and diplomatic positions for more than two decades, has been selected as the new dean of the School of Diplomacy and International Relations at Seton Hall University, starting July 1, 2013. Prior to his appointment, Bartoli served as dean of George Mason University's School for Conflict Analysis and Resolution (S-CAR).

Dr. Susan Allen Nan is a scholar-practitioner of conflict resolution and Associate Professor at the School for Conflict Analysis and Resolution (S-CAR). She has engaged long-term in conflict resolution in the Caucasus, as well as contributing to a variety of conflict resolution initiatives in Eastern Europe, Eurasia, the Caribbean, South America, and Africa.

Dr. Joyce Neu has been a part of the Mediation Support Unit at the official Track 1 level, but she has worked much more at the Track 2, unofficial level, as an NGO/academic person. She held posts such as chief mediator, unofficial advisor, consultant and advisor. Dr. Neu has been involved in peace processes in Somalia, Sudan, Uganda, Comoros, Central African Republic, Mali and Congo.

Dr. Miriam Anderson is an assistant professor of political science at Memorial University of Newfoundland. Her research encompasses peace processes and post-conflict reconstruction. She completed her dissertation on women's mobilization in contemporary peace processes at the University of Cambridge in 2010. Dr. Anderson worked as a human rights officer for the Organization for Security and Cooperation in Europe (OSCE) in Croatia from 1999 to 2002. She has also monitored elections in Bosnia-Herzegovina and Croatia and has volunteered with NGOs in Nicaragua and El Salvador.

achieving a compromise or a settlement of issues (Mitchell 2002). It should be noted that third-party negotiations can start long before the full-blown conflict has erupted and continue in some form in the post-conflict phase. Conflicts are complex; they are embedded in structures, institutions, and relationships that develop discrepancies and animosities over time. Once conflicts escalate, the parties can be drawn into a spiral of animosity, which become much more difficult to handle. Peacemaking processes can therefore be seen not only as a way to stop current conflicts, but also as a preventive activity that can break the path towards its recurrence.

Conflicts at different levels can be interrupted by certain conversational practices, such as dialogue, problem-solving workshops, mediation, or diplomacy that can maintain the conflict latent rather than actualized. In this space—created reciprocally by the parties to the conflict with the help of a facilitator—actors do not only participate in a dialogue to find solutions for specific issues, but they also build relationships through the processes of inquiry, exchange of ideas, and learning. Peacemaking processes suggest that a third party should attempt to move a conflict into a nonviolent mode so that sustainable solutions can be discussed. As Coleman and Ferguson (2014) posit "Constructive conflict negotiation has been found to improve the quality of leadership, decision making, and resource and risk management within organizations" (p. xvi).

Diamond and McDonald's (1996) framework of multitrack diplomacy provides an overview of some of the peacemaking "tracks" such as government, professional conflict resolution, business, private citizens, research, training and education, activism, religious, funding, and public opinion/communication. Whether peacemakers come from business, governmental sector, or any other track; they are all expected to introduce new ideas, innovation, inclusiveness, and mutual learning in a conflict system, which should lead to a de-escalation of conflict. This has been accomplished in many different settings leading to the prevention of violence and peaceful settlements of conflicts.

However, if we look at the statistics at the international level, there have been 216 peace agreements[2] brokered between 1975 and 2011 around the world, out of which an estimated 43 % fall back into conflict within five years of signing a negotiated peace accord (Collier 2008; Mack 2007). A key question is, how can peacemakers help avoid such negative outcomes and what is the role of culture in these processes?

Culture, Conflict, and Negotiation

In this section, we look at the role of culture in conflict and peacemaking through a broader lens, which can shed some light on difficult, recurring problems, and accommodate diverse cases. Cultures are systems of values, beliefs, scripts, and

---

[2]http://www.pcr.uu.se/digitalAssets/142/142371_peace-agreements-1975-2011final.pdf.

symbols that human beings use as their lens to make meaning, understand the world, and interact with others. As LeBaron argues, "cultures are like underground rivers that run through our lives and relationships, giving us messages that shape our perceptions, attributions, judgments, and ideas of self and other."[3] Humans are often so engulfed in their own systems of values, beliefs, and perceptions that they are often unaware of how those very perceptions, values, and beliefs can lead to conflicts.

The third-party negotiator's role is particularly complex because negotiators are entering sensitive, yet lesser-known cultural contexts as outsiders, whether at the level of organizations, institutions, communities, or states. Cultures are not always visible and obvious, but are rather latent and symbolic. This may represent a major challenge to a negotiators' job, which is to analyze and understand parties' cultural lenses and redefine those lenses in order to introduce change. Culture always permeates conflict and our own cultural lens can complicate things even more. Developing cultural fluency (Glazier 2003; Scott 1999) is a key tool for third-party negotiators, which suggests increased sensitivity and awareness of cultural nuances.

Cultural challenges should not be taken lightly; they are pervasive and complex, partially because they have to do with one's own expectations, language, and ideas. They are not exotic experiences that we come across in foreign and far away settings, but experiences that are part of our everyday lives and interaction. Conflict comes from a failure of making sense together and it suggests flawed interactional patterns. Conversely, conflict resolution is about rediscovering interactional patterns that allow for mutual sense-making to occur. For example, if we cannot make sense of a story about another group, we can potentially box ourselves into exclusionary, hostile narratives, which position the other as an enemy and a threat, thus creating the conditions for violence and human rights violations. These same culturally constructed narratives also hold within them a potential of constructing a better story (Monk and Winslade 2008), which should result from negotiation processes.

In times when numerous conflicts have to do with legal rights, power, resources, and identities, often the only way that we can understand these realities is through cultural artifacts, language, meanings, and ideas. However, we have to assume that culture is malleable and changing (Augsberger 1992). The cultural formations such as identity, narratives, or language represent a wider pool out of which both contentious and peaceful practices can be forged. In contentious situations, a culture of conflict and competition often emerges. Peacemaking, on the other hand, offers an alternative and engages parties in a process of cultural formation that enables new, cooperative, and constructive ways of addressing conflict. The role of negotiator then is to make sense of how a culture that promotes contention as socially acceptable behavior has emerged and offer alternatives thus, enabling transformation

---

[3]LeBaron, Michelle. "Culture and Conflict." Online Article. *Beyond Intractability*. Eds. Guy Burgess and Heidi Burgess. Conflict Information Consortium, University of Colorado, Boulder. Posted: July 2003 http://www.beyondintractability.org/essay/culture-conflict.

from the culture of contention to the culture of peace. As Colletta (2012) suggests: "Third party led negotiation is not simply deal making, but rather an effort to set in motion real political and societal transformation". War is an attempt to make sense of a new and changing reality through power and domination, whereas conflict resolution is a reverse process, which suggests making sense of the new reality through politics, dialogue, and conversation. In the end, there is no alternative to conflict resolution. Sooner or later, a political solution must be articulated culturally and in a way that makes sense to all parties involved.

It is people who create and change the culture which they are part of. Cultural constructs can be extremely constraining and peace needs to be allowed to emerge in these settings. Peace emerges when the culture is open to the transformative power of a new encounter, communication, and engagement. It was the openness of Nelson Mandela to learn the language of his enemy—Afrikaans—that enabled him to interact and engage meaningfully with the other. By learning Afrikaans, Mandela was able to welcome Afrikaner officers into his prison cell, and speak with them about his understanding of the new South Africa.[4] His political ideas about peace and reconciliation between White and Black South Africans gained meaning in his prison cell while talking to the guards. These conversations planted a momentum for his political platform based on unity and reconciliation. Peace processes require openness to a new kind of response and making sense of something new; there is an invitational element to it. Opportunities to engage in meaningful conversations are very rare in circumstances of conflict, distrust, and fear. The capacity that would allow us to change the cultural formations of conflict towards the cultural formations of peace requires tackling hostile and competitive patterns of behavior.

After analyzing the powerful role that culture has in conflict and peacemaking, we can now look at how negotiators understand the role of culture in their peacemaking efforts. While there are many lessons that can be learned from practitioners, we will address a few specific ones that are related to different cultural understandings of space, language, and time.

Lessons Learned

The Importance of Space

Cultural space and context can play an important role in peacemaking processes. Informal and safe spaces where parties can build trust and restore relationships are often key for peacemaking at various levels. Let us first consider a case of international level negotiations that led to peace in Mozambique. The process that led to direct negotiations to end the war in Mozambique was long and torturous. While

---

[4]See Interview with Fikile Bam who was on Robben Island with Mandela for ten years: http://www.pbs.org/wgbh/pages/frontline/shows/mandela/prison/bam.html.

contacts were established following Joaquim Chissano's appointment as President in 1986, it was only in July 1990 that the parties—the Government of Mozambique, led by Frelimo (Frente de Libertação de Mocambique) and the rebel group, Renamo (Resistência National Moçambicana)—were able to send delegations to Rome for the first direct talks. The talks were facilitated by the Community of Sant'Egidio in Rome, Italy, and observed by two of its members (the founder Prof. Andrea Riccardi and don Matteo Maria Zuppi), a representative of the Italian Government (Mario Raffaelli) and a Mozambican Roman Catholic Archibishop (H.E. Jaime Goncalves), the four being subsequently nominated formal mediators of the peace process.

The negotiations between two Mozambican parties, Frelimo and Renamo, took place in Rome. It was the city of Rome, as well as the *joie de vivre* of Italians whose joy of conversation, sharing a good meal, and being together that helped the Mozambican negotiation process.[5] The welcoming, hospitable, and safe environment provided to the parties resulted in open and engaging conversations, which eventually led to the signing of the peace agreement. The city of Rome, with its distinct culture, architecture, history, and beauty also contributed to the parties' relaxation and willingness to negotiate. Additionally, by bringing parties to a new and safe cultural setting away from violence and war, they were able to imagine and create new possibilities. Through displacement, Mozambicans were able to have culturally open conversation in Rome.

Safe space is not only important for processes at Track 1 or governmental level, but also at the level of communities and organizations. Managers have to create a space in which their employees will feel safe to express themselves and offer negative feedback. Conflicts often occur in business settings where culture is closed and animosities are perpetuated in secrecy. Informal gatherings and spaces where staff can meet and discuss issues casually may be useful for debunking tensions and misunderstandings that may not be easily expressed in more formal settings.

The Importance of Language and Communication

A breakthrough in the talks occurred when archbishop Goncalves and *Afonso Dhlakama*, the leader of Renamo, realized that they spoke the same dialect and their families came from the same village.[6] Common language became a key cultural platform for meaning making that allowed for trust-building and communication to occur. The level of competency in a language was also very important. Since one of the mediators and a party spoke the same dialect, the conversation among them became very intimate, open, and they could understand all the shared cultural nuances that an outside third party could not. They overcame previous animosities through these shared cultural identities, which were additionally facilitated by the

---

[5]Interview with Andrea Bartoli (01/12/2014).
[6]Interview with Andrea Bartoli (01/12/2014).

safe environment of Rome. However, it was not only speaking the same language, but also listening to each other that created an enormous amount of trust and bond between the two men.

The success of the Roman peace talks was a result of attentiveness to cultural nuances and intercultural communication. The mediators paid attention to the high-context culture of Mozambicans who needed time to build trust and relationships with the other before signing the peace agreement. Cultural constructs such as the same language provided a sense of commonality and belonging, which mediators used to push the negotiations forward. The peace agreement signed in Rome was a result of a process qualified as the special 'formula' by the UN Secretary General Boutros Ghali. He noted that the Community of Sant'Egidio "… worked with utmost discretion in Mozambique in order to bring both parties in contact with each other. It was very effective when it came to involving others who could contribute to a solution. The Community let its technique of informal discretion converge with the official work of governments and intergovernmental organizations".[7] Since this experiment, the expression "Italian formula" has been coined for this unique combination of government work and non-governmental peace efforts. The transparency, patience, and mediators' communication skills (through the archbishop of Beira), allowed the parties to come to an agreement themselves rather than through imposition of an outside solution. This is often not possible at the top level and with power mediators who are brought in the negotiations by a particular government or institution. Informal discretion, cultural sensitivity, and soft power of an NGO such as the Community of Sant'Egidio, which was first applied in their work with the poor and religious leaders around the world, enabled increased sensitivity to the parties' needs in the Mozambique peace process.

In organizational settings, managers need to learn how to best communicate not only with their employees of different cultural backgrounds, but also with their foreign partners. Culture affects communication in many subtle yet significant ways (Samovar et al. 2009). For example, there is a difference in cultural norms between Western and Japanese business cultures whereby the relationship between the employee and manager is more personal in Japan and some level of language proficiency is often needed to understand and express these subtleties. Communication and language can be seen as one of the key elements that managers must get to grips with in order to maintain effective collaboration with their overseas counterparts.

Issue of Time in Peacemaking Processes

One of the important lessons learned from practitioners is that Western cultural assumptions about doing things as efficiently and as quickly as possible cannot

---

[7]See: http://www.reteccp.org/biblioteca/disponibili/ccp/barbiero/barbiero3.html#anchor1.

always work in other cultural contexts. For example, the expectations in terms of length of negotiations may be measured in terms of centuries in cultural contexts such as Burma or India. In organizations, new managers often have to face a long process of cultural adaptation and resistance of the old organizational structures. Patience, listening, and allowing time to build trust and new ideas to get traction are key in such settings. It is by getting to know the facilitator or manager personally, and accepting him or her as the leader of the process that the people could commit to a certain assignment themselves.

One of the interviewees points out that although she worked for two decades in the Caucasus in South Ossetia, she still missed some cultural nuances and meanings related to time in negotiations at the community level.[8] She became aware of the challenges by working with a group of local partners who were coleading the process and knew the culture. Namely, she was facilitating a dialogue with an assumption that she gained through her core training as a mediator about the necessity of taking a break during negotiation talks. As the conversation was going on for more than two hours, she suggested a break. However, everyone else wanted to continue the conversation. After some time, she insisted on a break again, but the parties unanimously decided to continue the conversation that was now going into its fifth hour. It was not until one of the local partners told her that what kept the parties at the table was the fact that the conversation they were having was probably one of the most important conversations that they had in years. Therefore, they did not mind sitting and discussing issues for five hours straight. She eventually accommodated to their understanding of time. Respect for cultural nuances and sensitivities of parties in the conflict have been indispensable for the success of this and similar initiatives.

The Role of Women in Peacemaking and Its Cultural Implications: Burundi, Kenya, and South Ossetia

Gender is culturally constructed and gender-specific contributions are key for negotiations in any cultural context and at any level. Dominant patriarchal culture regulates norms and worldviews in many conflict and post-conflict settings. Violence and discrimination against women is not only a consequence of war, but can also preexist in social and cultural structures, unspoken traditions, and conventions performed in everyday behaviors, customs, and habits. Conflict resolution processes introduce change in such systems since they are integrative in nature and include gender balancing as part of their dynamics. Gender balancing entails equal access to the opportunities and development for both women and men. An important ingredient to gender balancing is the involvement of women in negotiations and today, more women are becoming involved and recognized for their

---

[8]Interview with Susan Allen Nan (12/5/2013).

efforts in negotiations processes. A good example is the Nobel Peace Prize of 2011 that was awarded to three women from Africa and the Arab world for their peace activism.[9]

Another example is the involvement of women in the negotiations leading up to the Arusha Peace Agreement[10] in 2000. Although women wanted to engage in formal negotiations as representatives of civil society, they were not able to do so until the UN, i.e., the UN Development Fund for Women (UNIFEM), helped them create the All-Women's Peace Conference. The All-Women's Peace Conference proposed a number of changes to the peace agreement regarding gender inclusivity and from that point on women had a large impact on the peace processes. Women did not have all of their demands fulfilled, but the key was that through their mobilization and inclusion in the process, they were able to create a strong women's lobby group in Burundi, which was able to get more concessions during the transition period and in the new constitution in 2005. They managed to secure the gender quota of 30 % in the legislative body, which has not only continued until now, but has even increased to almost 45 %. The peace process itself created conditions for a cultural shift from a deeply patriarchal system to a system which is not only more open and inclusive towards women, but also other 'minorities'.

Despite the growing recognition of the importance of women in negotiations, women still face many challenges. One of the challenges for women in the field of conflict resolution in general is that their multiple identities tend to be relegated to just their gender identity. By talking about the issues that are stereotypically thought of as women's issues, rather than talking about major and divisive issues of the conflict such as demobilization, disarmament, or responsibility, the peace processes can become "engendered". Women in Burundi make up more than 50 % of population and they should have a say in negotiations not only on so called "women's issues", but also other relevant issues. Prior to the establishment of the All-Women's Peace Conference, women were excluded from the main negotiations; they had an observer status as representatives of civil society towards the end of negotiations, but they were not able to actually speak. This is because women have not been generally considered as combatants or members of the fighting parties, and the purpose of mediation is to get people to put down their arms.[11] The conflicting parties are led by militant men who did not see women as full-fledged citizens, but rather as actors playing a supporting role.

Although excluded from the mediation process, Burundian women did not give up; they initiated a strong grassroots' anti-war movement that started as a response to the violence and were marching on the streets for peace, loudly demanding change, and working across party lines. Hutu and Tutsi women were working

---

[9]http://www.nytimes.com/2011/10/08/world/nobel-peace-prize-johnson-sirleaf-gbowee-karman.html?pagewanted=all&_r=0.

[10]See more on Arusha Peace Agreement at: http://unterm.un.org/dgaacs/unterm.nsf/8fa942046ff7601c85256983007ca4d8/d1e795e76bc4480c85256b0b0064661f?OpenDocument.

[11]Interview with Miriam Anderson (12/1/2013).

together in a very public way, and they were defining themselves in terms of gender and common humanity, which was an important alternative in an ethnically divided country. Women entered the peace negotiations not just to end the conflict, but also because they wanted a different kind of life in the post-conflict period. The processes of peacemaking and state building opened a window of opportunity for women in Burundi to voice their political views and achieve particular objectives such as: the protection of women and human rights, an increase of women's influence through representation, the criminalization of sexual violence, an establishment of health centers for women, etc. By becoming a part of political life, women became culturally visible and relevant, which created conditions for the conflict system to move towards democratization and positive change.

Despite these successes, most of the peacemaking processes around the world have very few women in key mediator roles. Even when the women are in key roles, as was the case in Kenya where two women served as leaders of the two negotiating teams representing two conflicting parties after the election crisis in 2007, there was no discussion about gender concerns during the talks facilitated by Kofi Annan. The women involved in mediation only played the role of professional political leaders. Moreover, women who were appointed to an official negotiating position tended to adopt a very masculine style of negotiations, which sometimes made them seem more hard-lined, positional, and argumentative.

The UN Security Council Resolution 1325 of October 2000 stipulates that women must be included in every phase of the peace process, from prevention to post-conflict peace building. One of the reasons for this inclusion is the recognition that women's perspectives can contribute to a cultural shift towards inclusiveness in negotiations and the resolution of conflict. However, appointing more women to official mediating positions just because they are women is not the answer. Women, as well as men, should be appointed based on their skills, experience, and ability to incorporate their feminine and masculine sides in a way that would facilitate the peace process.[12] The UN Resolution 1235 has given women a legal framework for action, but it is up to women to make it work so that their voice is heard and their ideas implemented.

Although there is still a very small number of women mediating at the Track One level, women at the grassroots level are brokering amazing agreements intended to facilitate everyday lives of their communities, such as establishing food corridors, providing safety, and access to services. These grassroots' women peace activists do not usually get publicity. Only recently, a Nobel Prize winner from Liberia, Leymah Gbowee, has been recognized for her exceptional work at the grassroots level in organizing and leading the women's peace movement that sought an end to the protracted conflict in Liberia.

One of the key lessons learned is that women should be fully integrated and play an active role throughout the whole peace process. Women can play different roles in peace processes and not just the roles defined by their gender. If women do not

---

[12]Interview with Joyce Neu (12/15/2013).

officially sit at the table, they can use back channels to communicate their message. For example, a mediator should make an effort to meet some of the women's groups that have very valuable perspectives on the conflict and how to resolve it. As Miriam Anderson[13] argues: "Women are more pragmatic than they are political. They take risks and deal with practical issues such as how to get the shooting to stop and how to get children to school."

In a dialogue in the South Caucasus, it was clear that women were in charge of the discussion. However, whenever a woman spoke there was always chitchat and background noise in the room; whenever a man spoke people were completely silent. A cultural assumption behind such behavior is that people showed more respect and attention to what men were saying. However, such an attitude also shows that people were more likely to engage in the conversation about peace if a woman spoke. Based on the observations of the dialogue sessions, one of the interviewees suggested that the conflict was fed by the "I defend my people" attitude, which is a masculine cultural expression, whereas conflict resolution was promoted by the "I care for my people" attitude, which is more of a feminine cultural formation.[14] Third parties in peacemaking processes need to be aware of these gender-specific cultural nuances and navigating through both may be seen as a challenge and an opportunity for the processes.

Conclusions

Culture permeates our lives in different ways—we cannot ignore it and we cannot fight it. What we can do is to be aware of the culture we work in and of our own cultural background. Third-party negotiators are cocreating a new reality with the people they engage. Being an outsider and having a different cultural background can be an advantage because it enriches the conversation through new perspectives and questions. It is this outside perspective that can stir the pot by introducing necessary change and innovation. However, this should be done respectfully and as an accompaniment that facilitates parties' conversation. A third party should offer a fresh outlook as a catalyst for new conversation by bringing in her or his own culture authentically and respectfully. The openness to interactive learning is a must in peacemaking processes. Learning from both failures and successes is a key for negotiating in ever evolving and complex conflict situations. Integrating cultural nuances into the negotiation practice should contribute to the efforts of moving towards a political rather than armed means of resolving conflicts, which will, at the same time, be more cost-effective and more humane.

---

[13]Interview with Miriam Anderson (12/1/2013).
[14]Interview with Susan Allen Nan (12/5/2013).

References

Augsberger, David W. (1992). *Conflict mediation across cultures: Pathways and patters*. Louisville: John Knox Press.

Boutros-Ghali, B. (1992). *An agenda for peace: Preventive diplomacy, peacemaking and peace-keeping: Report of the secretary-general pursuant to the statement adopted by the summit meeting of the security council on 31 January 1992*. New York: United Nations.

Coleman, P. T., & Ferguson, R. (2014). *Making conflict work: Harnessing the power of disagreement*. New York: Houghton Mifflin Harcourt.

Colletta, N. (2012). Mediating ceasefires and cessation of hostilities agreements in the framework of peace processes. In A. Bartoli, S. A. Nan, & Z. Mampilly (Eds.), *Peacemaking: From practice to theory* (pp. 135–147). New York: Praeger Publishers.

Collier, P. (2008). *The bottom billion: Why the poorest countries are failing and what can be done about it*. Oxford: Oxford University Press.

Diamond, L., & McDonald, J. (1996). *Multi-track diplomacy: A systems approach to peace*. London: Kumarian Press.

Glazier, J. A. (2003). Developing cultural fluency: Arab and Jewish students engaging in one another's company. *Harvard Educational Review, 73*(2), 141–163. http://her.hepg.org/index/TR2H742325553M76.pdf

Mack, A. (2007). Global political violence: Explaining the post-cold war decline. In *Coping with crisis working paper series*. New York: International Peace Academy.

Mitchell, C. R. (2002). What does conflict transformation actually transform? *Peace and Conflict Studies, 9*(1), 1–24. http://shss.nova.edu/pcs/journalsPDF/V9N1.pdf

Monk, G., & Winslade, J. (2008). *Practicing narrative mediation: Loosening the Grip of Conflict*. Jossey-Bass.

Nan, S. A., Mampilly, Z. C., & Bartoli, A. (Eds.). (2011). *Peacemaking: From practice to theory*. Westport, Conn.: Praeger.

Samovar, L. A., Porter, R. E., & McDanie, E. R. (2009). *Communication between cultures*. Boston: Cengage Learning.

Scott, J. C. (1999). Developing cultural fluency: The goal of international business communication instruction in the 21st century. *Journal of Education for Business, 74*(3), 140–43. http://www.tandfonline.com/doi/full/10.1080/08832329909601676

The Charter of the United Nations. Accessed online 29 October 2011. http://www.un.org/en/documents/charter/chapter1.shtml

The Community of Sant'Egidio website. Accessed online on 2 November 2011. http://www.santegidio.org/archivio/pace/mozamb_19900710_EN.htm; http://www.gppac.net/documents/pbp/11/6_egidio.htm

The Joint Communiqué accessed online on 2 November 2011 on the United States Institute of Peace' Digital Collection of Peace Agreements webpage. http://www.usip.org/files/file/resources/collections/peace_agreements/mozambique_07101990.pdf

University of Uppsala's Peace Agreements Dataset. Accessed online 19 October 2011. http://www.pcr.uu.se/publications/UCDP_pub/UCDP%20Peace%20Agreement%20Dataset.xs

Chapter 8
Assessing Cross-Cultural Competence: A Working Framework and Prototype Measures for Use in Military Contexts

Meghan W. Brenneman, Jennifer Klafehn, Jeremy Burrus, Richard D. Roberts and Jonathan Kochert

The ability to operate effectively in unfamiliar cultures is of paramount importance to the U.S. Army and the Soldiers who carry out missions overseas. Numerous statements illustrate how Army leadership has grown to recognize the essential role that culture plays in strategic mission planning and accomplishment. For example, in regard to U.S. operations in Iraq, former Lieutenant General Peter Chiarelli noted that, "understanding the effect of operations as seen through the lens of the Iraqi culture and psyche is a foremost planning consideration for every operation" (Chiarelli and Michaelis 2005 as cited in Abbe and Halpin 2009–2010, p. 20). This sentiment was underscored more recently in a memorandum from Defense Secretary Pannetta (2011), who emphasized the general importance of cultural capabilities for mission success.

M.W. Brenneman (✉) · J. Klafehn
Educational Testing Service—Center for Academic and Workforce Readiness and Success, 660 Rosedale Road, Princeton, NJ 08541, USA
e-mail: mbrenneman@ets.org

J. Klafehn
e-mail: jklafehn@ets.org

J. Burrus · R.D. Roberts
Professional Examination Service, 475 Riverside Drive, Suite 600, New York, NY 10115, USA
e-mail: Jburrus@proexam.org

R.D. Roberts
e-mail: RRoberts@proexam.org

J. Kochert
Army Research Institute, 6010 Frankford St—Office 221, Aberdeen Proving Grounds, Natick, MD 21005, USA
e-mail: jonathan.f.kochert.civ@mail.mil

© Springer International Publishing Switzerland 2016
J.L. Wildman et al. (eds.), *Critical Issues in Cross Cultural Management*,
DOI 10.1007/978-3-319-42166-7_8

These quotes emphasize the fact that mission success and, by extension, national security are largely dependent on Soldiers' ability to effectively interact with members of unfamiliar cultures. Furthermore, Soldiers must be able to interact not only with the wide variety of individuals and cultural groups comprising their theater of operations, but also with third-party militaries, coalition partners, and individuals from other U.S. services and organizations.

The ability to interact successfully with members of unfamiliar cultures has been labeled *cross-cultural competence* (3C). Currently, the Department of Defense (DoD) defines 3C as, "a set of culture-general knowledge, skills, abilities, and attitudes developed through a continuing process of education, training, and experience that provide the ability to operate effectively in interactions with other cultures" [DoD Directive (DoDD) 5160.41E]. But how does one develop this set of cultural knowledge, skills, abilities, and attitudes? The focus of this chapter is to introduce a working framework used to guide our development of a comprehensive 3C assessment system and provide some examples of the measures that comprise the system.

Statement of the Problem

Improved selection and/or training methods are needed to ensure that Soldiers working with people from unfamiliar cultures are cross-culturally competent. Both selection and training require a valid and reliable system for assessing 3C in Soldiers. However, despite the growing recognition of the importance of 3C, a comprehensive assessment that measures all facets of 3C has yet to be developed. Although individual assessments exist that measure constructs that are very closely related to 3C, these assessments tend to be self-report in nature, and, as such, their validity may be compromised by test-takers' lack of accurate self-knowledge, response styles, and/or faking (e.g., Kruger and Dunning 1999; Ziegler et al. 2011). For instance, individuals who lack 3C may actually overestimate their level of 3C on a self-report questionnaire simply because they are unaware of how low their 3C truly is (see Kruger and Dunning 1999 for a more detailed discussion). This phenomenon largely occurs because self-awareness, a component of 3C, is also necessary in evaluating one's level of 3C. To explain using a concrete 3C example, one can only evaluate the ability to negotiate with people from other cultures if he or she already knows what it takes to successfully negotiate with people from other cultures. However, asking an unskilled negotiator to evaluate his or her negotiation ability would likely result in a response that is either a guess or a constructed answer based on naïve theories of skilled negotiation. Furthermore, faking may be an issue with self-report measures, in that those who are motivated to present themselves in a positive light may present an overly optimistic view of themselves by inflating their responses to self-report items (e.g., Ziegler et al. 2011).

Both faking and a lack of self-knowledge can result in Soldiers being selected for missions for which they are either underprepared, unqualified, or both. The goal of the chapter is to describe a current project aimed at addressing this problem through the development of a comprehensive assessment system of 3C. This assessment system, in addition to being grounded in emerging theory, is composed of innovative measures that are designed to be less vulnerable to issues related to self-awareness and faking. This chapter serves as an introduction to the framework that inspired this assessment system, an explanation of the process by which the assessment system was developed, and a presentation of the measures that ultimately comprise the system. The chapter is organized as follows: first we introduce a comprehensive review of the literature surrounding 3C; next, we provide a synthesis of existing frameworks of 3C; third, we provide a detailed explanation of constructs related to 3C, as well as corresponding measures or item types that have demonstrated greater resistance to faking or bias. Finally, we conclude with a number of considerations researchers should bear in mind when developing assessments to measure 3C and other closely related noncognitive skills.

Cross-Cultural Competence

Culture, in general, can be thought of as comprising three components that are learned and shared by a group of people. These components include: (1) artifacts people make and use, (2) behavior, and (3) ideas (Caligiuri et al. 2011). These components are believed to be relatively stable in nature, although they can change depending on circumstances (Caligiuri et al. 2011). Figuratively, culture is often explained using the iceberg metaphor (e.g., Hall 1976), such that the majority of what individuals understand as representing culture or cultural influence is unseen by human observers or occurs "below the surface" (see Fig. 8.1). The part of culture that is observable or manifests "above the surface" includes the norms, artifacts, and behaviors. Just below the surface are cultural values and interests. Finally, at the deepest point, resides the set of assumptions held by the members of the culture. It is thought that cultural assumptions influence values and interests, which, in turn, influence norms, artifacts, and behaviors.

The fact that most of culture's effects are unseen (i.e., "below the surface") is one reason why cross-cultural interactions can be so complex. Within a military context, the idea of what constitutes a culturally competent Soldier muddles the definition even more. A Soldier who is interacting with a person from a foreign culture and unaware of such underlying cultural differences might perceive that person to be unreasonable or, even worse, irrational. This misconception may lead the Soldier to feel that his or her time and energy should not be spent attempting to work towards an effective solution. After all, it is pointless to reason with someone who is unreasonable or irrational. In addition, these differing cultural values and assumptions may further contribute to a sense that the person (and group of people with whom he or she is affiliated) is fundamentally "different" than the Soldier.

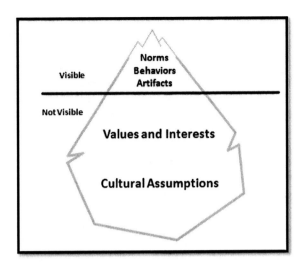

Fig. 8.1 Graphical depiction of cultural iceberg metaphor

Decades of psychological research have demonstrated that even these seemingly trivial group differences can trigger competitive and discriminatory behavior (e.g., Tajfel and Turner 1979).

Unlike Soldiers who are culturally unaware, a cross-culturally competent Soldier is capable of understanding culture and cultural influence as it occurs both above and below the surface. For example, a culturally competent Soldier would not only recognize differences in how Muslim women dress, but he/she would also understand that such restrictions on attire are rooted in deeply held beliefs prescribed in the Quran. Additionally, the Soldier may even understand the deeper reasoning and moral arguments for why attire restrictions are addressed in the Quran. This nuanced level of cultural understanding allows Soldiers to be more likely to know not only what people from other cultures tend to do, but also the reasons why they tend to do it. Such deeper, multilevel knowledge base should then help Soldiers not only to properly interpret the behavior of people from unfamiliar cultures, but also to more accurately predict future behavior. Cross-cultural competence, however, involves more than just knowing about cultural norms, behaviors, artifacts, values, and assumptions. It also involves the ability to apply cultural knowledge, to adapt to unfamiliar cultures, and to work effectively with people within those cultures.

3C represents a cross-cultural application and/or extension of previous concepts in psychology that have attempted to define the ability to work with others as a separate form of intelligence. These constructs include social intelligence (Thorndike 1920), successful intelligence (Sternberg 1999), and emotional intelligence (Mayer et al. 2008). More recently, Earley and Ang (2003), borrowing upon these concepts, developed a framework for the construct cultural intelligence (CQ), which they defined as the ability to effectively adapt to other cultures (for a recent review, see Morris et al. (2014). It is worth noting that there have been very few attempts to integrate these various "personal" intelligences, and that CQ may exist as a sub-component of one or more of these other, well-established intelligences or as a relatively independent construct (Morris et al. 2014).

Although the framework developed by Earley and Ang (2003) represents one significant theory upon which the current project's 3C framework development could be based, other frameworks have recently been developed that may be more useful for the purposes of the current effort as they have been developed specifically for a military population. Four such frameworks provide currency for the purposes of building an assessment system by being based on the military-relevant literature reviews, as well as interviews and critical incidents elicited from military personnel. Below, we review and synthesize these 3C frameworks. Following this synthesis, we discuss components of our framework in greater detail.

Review of Existing Military Frameworks

In developing a comprehensive framework of 3C, four frameworks (Abbe et al. 2008; Caligiuri et al. 2011; McCloskey et al. 2010; Reid et al. 2012) were selected that had been developed specifically with a military population in mind. In the section that follows, we briefly summarize each of these frameworks and provide a synthesis of overlapping competencies across these frameworks.

Abbe et al. (2008)

Abbe and colleagues developed a 3C framework by integrating previous research on intercultural effectiveness and organized it to maximize relevancy to Army leadership. Intercultural effectiveness was defined as job performance and work adjustment, personal adjustment, and interpersonal relationships of Soldiers or expatriates working in new cultures. Abbe et al.'s (2008) framework is depicted in Fig. 8.2.

On the far left side of the framework are antecedent variables (e.g., Big Five personality traits, tolerance for ambiguity, self-monitoring, self-efficacy). These variables, which facilitate the development of 3C, have been shown to be related to intercultural effectiveness and are thought to be relatively stable (though based on meta-analytic evidence, these variable may be subject to greater mean level change than originally thought; see e.g., Roberts et al. 2006).

Cross-cultural competence is depicted in the middle section of the framework. Compared to the antecedent variables, the competencies comprising 3C reflect

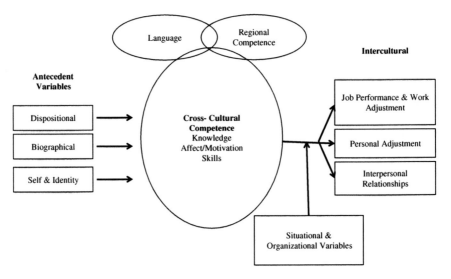

Fig. 8.2 3C framework proposed by Abbe et al. (2008)

"what individuals know, do, and feel with regard to cross-cultural experiences" (p. 12). Furthermore, these variables are conceptualized as being more dynamic in nature than the antecedent variables in that they can change over time (either as a function of natural development or through some form of intervention).

The framework also includes culture-specific language and knowledge (referred to as regional competence in Fig. 8.2). Abbe et al. note that, although variables such as culture-specific language and knowledge have previously been viewed as the most crucial variables for intercultural competence (e.g., Graf 2004; Guthrie and Zektick 1967), research suggests that they are not as important as one might assume. For instance, a meta-analysis conducted by Mol et al. (2005) revealed that the sample weighted mean correlation between local language ability and expatriate job performance was lower ($r = 0.15$) than it was for constructs such as cultural sensitivity ($r = 0.24$), cultural flexibility ($r = 0.21$), ego strength ($r = 0.20$), tolerance for ambiguity ($r = 0.27$), social adaptability ($r = 0.24$), and interpersonal interest ($r = 0.20$). In other words, language ability did not predict expatriate job performance as well as other individual difference variables that might be considered part of 3C.

Finally, the framework includes situational and organizational variables that moderate the relationship between 3C and intercultural effectiveness. That is, Abbe suggested that cross-cultural interactions are influenced not only by characteristics of the individual, but also by characteristics of the context or situation in which that individual is engaged. One potentially important situational variable is the amount of distance between one's own culture and the culture in which one is operating. For example, two people working together from two cultures that both value hierarchy and status have a better chance of achieving a positive outcome than two people from two cultures that have very different perspectives on hierarchy and status.

Reid et al. (2012)

Reid et al. constructed a 3C framework by merging common elements of two recently published reports: one report (and coinciding framework) was developed by the Defense Equal Opportunity Management Institute (DEOMI; Defense Equal Opportunity Management Institute 2011), while the other was developed by Applied Research Associates, Inc. (ARA; Applied Research Associates, Inc. 2011). Similar to Abbe et al. (2008), this framework includes constructs that are akin to antecedents, though Reid et al. refer to them as *enablers*. Enablers represent "characteristics—some of which stem from personality traits—that generally predispose individuals to act in a certain manner" (p. 4).

Their final framework consists of six core competencies and ten enablers. Enablers are not exclusively linked to individual core competencies; rather, several enablers are theorized to influence more than one competency (e.g., the enabler self-efficacy is theorized to influence all six competencies). The framework also includes several "secondary cross-cultural competencies", which are represented as facet-like components of the core competencies. Core competencies, enablers, and secondary competencies are listed in Table 8.1.

This framework also incorporates a developmental component that depicts Soldiers' progression from lower to higher levels of competency. First, the Soldier becomes aware of and/or recognizes cross-cultural issues ("baseline" competency). Next, they continue to refine and develop their knowledge and skills ("intermediate" competency). Finally, Soldiers have developed an advanced understanding of the influence of culture on oneself and others, and are able to apply their knowledge and skills in cross-cultural interactions ("advanced" competency).

Recently, Gabrenya et al. (2011) conducted a validation study of the DEOMI framework upon which much of the Reid et al. framework was developed. In comparing this framework to several military and other applied psychology models of 3C, they concluded that the DEOMI framework demonstrated acceptable content validity evidence. However, two competencies and four enablers were not well supported, such that these competencies and enablers were not included as 3C competencies and enablers by other prominent 3C frameworks. The less well-supported competencies included the *employment of human and material resources* component of the communication competency and the *adjusting or integrating cultural differences (according to operational demands)* component of cultural adaptability. The less well-supported enablers included *the avoid stress-induced perspectives that oversimplify cultures* and *acts as a calming influence* components of stress resilience, the *demonstrates ability to maintain personal values independent of situational factors* component of self-identity, and *optimism*.

Table 8.1 3C framework put forth by Reid et al. (2012)

Competency 1: Cultural reasoning		Competency 2: Intercultural interaction	
Enablers	*Secondary competencies*	*Enablers*	*Secondary competencies*
Inclusiveness	Applies cultural explanation of behaviors; sense making	Patience	Self-monitoring
Tolerance for uncertainty	Cognitive complexity	Inquisitiveness	Cognitive complexity
Self-efficacy	Suspends judgment	Willingness to engage	Nonverbal and verbal communication skills
		Openness to experience	Language skills
		Self-efficacy	Communication planning
			Trust building
			Negotiation skills
Competency 3: Cultural perspective taking		**Competency 4: Cultural learning**	
Enablers	*Secondary competencies*	*Enablers*	*Secondary competencies*
Tolerance for cultural uncertainty	Recognize existence of other world views	Inquisitiveness	Cultural knowledge
Self-efficacy	Cultural scripts based on cross-cultural mental models	Openness to experience	Learning through observation
	Suspends judgment	Self-efficacy	Rules about survival language
	Cultural explanations of behaviors; sensemaking		Cognitive complexity
	Cognitive flexibility		Understanding of own and other cultures
Competency 5: Self-regulation		**Competency 6: Self-awareness**	
Enablers	*Secondary competencies*	*Enablers*	*Secondary competencies*
Resilience	Self-monitoring	Leveraging personality attributes	Understands self in cultural context
Emotional stability	Reflection and feedback	Self-efficacy	Understands factors that shape worldview
Self-efficacy	Emotion regulation		Understands self in a cross-cultural context
	Emotion understanding		
	Attitudes toward cultures		

McCloskey et al. (2010)

McCloskey and colleagues relied on interviews of Soldiers in creating their developmental framework of 3C. Prior to conducting the interviews, they developed a list of 29 knowledge, skills, attitudes, and abilities (KSAAs) by reviewing the research literature and analyzing Soldier critical incidents and team ranking exercises. This list was condensed to 17 KSAAs by comparing the original set of KSAAs to 40 cultural learning statements developed by a group of researchers at the DoD (McDonald et al. 2008). They then took 400 statements from the interviews that were representative of the KSAAs and documented when the level of 3C influenced the success of the mission.

Next, 70 Soldiers completed simulation interviews. In a simulation interview, Soldiers are presented with several scenarios regarding a cross-cultural interaction and asked how they would respond. Responses were coded for the presence or absence of KSAAs and were also coded for overall level of competency. As a result of the coding, the 17 KSAAs were reduced to 16 (two overlapped in content) and were grouped into five overall components of 3C. The final five components are *cultural maturity, cognitive flexibility, cultural knowledge, cultural acuity,* and *interpersonal skills.* These components and their corresponding KSAAs are listed in Table 8.2.

McCloskey et al. also used the overall competency ratings to categorize respondents into *pre-competent, beginner, intermediate,* and *advanced* levels of competence. They then conducted an analysis to map factors according to developmental levels. This mapping is portrayed in Fig. 8.3. The figure illustrates that pre-competent Soldiers demonstrate low levels of KSAAs on each of the five factors. Beginner Soldiers demonstrate higher levels of all KSAAs than pre-competent Soldiers, with cultural maturity increasing at a demonstrably higher rate. Intermediate Soldiers increase on all factors, with the most pronounced increase occurring in interpersonal skills. Finally, advanced Soldiers demonstrate high levels of performance on all five factors.

Table 8.2 3C framework put forth by McCloskey et al. (2010)

Cultural maturity	Cognitive flexibility	Cultural knowledge	Cultural acuity	Interpersonal skills
Emotional self-regulation	Flexibility	Awareness	Perspective taking	Self-monitoring
Self-efficacy	Uncertainty tolerance		Sensemaking	Rapport building
Dedication	Openness		Big picture mentality	Relationship building
Willingness to engage				Manipulation/persuasion
Emotional empathy				

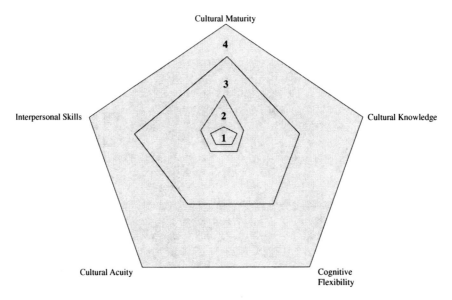

Fig. 8.3 Developmental model of 3C as proposed by McCloskey et al. (2010) *Note* Pentagon numbers represent overall competency level, such that *1* pre-competent, *2* beginner, *3* intermediate, and *4* advanced

Caligiuri et al. (2011)

Caligiuri and colleagues viewed 3C as consisting of two basic components: *cultural learning* and *cultural agility*. Cultural learning involves understanding new and unfamiliar cultures, whereas cultural agility is applying this new understanding to interactions with people from different cultures. Although they do not put forth a specific 3C "framework" as did the other authors covered by this review, they do present a list of 3C "facilitators," with each facilitator comprising several dimensions. These facilitating factors and their corresponding dimensions are listed in Table 8.3.

Caligiuri et al. also presented a five-stage model (adapted from Nolan 1999) that represents how people are thought to adjust to other cultures over time. The five stages are as follows:

1. **Identifying**—becoming aware that there are different cultures other than one's own
2. **Understanding**—learning rules that govern how other cultures work
3. **Coping**—interacting successfully with other cultures
4. **Managing**—learning how to manage other cultures in acceptable ways
5. **Integrating**—incorporating elements of other cultures into one's own way of thinking.

This model is developmental in that Soldiers progress from one stage to another as they gain more cross-cultural experience and training. For example, Soldiers who

Table 8.3 3C facilitators and dimensions put forth by Caligiuri et al. (2011)

Knowledge and cognition	Skills and abilities	Affect and motivation	Personality or dispositional traits
Self-awareness	Cognitive ability	*Willingness and motivation to...*	Openness, intellectual curiosity, and curiosity about others
Geopolitical history	Communication	Develop oneself	Sociability and extraversion
Global history	Influence	Gain the skills to be effective in intercultural and multicultural situations	Emotional strength and stability
Cultural Knowledge	Diplomacy	Gain the skills to be effective in intercultural and multicultural situations	Flexibility
Regional knowledge	Language skills	Suspend judgment	Tolerance of ambiguity
		Operate without racism (and other isms)	

are novices in cross-cultural interactions may only conduct stage one activities in their interactions (e.g., identifying differences between their own and other cultures), whereas Soldiers with very high 3C should be able to conduct stage five activities (e.g., taking the perspective of someone from a different culture).

Although they do not designate the facilitators as antecedents or competencies, the authors do speculate as to how the facilitators are acquired. The *personality and dispositional traits* facilitators are said to be relatively stable personality characteristics that are difficult to change. As such, they may be thought of as conceptually equivalent to several of the antecedents put forth by other frameworks (e.g., Abbe et al. 2008; McCloskey et al. 2010). Furthermore, the *affect and motivation* facilitator is thought to be acquired by both personality and learning, the *skills and abilities* facilitator is thought to be acquired by learning that may be influenced by personality, and the *knowledge and cognition* facilitator is thought be to acquired strictly through learning. Because each of these three facilitators can be at least partially acquired through learning, the most straightforward way to compare the Caligiuri et al. framework with the other three frameworks is to consider the personality and dispositional traits to be antecedents and the other three facilitators to be competencies.

Framework Synthesis

In developing a comprehensive, yet parsimonious 3C framework, we attempted to synthesize the four frameworks, combining constructs we identified as evidencing substantial overlap. For instance, we noted several of the antecedents/enablers and competencies overlapped across frameworks. Furthermore, a comparison of the frameworks demonstrated that extant 3C frameworks, in general, are subject to the "jangle fallacy" (Kelley 1927). That is, two or more concepts representing the same construct are labeled differently. In fact, in their recent critique of theory and research in 3C, Gabrenya et al. (2011) stated that one of the greatest challenges the field faces is overlap among constructs, citing Spitzberg and Changnon (2009), who identified 326 factors associated with interpersonal, communicative, and intercultural competence from the literature.

Our review revealed a large amount of overlap among the theorized antecedents and competencies of 3C. In fact, frameworks developed for civilian populations (i.e., students and the business community; i.e., research coming out of educational and industrial psychology) demonstrated remarkable overlap with frameworks developed for the Army (see e.g., Morris et al. 2014). Overall, nearly every competency in these frameworks could be categorized as knowledge/cognition, behavior/skills, or motivation.

Our framework synthesis is presented in Tables 8.4 and 5. We arrived at this synthesis by examining the different definitions of antecedents, dimensions, and constructs to determine overlap. We then combined the antecedents and competency components that demonstrated overlap, and attempted to define overarching, superordinate dimensions. The term "core competency" was borrowed from Reid et al. to describe these overarching dimensions. Our goal was to accurately capture the information in all four frameworks, while minimizing the presence of redundant constructs. Another goal was to provide an indication of the extent to which extant frameworks agreed upon the importance of each component. This is represented by the "Xs" in Tables 8.4 and 5. For example, *Tolerance for Ambiguity* is one component that was mentioned in every framework we reviewed. This congruence across existing frameworks provides some confidence in the relevance of *Tolerance for Ambiguity* to 3C when compared with other, less frequently mentioned constructs, such as *Need for Closure* or *Frame Shifting*. While other organizing methods are possible, the current synthesis provides a relatively simple, informative, and consensual view of the literature.

Table 8.4 Synthesis of antecedents of four reviewed frameworks

Antecedent	Reid	Abbe	McCloskey	Caligiuri
Openness	X	X	X	X
Self-efficacy	X	X	X	
Cognitive ability				X
Agreeableness	X	X		
Conscientiousness		X		
Emotional stability	X	X		X
Extraversion		X		X
Prior experiences		X		
Bicultural identity		X		

Table 8.5 Synthesis of competencies of four reviewed frameworks

Core competency	Components	Reid	McCloskey	Abbe	Caligiuri
Knowledge/cognition	Cross-cultural schema	X		X	
	Cultural awareness	X	X	X	
	Emotional understanding	X			
Behavior/skills	Self-monitoring	X	X	X	X
	Verbal/nonverbal communication skills	X			X
	Trust building	X	X		
	Negotiation skills	X			X
	Self-regulation	X	X	X	
	Frame shifting			X	
	Flexibility	X	X		X
	Influence	X	X		X
	Perspective taking		X	X	
	Cognitive complexity	X	X	X	
Motivation	Willingness		X		X
	Need for closure			X	
	Tolerance for ambiguity	X	X	X	X
	Non-ethnocentrism	X		X	
	Big picture mentality		X		

Note Willingness includes willingness to: engage, communicate, develop oneself, gain skills, suspend judgment, operate without racism or other isms

A Working Model to Assess Cross-Cultural Competency

Informed by our review of the extant literature, we then developed a 3C working model to serve as a guide for our assessment development, data collection, and analysis (see Fig. 8.4). Our approach was to break the process of working with someone from a different culture into steps and align antecedents and competencies from existing frameworks with each step. The major difference between this new framework and previous frameworks is a shift in focus from the characteristics or traits cross-culturally competent people "*have*" to what cross-culturally competent people actually *do*. Conceptualizing 3C through a performance-based lens is advantageous for a number of reasons. First, assessments of performance, in general, are not only more objective from a measurement and scoring stance, but also tend to be easier to develop than assessments of broad latent traits and dispositions (Kyllonen et al. 2014). Second, depicting 3C as a dynamic process as opposed to a static set of competencies encourages researchers and practitioners to consider how 3C may be more efficiently developed or trained. Finally, the "30,000 foot view" adopted by most traditional 3C frameworks allows for little to no exploration of the

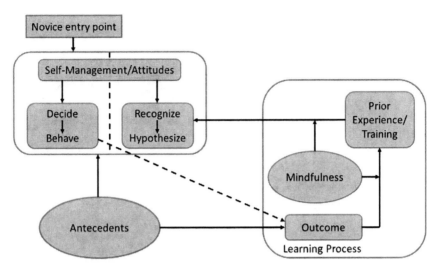

Fig. 8.4 3C Working Framework

finer-grained details that characterize cross-cultural interactions. In contrast, we believe our framework offers a more nuanced depiction of 3C that may help to strategically guide cross-cultural research questions in the future.

The four steps that comprise the process component of the Cross-Cultural Competence (3C) Working Framework are briefly defined below. Although these steps are presented in a deliberate, linear fashion, we theorize that several may occur automatically depending on the individual. For example, on the one hand, a Soldier who has had sufficient time and experience to develop his or her 3C may progress rapidly through each of these steps during a cross-cultural interaction. On the other hand, a Soldier relatively low in 3C may only reach the *Recognize* step of the model (or not reach it at all) during a similar interaction.

- Step 1: **Recognize**—noticing that the situation one encounters or anticipates encountering may be influenced by cultural differences
- Step 2: **Hypothesize**—gathering information about the local culture and developing hypotheses about why the situation is unfolding in the way that it is
- Step 3: **Decide**—planning, prioritizing, and selecting among behavioral strategies based on what one has learned or predicts will happen
- Step 4: **Behave**—taking the course of action decided upon in the previous step (in some cases, the course of action may be inaction).

Beyond these four steps, there are a few additional elements/features of the process model that are worthwhile to mention here. First, the model depicts the Recognize and Hypothesize steps as grouped together. This grouping was purposeful, as it was theorized that an individual could not engage in hypothesis generation without first recognizing that the situation he or she had encountered required some kind of deductive reasoning to navigate successfully. The same dependency was theorized for the Decide and Behave steps. Specifically, it was suggested that individuals typically do not behave without first deciding how or in what way they will behave given the situation. This relationship is believed to hold true even if the decision to behave is made subconsciously or is the product of a learned response, as the response itself was, at some point, influenced by a conscious decision to react in a particular way.

A second feature of the process model is the moderation of the four steps by a grouping of factors labeled "Self-Management/Attitudes". These factors, in general, reflect less malleable individual differences, such the extent to which one holds an ethnocentric worldview. While these factors are not foundational to the 3C model, they do reflect what individuals are "bringing to the table" that could influence the rate and success of progression through each of the four steps. As such, they were included in the model as moderating variables to illustrate (and perhaps help explain) differences in the way individuals process and integrate information in the development of 3C.

Once the fourth step has been executed and a behavior occurs, there is either a positive, negative, or neutral outcome that transpires in response to that behavior. In this framework, outcomes are conceptualized similarly to Abbe et al.'s (2008) view of outcomes as related to performance, adjustment, and personal relationships. This conceptualization was chosen in order to remain consistent with the majority of the reviewed frameworks, which propose behaviors, such as effective communication, to be 3C skills rather than outcomes themselves. Because outcomes provide individuals with direct feedback regarding the effectiveness of their behavior, they have the potential to be converted into learning experiences ("Prior Experiences/ Training"). These experiences are crucial for the continued development of 3C, however, they are only useful to the extent that the individual is aware (and cares) they occurred (see Deardorff 2006; Thomas et al. 2008). Thus, to improve upon one's 3C, one must be mindful of the ways in which their experiences (e.g., personal, professional) can influence and inform their understanding of cross-cultural situations.

Assessment Frameworks

Although 3C has received much attention recently, an initial evaluation of existing 3C assessments revealed that there are very few adequate measures of 3C. Gabrenya et al. (2011) acknowledged the efforts researchers have devoted to developing measures, yet identified seven overlapping problems with existing measures in their review of the Defense Language Office's (DLO) competency framework. Regarding the current measures of 3C:

(1) [N]early all use self-report methods that appear unsuitable for assessing most competencies; (2) only declarative, cognitively accessible, and self-referent information is usually

obtained; (3) the potential for faking ranges from subtle to severe; (4) affective states or processes are poorly assessed; (5) behavior is rarely measured; (6) the instruments map poorly to DLO Framework competencies; and (7) few were found to be adequately validated using performance criteria (p. 8).

The considerations highlighted by Gabrenya et al. indicate there is a critical need to develop alternative measurement approaches to assess cultural competence that do not rely solely on self-report. In the passages that now follow we review a range of established and newly designed measures to assess 3C. Innovative assessment methods include forced-choice, biographical data, situational judgment tests, and several performance-based tasks. We cover each of these methods, along with sample items next.

Forced-Choice

Forced-choice methodology requires the respondent to select between blocks of two or more statements from different dimensions that are of equal social desirability (Brown and Maydeu-Olivares 2011). One of the most well-known forced-choice assessments is the Tailored Adaptive Personality Assessment System or TAPAS, which has been used by the U.S. Army since 2009 (Drasgow et al. 2012). TAPAS employs a two-alternative forced-choice format wherein two personality statements are presented (e.g., "I always get my work done on time" and "I get along well with my co-workers") and the respondent must choose which of the two statements is "more like me".

There is some evidence to suggest that forced-choice tests are less fakeable than standard rating scales and show stronger relationships with performance (e.g., Jackson et al. 2000; Martin et al. 2002). However, forced-choice measures may have ipsative or partly ipsative properties (Hicks 1970). That is, scores on forced-choice measures may be appropriate for comparing the relative level of different traits within an individual, but inappropriate for comparing the relative level of a trait across different people. Essentially, forced-choice tests are inherently built around the assumption that personality dimensions are not independent. This poses a problem for test-takers who score highly across multiple personality dimensions or for test users who want to select individuals based on high scores on more than one personality dimension.

However, Stark et al. (2011) propose a number of IRT-based processes for constructing forced-choice items that ameliorate these issues of ipsativity. For example, in the sequential approach to developing a multi-dimensional pairwise preference (MDPP) measure, one first determines both social desirability and item parameters of a large number of items presented in conventional format. Social desirability ratings and item parameters may then be used to develop pairs of statements that act as a pair-comparison judgment (e.g., "I work hard" versus "I think up new ideas"). An important feature is that, within most pair comparisons, items are drawn from two different personality domains (e.g., an item measuring

---

Of these three statements, which one is MOST LIKE YOU and which one is LEAST LIKE YOU?

    A. When I get scared, I feel it physically.

    B. When I am in a bad mood, I can identify what led to it.

    C. It is easy for me to calm down after a heated argument.

Fig. 8.5 Sample forced-choice assessment item

Conscientiousness is compared to an item measuring Agreeableness). For some pairs, however, the items belong to the same domain (e.g., both items measure Conscientiousness). In this sense, it is possible to compute scores that also have a normative value (i.e., can be used to differentiate between people). Empirical evidence to date suggests that tests constructed and scored using the MDPP method appear resistant to faking, and that normative rather than ipsative information can be recovered from this process. Thus, an empirically-based procedure for item selection and test development combined with new statistical modeling techniques seems to produce the best of both worlds: fake-proof tests that also lack the ipsativity concerns corresponding with earlier operationalizations of forced-choice measurement.

Given that the Army already utilizes the TAPAS to assess personality in Soldiers, we sought to develop additional forced-choice assessments for other constructs of interest. For example, we have developed forced-choice assessments for the following constructs: emotional intelligence and ethnocentrism/ethnorealitivism. Below is an example from the Three-Branch Emotional Intelligence Forced-Choice Assessment (TEIFA). Preliminary validity evidence, collected with Amazon Mechanical Turk workers, suggests that this instrument functions particularly well for the assessment of typical emotional intelligence (Anguiano-Carrasco et al. 2015) (Fig. 8.5).

Situational Judgment Tests

Situational judgment tests (SJTs) present test-takers with realistic, hypothetical scenarios, and ask them to identify the most appropriate response or to rank the responses in terms of their perceived effectiveness (Lievens et al. 2008). SJTs have a long history in the military since their first use in World War II. SJTs represent fairly straightforward, economical simulations of relevant academic- (or job-) related tasks (Kyllonen and Lee 2005).

SJTs have several advantages over traditional self-assessment instruments. First, SJTs may be developed to elicit more subtle and complex judgment processes than is possible with conventional tests. Carefully constructed, the methodology of the

SJT enables the measurement of many relevant attributes of applicants, including social competence, emotion management, communication skills, critical thinking, leadership, teamwork, to name a few (e.g., MacCann and Roberts 2008; Oswald et al. 2004; Waugh and Russell 2003). As such, SJTs can potentially overcome the validity ceiling attributable to conventional cognitive assessments in personnel selection. Second, SJTs in general appear to be associated with less adverse impact than IQ tests and are positively received by test-takers (Patterson et al. 2012). Third, in a workforce setting, SJTs can be used during training sessions to provide employees with feedback on certain competencies important to the organization. For example, if a company is interested in strong communication skills within their IT department, a training session could be developed using participants responses to various scenarios that involve using communication skills. Finally, SJTs appear to be less susceptible to faking when compared to self-assessments, for which score improvement due to incentives can be up to a full standard deviation. Yet, there remains a lot of speculation on the nature of how fake-resistant SJTs actually are (McDaniel and Nguyen 2001).

Using critical incidents gathered from military personnel, we have developed SJT items for the following constructs: coping, emotion management, military knowledge and behavior, and cultural fundamental attribution error. Below are a few example items we have developed in our battery (Figs. 8.6, 7 and 8).

You are feeling stressed about the amount of work your boss has given you. You have many deadlines that you will likely not be able to meet. How do you think, feel, or act when you are stressed from having too much work to do? *Rank each option from 1(Most like me) to 4 (Least like me).*

  A. I treat myself to a nice meal.
  B. I tell myself that my boss has a lot of trust in me if he/she gave me so much work.
  C. I blame myself for having put off my work.
  D. I make a list of all the things I have to do at work.

Fig. 8.6 Sample situational judgment test item assessing coping with stress

---

Miguel served as an interpreter to a foreign military group. While interpreting Miguel stood very close to Soldiers, spoke animatedly and used a lot of hand gestures. Some of the Soldiers complained that Miguel was invading their personal space.

How important was this factor in Miguel's behavior?
  o Miguel's cultural has less "personal space"
  o Miguel is a very social person and was excited to be chosen as the interpreter
  o Miguel was taught to do this to build rapport with Soldiers by his instructor

---

Fig. 8.7 Sample situational judgment test item assessing cultural fundamental attribution error

A Major was working as an advisor to the foreign military forces and wanted to build a trusting relationship with his foreign counterpart. The Major demonstrated an interest in the country's history and people, and encouraged his counterpart to teach him about historical events.

How effective was the Major's behavior?

Very Ineffective	Ineffective	Somewhat Ineffective	Somewhat Effective	Effective	Very Effective
1	2	3	4	5	6

How likely would you be to act like the Major in this situation?

Very Unlikely	Unlikely	Somewhat Unlikely	Somewhat Likely	Likely	Very Likely
1	2	3	4	5	6

Fig. 8.8 Sample situational judgment test item assessing effective behavior

Biographical Data

Biographical data has long been used as an assessment method to more closely understand the life and work experiences of respondents. Biographical data, or biodata, have been explored for college admissions in the United States (Oswald et al. 2004), Chile (Delgalarrando 2008), and other countries. Biodata has also been a standard methodology for assessing constructs such as opportunity to learn and socio-economic status in large-scale national and international group-level comparative studies (e.g., the National Assessment of Educational Progress, Programme for International Student Assessment, and Trends in International Mathematics and Science Study; Naemi et al. 2013).

Biodata instruments have an advantage over personality and interest inventories in that they can directly capture the past behavior of a person and in greater detail than would otherwise be elicited via self-report methods (Mael 1991). In other words, these measures deal with facts about the person's life rather than subjective judgments. Biodata are obtained by asking standardized questions about individuals' past behaviors, activities, or experiences. Respondents are typically offered multiple-choice response options or are asked to answer questions in an open-ended format (e.g., state frequency of behaviors).

Jackson et al. (2010) demonstrated that the biodata approach can be effective when assessing individuals' personality. In this particular study, the researchers attempted to identify the behavioral component of Conscientiousness as well as specify a relatively large pool of behaviors that represented it. They developed and validated the Behavioral Indicators of Conscientiousness (BIC) and showed that the lower order structure of conscientious behaviors (as assessed by the BIC) was nearly identical to the lower- order structure obtained from extant self-report measures. Furthermore, the researchers used a daily diary method to validate the BIC against frequency counts of conscientious behavior and found that behaviors assessed with the BIC were strongly related to behaviors assessed daily through a diary method. The findings of Jackson et al. (2010) support the broader conclusion that, "reports of past behavior are at least partially valid, mitigating a criticism often applied to self-reports of behavior" (p. 7).

Another noteworthy finding is that measures of biodata show incremental validity beyond SAT scores and Big Five personality scores (Oswald et al. 2004). Biodata may offer a less fakeable method of assessment than standard self-report scales, as there are several test characteristics that can be implemented to minimize faking (e.g., Dwight and Donovan 2003; Schmitt et al. 2003). These include asking test-takers to elaborate on the biodata details (e.g., "What was the name of the last

Table 8.6 Item examples of biographical data

Scale	Description of scale	Sample item	Number of items	Response format
Travel experience	The amount of times individuals have traveled to other countries, states	If you have ever traveled to different countries, how many have you traveled to for personal (non-business) reasons?	5	5 pt
Openness to new experience	How stressful new situations are for the respondent	How stressful do you find visiting new places to be?	5	5 pt
Behavioral flexibility	Behavioral change when encountering new situations	How much have you changed your behavior when you encounter new people from other cultures?	5	6 pt
Cultural openness	The level of enjoyment in engaging with activities related to other cultures	In the past, how much have you liked interacting with people from different backgrounds?	6	6 pt
Cultural coursework	The number of classes taken related to other cultures or languages	How many cultural clubs (e.g. Spanish Club) were you a member of in high school?	7	Numeric Open ended
Cultural immersion	The amount other ethnicities represented at respondent's different environments growing up	When you were growing up, about what percent of people in your neighborhood shared your ethnicity?	5	5 pt
Prior cultural opportunities	Prior opportunities for cultural experiences	In the past, how much opportunity did you have to befriend someone of a different cultural background?	5	6 pt

foreign movie you saw?") or triangulating results obtained with alternative measurement approaches (e.g., other-reports).

For our assessment, it is important to understand how individuals' past behaviors, activities, or experiences have helped to shape their current level of cultural
competence. For example, if you have had the opportunity to travel to more
countries as a child or had a diverse group of friends growing up, does that, in turn,
make you a more culturally competent Soldier today? We developed a 38-item
biodata assessment to represent the following seven dimensions: travel experience,
openness, behavioral flexibility, listening skills, prior cultural opportunity, cultural
immersion, and cultural courses taken. Table 8.6 provides sample items for each of
these dimensions included in the biodata instrument.

Performance Tasks

Finally, a wide range of performance-based assessments can be used to measure the
application of knowledge, skills, and work habits within a cross-cultural setting.
These performance tasks include a range of innovative assessment types, including
an Implicit Associations Test for ethnocentrism and an image task designed to
measure situational awareness. In the sections that follow, we provide examples of
several of these performance tasks.

Implicit Association Test

The implicit association test (IAT; Greenwald et al. 1998) has become a popular
method for researching noncognitive factors, particularly implicit attitudes that
individuals would be unlikely to disclose on a self-report inventory (e.g., racial bias;
see Greenwald et al. 2006). IATs record the reaction time it takes to classify
stimulus pairs (e.g., word and picture), which is then treated as an indirect measure
of whether a participant sees the stimuli as naturally associated. IATs thus measure
the strength of implicit associations and have been used in prior research to gauge
attitudes, stereotypes, self-concepts, and self-esteem (Greenwald et al. 2002;
Greenwald and Farnham 2000).

Again using the 3C working framework, we recently developed an IAT to
measure individuals' implicit preference for American culture. In the first stages of
the IAT, respondents are asked to separately classify words as either positive (e.g.,
"wonderful") or negative (e.g., "terrible") and images as either American (e.g., the
Statue of Liberty) or Non-American (e.g., the Great Pyramids). In the stage that
follows (i.e., the assessment stage), respondents are presented both words and
images and are asked to categorize each into one of two groupings, such as
"American and Positive" versus "Non-American and Negative", or "American and
Negative" versus "Non-American and Positive". By examining accuracy and

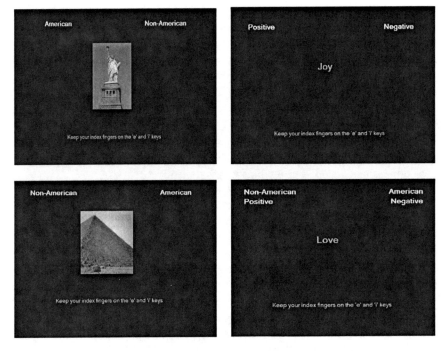

Fig. 8.9 Screen shots from ethnocentrism IAT

latency in the categorizations, we can assess an individual's implicit association of American images with positive words, and Non-American images with negative words. Our hypothesis is if participants have strong associations (i.e., high accuracy, low latency) between Non-American images and negative words, this could indicate a higher level of implicit ethnocentrism. Because this test is a performance measure based on the accuracy and latency of one's responses, it is less prone to faking than a self-reported measure of ethnocentric bias and attitudes (Fig. 8.9).

Situational Awareness Task

Nolan et al. (2014) state that it is extremely difficult to teach Soldiers everything they need to know about a culture prior to deployment. Despite this challenge, however, it is still essential that Soldiers possess the necessary skills that will enable them to uncover salient cultural differences and to act or react appropriately when interacting with others. These skills, collectively referred to as situational awareness, facilitate the identification of culturally relevant cues in new or unfamiliar environments. Situational awareness is particularly important for Soldiers, as they frequently interact with unfamiliar cultural groups in carrying out their mission.

To assess situational awareness, we have developed a performance-based task called the Cultural-General Recognition (CGR) Task. The CGR Task presents Soldiers with a number of photographs of people and places from around the world. The photographs were selected to represent themes that are universal to every culture (e.g., gender roles, success/well-being, degree of equality). For each image, Soldiers are cued as to the culturally universal theme referenced in that image, and are then asked to drop a pin on objects in the scene that they believe are reflective of that theme. For example, if the cultural theme being referenced in the photograph is "Political Structure/Governance", Soldiers may place a pin on a police officer. Following each photograph, Soldiers are taken to a page that presents vignetted references of areas in the photograph where pins were placed. On this page, Soldiers will briefly describe what they pinned to ensure accuracy. Figure 8.10 provides a sample CGR item.

Public and Private Space

All cultures have notions of privacy. Some cultures have very clear notions of privacy; others, the boundaries between what is private and public are blurred. Look at the image below. Select up to ten things that relate to how private vs public space are viewed in this situation.

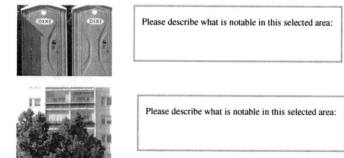

Fig. 8.10 Sample Item from the cultural-general recognition task

Conclusion and Next Steps

In this chapter, we have introduced a working framework and some initial proto-
types developed for a corresponding assessment battery clearly targeting a military
context. Our work is ongoing, and there remain additional considerations as we
continue to develop and refine assessments. Some of these considerations include:

1. *What is the best use case for the current battery?* The debate on whether an
   assessment of cross-cultural competence should be used for selection or training
   remains one that we are grappling with. From a selection standpoint, the
   assessment would allow organizations such as the U.S. Army to distinguish
   between individuals who are likely to perform adequately in cross-cultural
   contexts from those who are less skilled or whose performance may be problematic in such contexts. At the same time, however, it is unlikely that the
   assessment, at least in its current state, will be able to validly differentiate
   between individuals with average and above average levels of 3C given that the
   criteria upon which the assessment will be validated cannot sufficiently capture
   the nuanced differences in interpersonal performance that would otherwise make
   such differentiation feasible (cf. MacCallum et al. 2002; Oakes 1982). Under
   these circumstances, the assessment may function more practically as a training
   aid or intervention designed to develop or hone cross-cultural skills in individuals who have attained at least minimal levels of 3C. Thus, the response to
   this question is not a mutually exclusive one, but rather one that is dependent on
   the context and purpose for which the assessment intends to be used. While the
   eventual validation of the assessment will likely help clarify whether it is better
   suited as a selection or training tool, it will ultimately be at the discretion of the
   user (i.e., the U.S. Army) to determine when, where, and for whom an
   assessment of 3C will have the greatest impact.
2. *Is it necessary for a Soldier to excel in every step of the framework to be
   considered high in 3C?* We suspect that the answer to this question is "no" and
   that strength in some steps can compensate for weaknesses in others (i.e., a set
   of claims entirely consistent with a compensatory model). Similar compensatory
   relationships among skills or competencies have been demonstrated in constructs such as metacognition (Flavell 1979; Swanson 1990), such that those
   with strong metacognitive skills are able to overcome deficits in knowledge,
   especially in novel or unfamiliar contexts. However, even individuals who rely
   heavily on metacognition require basic levels of cognitive ability for their
   metacognitive skills to function effectively. Likewise, it may be the case that
   some steps of the 3C framework are required (e.g., recognize) for performance
   to be considered cross-culturally competent.
3. *Do cross-cultural interactions always take place in the order presented here?*
   Once again, we suspect that the answer is "no". For example, it may be the case
   that for many interactions, the *hypothesize* stage must take place before the
   recognize stage. At the same time, there may be interactions for which steps
   occur simultaneously or not at all. In situations where there are few to no

alternatives to act according to what one recognizes or hypothesizes as in keeping with cultural norms, also known as a strong situation (Meyer et al. 2011), the multi-step process is reduced to a single step: behave. This outcome is likely to occur more frequently in military contexts where official orders take precedence over individual preferences or judgments. With that being said, those leaders who are responsible for issuing such orders should take into account the cultural relevance of their decisions, not only as they impact the immediate goals of their unit, but also the broader mission at hand.

4. *How is motivation relevant to 3C and the 3C process?* In our framework, we posit that motivation may act as a mediator between antecedents and competencies, such that antecedents influence competencies only to the extent that one is motivated or willing to act upon them. For example, on the one hand, an individual who is high in openness to experience (an antecedent) is more likely to be motivated to engage in cross-culturally relevant behaviors, such as perspective taking (a competency), which, in turn, is more likely to lead to the actual performance of such behaviors in cross-cultural contexts. On the other hand, individuals who are low in openness generally lack the motivation or willingness to engage in cross-cultural behaviors, which, in turn, leads to their avoidance, disengagement, or withdrawal from cross-cultural contexts. Though this particular mediated relationship has yet to be empirically demonstrated, similar connections between behavior and behavioral intentions have been observed in other domains of research (e.g., Fishbein and Ajzen 2010).

5. *Is the current battery restricted only to military contexts?* We acknowledge that cultural competence is important for contexts outside of the military. Indeed, culture's influence is not only pervasive, but has become a common feature in environments where interpersonal interactions are necessitated, such as schools, workplaces, and local communities. With modifications, we anticipate the current battery as being applicable across a wide range of contexts in which cross-cultural interactions play an important role in performance.

Finally, since developing our framework, the bulk of the work has been dedicated to the development of the assessments themselves, yet we acknowledge we have much more work to go. In addition to item generation and refinement, the development process also involves analyzing existing critical incidents, interviewing and collecting data from Soldiers, and conducting large-scale studies with civilian populations (particularly Amazon Mechanical Turk workers). Our ultimate goal is to develop a comprehensive, reliable, and valid assessment of 3C with the hope that Soldiers, as well as any other professional group for whom cross-cultural performance is important, can be more effective when interacting with others and, in turn, more successful in accomplishing their respective stated missions, broadly writ.

Acknowledgments We would like to thank Lauren Carney, Chelsea Ezzo, Patrick Barnwell, Cristina Anguiano Carraso, Teresa Jackson, Carolyn MacCann, and Anna Lipenvich for their guidance and assistance with this chapter. This research was supported in part by U.S. Army Research Institute (ARI) Contract W5J9CQ-12-R-0002 to the Educational Testing Service (ETS).

All statements expressed in this article are the authors' and do not reflect the official opinions or policies of the U.S. government, ARI, or any of the authors' host affiliations. Correspondence concerning this article should be addressed to: mbrenneman@ets.org.

References

Abbe, A., Gulick, L. M. V., & Herman, J. L. (2008). *Cross-cultural competence in army leaders: A conceptual and empirical foundation (Study Report 2008–01)*. Arlington, VA: U.S. Army Research Institute for the Behavioral and Social Sciences.

Abbe, A., & Halpin, S. M. (2009-2010). The cultural imperative for professional military education and leader development. *Parameters, 10*, 20-31.

Anguiano-Carrasco, C., MacCann, C., Geiger, M., Seybert, J. M., & Roberts, R. D. (2015, in press). Development of a forced-choice measure of typical-performance emotional intelligence. *Journal of Psychoeducational Assessment*.

Baker III, J. A., Hamilton, L. H., & Iraq Study Group. (2006). *The Iraq study group report*. New York: Vintage.

Brown, A., & Maydeu-Olivares, A. (2011). Item response modeling of forced-choice questionnaires. *Educational and Psychological Measurement, 71*(3), 460–502.

Caligiuri, P., Noe, R., Nolan, R., Ryan, A. M., & Drasgow, F. (2011). *Training, developing, and assessing cross-cultural competence in military personnel* (Technical Report No. 1284). Arlington, VA: U.S. Army Research Institute for the Behavioral and Social Sciences.

Chiarelli, P. W., & Michaelis, P. R. (2005). Winning the peace: The requirement for full-spectrum operations. *Military Review, 85*, 10.

Deardorff, D. K. (2006). Identification and assessment of intercultural competence as a student outcome of internationalization. *Journal of Studies in International Education, 10*, 241–266.

Delgalarrando, M. G. (2008, July). *Validan plan de admisión complementaria a la UC*. El Mercurio, Santiago, Chile.

Department of the Army. (in progress). *Army language, regional expertise, and culture strategy*. Arlington, VA: Headquarters, Department of the Army.

Drasgow, F., Stark, S., Chernyshenko, O. S., Nye, C. D., Hulin, C., & White, L. A. (2012). *Development of the Tailored Adaptive Personality Assessment System (TAPAS) to support Army selection and classification decisions*. Fort Belvoir, VA: US Army Research Institute for the Behavioral and Social Sciences.

Dwight, S. A., & Donovan, J. J. (2003). Do warnings not to fake reduce faking? *Human Performance, 16*(1), 1–23.

Earley, P. C., & Ang, S. (2003). *Cultural intelligence: An analysis of individual interactions across cultures*. Palo Alto, CA: Stanford University Press.

Fishbein, M., & Ajzen, I. (2010). *Predicting and changing behavior: The reasoned action approach*. New York: Psychology Press (Taylor & Francis).

Flavell, J. H. (1979). Metacognition and cognitive monitoring: A new area of cognitive-developmental inquiry. *American Psychologist, 34*, 906–911.

Gabrenya, W. K, Jr., Moukarzel, R. G., Pomerance, M. H., Griffith, R. L., & Deaton, J. (2011). *A validation study of the Defense Language Office Framework for Cultural Competence and an evaluation of available assessment instruments (Technical Report #13-12)*. Patrick AFB, Florida: DEOMI Press.

Graf, A. (2004). Assessing intercultural training designs. *Journal of European Industrial Training, 28*, 199–214.

Greenwald, A. G., Banaji, M. R., Rudman, L. A., Farnham, S. D., Nosek, B. A., & Mellott, D. S. (2002). A unified theory of implicit attitudes, stereotypes, self-esteem, and self-concept. *Psychological Review, 109*, 3–25.

Greenwald, A. G., & Farnham, S. D. (2000). Using the Implicit Association Test to measure self-esteem and self-concept. *Journal of Personality and Social Psychology, 79*, 1022–1038.

Greenwald, A. G., McGhee, D. E., & Schwartz, J. K. L. (1998). Measuring individual differences in implicit cognition: The implicit association test. *Journal of Personality and Social Psychology, 74*, 1464–1480.

Greenwald, A. G., Nosek, B. A., & Sriram, N. (2006). Consequential validity of the Implicit Association Test: Comment on Blanton and Jaccard. *American Psychologist, 61*(1), 56–61.

Guthrie, G. M., & Zektick, I. N. (1967). Predicting performance in the Peace Corps. *Journal of Social Psychology, 71*, 11–21.

Hall, E. T. (1976). *Beyond Culture*. Garden City, N.Y: Anchor Press.

Hicks, L. E. (1970). Some properties of ipsative, normative, and forced-choice normative measures. *Psychological Bulletin, 74*(3), 167–184.

Jackson, J. J., Wood, D., Bogg, T., Walton, K. E., Harms, P. D., & Roberts, B. W. (2010). What do conscientious people do? Development and validation of the Behavioral Indicators of Conscientiousness (BIC). *Journal of Research on Personality, 44*(4), 501–511.

Jackson, D. N., Wroblewski, V. R., & Ashton, M. C. (2000). The impact of faking on employment tests: Do forced-choice offer a solution? *Human Performance, 13*, 371–388.

Kelley, E. L. (1927). *Interpretation of educational measurements*. Yonkers, NY: World.

Kruger, J., & Dunning, D. (1999). Unskilled and unaware of it: How difficulties in recognizing one's own incompetence lead to inflated self-assessments. *Journal of Personality and Social Psychology, 77*, 1121–1134.

Kyllonen, P. C. (2008). *The research behind the ETS personal potential index (PPI)*. Princeton, NJ: Educational Testing Service

Kyllonen, P. C., & Lee, S. (2005). Assessing problem solving in context. In O. Wilhelm & R. W. Engle (Eds.), *Handbook of understanding and measuring intelligence* (pp. 11–25). Thousand Oaks, CA: Sage.

Kyllonen, P. C., Lipnevich, A. A., Burrus, J., & Roberts, R. D. (2008). *Personality, motivation, and college readiness: A prospectus for assessment and development*. Princeton, NJ: Educational Testing Service.

Kyllonen, P. C., Lipnevich, A. A., Burrus, J., & Roberts, R. D. (2014). Personality, motivation, and college readiness: A prospectus for assessment and development. *Educational Testing Service Research Report No: RR-13-14*. Princeton, NJ: Educational Testing Service.

Lievens, F., Peeters, H., & Schollaert, E. (2008). Situational judgment tests: a review of recent research. *Personnel Review, 37*(4), 426–441.

MacCallum, R. C., Zhang, S., Preacher, K. J., & Rucker, D. D. (2002). On the practice of dichotomization of quanitative variables. *Psychological Methods, 7*(1), 19–40.

MacCann, C., & Roberts, R. D. (2008). New paradigms for assessing emotional intelligence: Theory and data. *Emotion, 8*, 540–551.

Mael, F. A. (1991). A conceptual rationale for the domain and attributes of biodata items. *Personnel Psychology, 44*, 763–927.

Martin, B. A., Bowen, C. C., & Hunt, S. T. (2002). How effective are people at faking on personality questionnaires? *Personality and Individual Differences, 32*(2), 247–256.

Mayer, J. D., Roberts, R. D., & Barsade, S. G. (2008). Human abilities: Emotional intelligence. *Annual Review of Psychology, 59*, 507–536.

McCloskey, M. J., Behymer, K. J., Papautsky, E. L., Ross, K. G., & Abbe, A. (2010). *A developmental model of cross-cultural competence at the tactical level (Technical Report 1278)*. Alexandria, VA: U.S. Army Research Institute.

McDaniel, M. A., & Nguyen, N. T. (2001). Situational judgment tests: A review of practice and constructs assessed. *International Journal of Selection and Assessment, 9*, 103–113.

McDonald, D. P., McGuire, G., Johnston, J., Selmeski, B., & Abbe, A. (2008). *Developing and managing cross-cultural competence within the Department of Defense: Recommendations for learning and assessment*. Paper submitted to the Defense Language Office, Arlington, VA.

Mol, S. T., Born, M. P., Willemsen, M. E., & Van der Molen, H. T. (2005). Predicting expatriate job performance for selection purposes: A quantitative review. *Journal of Cross-Cultural Psychology, 36*(5), 590–620.

Morris, M. W., Savani, K., & Roberts, R. D. (2014). Intercultural training and assessment: Implications for organizational and public policies. *Policy Insights from Behavioral and Brain Sciences, 1*, 63–71.

Naemi, B., Gonzalez, E., Bertling, J., Betancourt, A., Burrus, J., Kyllonen, P. C., et al. (2013). Large-scale group score assessments: Past, present, and future. In D. H. Saklofske, C. B. Reynolds, & V. L. Schwean (Eds.), *Oxford handbook of child psychological assessment* (pp. 129–149). Cambridge, MA: Oxford University Press.

Nolan, R. (1999). *Communicating and adapting across cultures.* Westport, CT: Bergin & Garvey.

Nolan, R., LaTour, E., & Klafehn, J. L. (2014). *Framework for rapid situational awareness in the field.* (Technical Report 1338). Fort Belvoir, VA: U.S. Army Research Institute for the Behavioral and Social Sciences.

Oakes, M. (1982). Intuiting strength of associate from a correlation coefficient. *British Journal of Psychology, 73*(1), 51–56.

Oswald, F. L., Schmitt, N., Kim, B. H., Ramsay, L. J., & Gillespie, M. A. (2004). Developing a biodata measure and situational judgment inventory as predictors of college student performance. *Journal of Applied Psychology, 89*, 187–207.

Panetta, L. (2011, August). Secretary of defense memorandum.

Patterson, F., Ashworth, V., Zibarras, L., Coan, P., Kerrin, M., & O'Neill, P. (2012). Evaluations of situational judgement tests to assess non-academic attributes in selection. *Medical Education, 46*(9), 850–868.

Rasmussen, L. J., Sieck, W. R., Crandall, B. W., Simpkins, B. G., & Smith, J. L. (2013). *Data collection and analysis for a cross-cultural competence model.* Fairborn, OH: Applied Research Associates Inc.

Reid, P., Steinke, J. C., Mokuolu, F., Trejo, B., Faulkner, D., Sudduth, M. M., & McDonald, D. P. (2011). *A proposed developmental sequence for cross-cultural competence training in the Department of Defense.* Melbourne, Florida: Defense Equal Opportunity Management Institute.

Reid, P., Kaloydis, F. O., Sudduth, M. M., & Greene-Sands, A. (2012). *Executive summary: A framework for understanding cross-cultural competence in the Department of Defense.* DEOMI Technical Report No. 15–12. Washington, D.C.

Roberts, B. W., Walton, K. E., & Viechtbauer, W. (2006). Patterns of mean-level change in personality traits across the life course: A meta-analysis of longitudinal studies. *Psychological Bulletin, 132*(1), 1–25.

Schmitt, N., Oswald, F. L., Kim, B. H., Gillespie, M. A., & Ramsay, L. J. (2003). Impact of elaboration on socially desirable responding and the validity of biodata measures. *Journal of Applied Psychology, 88*, 979–988.

Spitzberg, B. H., & Changnon, G. (2009). Conceptualizing intercultural competence. In D. K. Deardorff (Ed.), *The Sage handbook of intercultural communication* (pp. 2–52). Thousand Oaks, CA: Sage.

Stark, S., Chernyshenko, O. S., & Drasgow, F. (2011). Constructing fake-resistant personality tests using item response theory: High stakes personality testing with multidimensional pairwise preferences. In M. Ziegler, C. MacCann, & R. D. Roberts (Eds.), *New perspectives on faking in personality assessments.* NY: Oxford University Press.

Sternberg, R. J. (Ed.). (1999). The theory of successful intelligence. *Review of General Psychology, 3*, 292–316.

Swanson, H. L. (1990). Influence of metacognitive knowledge and aptitude on problem solving. *Journal of Educational Psychology, 82*, 306–314.

Tajfel, H., & Turner, J. (1979). An integrative theory of intergroup conflict. In W. G. Austin & S. Worchel (Eds.), *The social psychology of intergroup relations* (pp. 33–47). Monterey, CA: Brooks/Cole.

Thomas, D. C., Elron, E., Stahl, G., Ekelund, B. Z., Ravlin, E. C., Cerdin, J.-L., & Lazarova, M. B. (2008). Cultural intelligence: Domain and assessment. *International Journal of Cross-Cultural Management, 8*(2), 123–143.

Thorndike, E. L. (1920). A constant error in psychological ratings. *Journal of Applied Psychology, 4*(1), 25–29.

Waugh, G. W., & Russell, T. L. (2003). *Scoring both judgment and personality in a situational judgment test.* Paper presented at the 45th Annual Conference of the International Military Testing Association. Pensacola, FL.

Ziegler, M., MacCann, C., & Roberts, R. D. (2011). *New perspective on faking in personality assessment.* New York: Oxford University Press.

Chapter 9
Expecting the Unexpected: Cognitive and Affective Adaptation Across Cultures

Zachary N.J. Horn, Tara A. Brown, Krista L. Ratwani
and Gregory A. Ruark

Success in international operations requires understanding how individuals, teams, and organizations learn to operate in unfamiliar cultures. This need exists across all industries, as the emphasis on global teamwork and competition continues to increase in frequency and complexity (Baard et al. 2014). Organizations can gain a competitive advantage by learning how leaders can facilitate—and even accelerate—readiness for cross-cultural operations; however, such interventions must be tailored to the unique challenges of adapting quickly to unfamiliar cultures. This chapter summarizes an in-depth exploration into the knowledge, skills, attitudes (KSAs), and experiences that help individuals and teams adapt to cross-cultural operations. Similarly, we identify leader strategies that can help mitigate challenges and facilitate adaptability to international collaborations. To conduct this research, we turned to one of the world's largest organizations that continuously evolve its strategic approach to conducting rapid, high stakes operations in new and unfamiliar cultures: the U.S. military.[1]

---

[1]The findings summarized in this chapter are not to be construed as an official Department of the Army position.

Z.N.J. Horn (✉)
Stitch Fix, 3977 Casanova Dr., San Mateo, CA 94403, USA
e-mail: zackhorn@gmail.com

T.A. Brown
Aptima, Inc., 9026 Kingsley Lane, Fishers, IN 46037, USA
e-mail: tbrown@aptima.com

K.L. Ratwani
Aptima Inc., 1726 M St. NW, Suite 900, Washington, DC 20036, USA
e-mail: kratwani@aptima.com

G.A. Ruark
U.S. Army Research Institute for the Behavioral and Social Sciences,
6000 6th Street, FT Belvoir, VA 22060, USA
e-mail: gregory.a.ruark.civ@mail.mil

© Springer International Publishing Switzerland 2016
J.L. Wildman et al. (eds.), *Critical Issues in Cross Cultural Management*,
DOI 10.1007/978-3-319-42166-7_9

The focus of current American military operations has changed over the last few years as emphasis has shifted from warfighting missions to those of full spectrum operations and persistent conflict. Because of this change in focus, Soldiers need to prepare for cross-cultural interactions during deployment, as "understanding and empathy will be important weapons of war...[and] cultural awareness and the ability to build ties of trust will offer protection to troops more effectively than body armor" (Scales 2009, p. S27). As a result, cultural awareness and competency are critical for effective performance and mission success in irregular warfare, counterinsurgency, nation building, and other such operations (Scales 2009). Such competence requires a great deal of cultural knowledge, as it "goes beyond words to include understanding gestures, body language, cultural norms, social networks, perspectives, and so on" (Laurence 2011, p. 293). Thus, Soldiers must work hard to understand how cultural norms impact the behaviors and beliefs of individuals. By developing this understanding, military personnel will be more likely to succeed across different cross-cultural situations.

Cross-cultural interactions are challenging, and a lack of cultural understanding likely will impede interactions with locals. For the last few years, the Army has been identifying competencies that help Soldiers remain effective in cross-cultural situations (e.g., Abbe et al. 2008). Complicating this effort, Soldiers also must be able to adapt when transitioning to a new cultural context and/or new mission. This transition may be in the form of entering a new area of operations in a different country, traversing an unfamiliar village with different religions, or even transitioning from warfighting to peace-keeping operations. The challenge is that Soldiers do not enter a new situation as a clean slate. They bring knowledge, skills, attitudes, experiences, and personal characteristics that enhance or inhibit adaptation to each new cultural situation. To achieve mission success, Soldiers must actively seek information about the new situation and integrate this knowledge with past experiences. They must put aside prior assumptions and feelings and think critically about the new situation. Given this need, those adapting to new cultures should be trained on *how* to think and not *what* to think (Abbe et al. 2008).

This chapter addresses the drivers of cross-cultural adaptability and *how* leaders facilitate such adaptation in their team members. Similar to most organizations, military personnel must be provided with guidance on how to successfully adjust to new cultural expectations. This guidance most often comes from leaders, who are in a unique position to provide this guidance and reinforce the success of their team members. U.S. Army Chief of Staff, Gen. Ray Odierno, noted that the Army holds a "leader-centric view of being adaptable, flexible, and able to adapt to the situation on the ground" (Vergun 2014, February 12). While leaders themselves must be flexible and adaptable, they are also responsible for ensuring the adaptability of their unit members. By learning how to recognize signs that personnel are not effectively adapting to different cultures, leaders can subsequently take action to manage the cognitive, affective, and situational factors that enable team member to adapt across cultures. The research summarized in this chapter was funded by the U.S. Army Research Institute for the Behavioral and Social Sciences (Contract number W911NF-13-C-0067) to identify these factors and develop leader strategies to establish and maintain adaptability across cultures.

Adapting Across Cultures

For leaders to effectively monitor, assess, and influence the adaptive success of team members in new cultural settings, it is critical to (1) understand what is meant by "adaptation," and (2) recognize that there are many cultural and individual factors that may influence cross-cultural adaptation. Adaptation can be defined as the "cognitive, affective, motivational, and behavioral modifications made in response to the demands of a new or changing environment, or situational demands" (Baard et al. 2014, p. 50). This definition highlights the cognitive, affective/motivational, and behavioral pathways along which adaptation occurs. While this definition comes from the general adaptation literature, it is also relevant when considering cross-cultural adaptation more specifically. Some of the cues, situational demands, and factors affecting adaptation may be culture-specific; however, the adaptation process applies across cultures. Leaders need to be aware of the relatively stable (e.g., cultural knowledge, personality characteristics) and malleable (e.g., perspective taking skills; motivation level) factors that contribute to an individual's ability to adapt successfully to new or changing cultures and how they may influence this process.

Phases of Adaptation

The organizational psychology literature and military doctrine make it clear that "being adaptable" when encountering new or changing situations is critical to effectiveness at all levels: individual, team (unit), and organization (Burke et al. 2006; U.S. Department of the Army 2012). While agreement exists on the importance of adaptability, Baard et al. (2014) noted that research on adaptability originated from different perspectives, which influences how the construct is viewed: an individual differences perspective (e.g., Pulakos et al. 2000, 2002), a learning/developmental perspective (e.g., Kozlowski et al. 2001), and a dynamic process perspective (e.g., Burke et al. 2006). From an individual differences perspective, adaptability is represented as a set of relatively stable characteristics about an individual (e.g., cognitive ability, openness) that allow an individual to be more adaptable across different situations. In contrast, researchers adopting a learning perspective of adaptation focus on identifying training and learning experiences that will facilitate the development of adaptive domain-specific expertise and skills (e.g., Bell and Kozlowski 2008; Smith et al. 1997). Finally, a dynamic process perspective conceptualizes adaptation as an unfolding sequence of phases through which individuals must progress to successfully adapt (e.g., Burke et al. 2006).

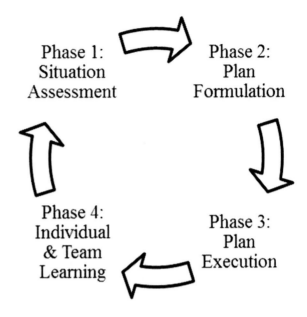

Fig. 9.1 Adaptive cycle (adapted from Burke et al. 2006)

Phase 1: Situation Assessment

Phase 2: Plan Formulation

Phase 4: Individual & Team Learning

Phase 3: Plan Execution

The model put forth by Burke et al. (2006; Fig. 9.1) comprises a four-phase adaptive cycle. During the first phase, *situation assessment*, individuals scan their environment for signs (cues) that may impact the outcome of the team's task or mission. Individuals must be able to recognize cues that may signal a change is needed and interpret those changes appropriately in light of their expectations and current performance goals. In the second phase, *plan formulation*, individuals use the knowledge they gained during the first phase to determine what to do moving forward. For example, what course of action should be taken? What adjustments need to be made? If an individual fails at Phase 1, they are likely to fail at developing an effective plan at Phase 2. Phase 3, *plan execution*, requires individuals to implement the plan they developed in Phase 2. It is possible for individuals to effectively assess a situation and develop an effective plan but fail to execute it properly. In Phase 4, *individual and team learning*, individuals and teams reflect upon and learn from the results of their assessment and actions, which can improve success in future situations. Team members who are provided opportunities to reflect on, discuss, and constructively critique past behaviors and performance are likely to learn more, which could help improve adaptability in the future.

Integrated Model of Adaptability

While the three perspectives on adaptation (individual differences, learning, and dynamic process perspectives) diverge in focus, they are not incompatible. In fact, when integrated, the result is a more complete picture of the adaptation space (Baard et al. 2014). That is, adaptation is a process that individuals move through when facing novel or changing conditions, but an individual's ability to successfully move through this process is likely driven by multiple stable characteristics as well as trainable knowledge and skills. In their full model, Burke et al. (2006) identified a subset of KSAs with team processes that may result from individuals and teams implementing the adaptation process. This work provides a basis for integrating across adaptation perspectives, which allows for a more comprehensive, synergistic model of adaptation. However, this model proposes sequential movement through the adaptive phases: (a) situation assessment, (b) plan formulation, (c) plan execution, and (d) learning. In reality, the process is likely to be more dynamic (e.g., individuals continue to assess the environment for new cues while they are developing a new plan). Additionally, this model suggests that individual characteristics directly influence only the initial phase of adaptation (situation assessment), while team processes and states drive the subsequent phases. However, as individuals adapt to changing situations, it is likely that their individual characteristics, biases, and experiences join with team-level states and processes to directly impact each of the phases of adaptation. Recent work by Ratwani et al. (2014; under review) extends the Burke et al. (2006) model by (a) making explicit the dynamic nature of the adaptive phases; (b) considering the individual-level cognitive and affective factors that may influence each phase of the adaptation process (i.e., not only the initial situation assessment); and (c) addressing how the relationship between individual characteristics and adaptation may vary as a result of situational and leader/team factors. Such extensions allow for integration of these three perspectives on adaptation.

Ratwani et al. (2014) integrated model of adaptation is presented in Fig. 9.2. As illustrated, both cognitive and affective barriers (factors that hinder adaptation) and

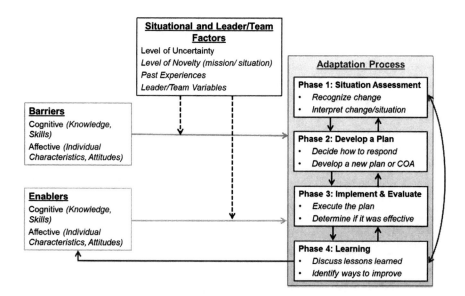

Fig. 9.2 Integrated model of cognitive and affective adaptation

enablers (factors that help adaptation) impact the adaptation process—a relationship which may vary based on the situation and historical experiences of the individual. As individuals progress through the adaptation process, learning occurs and influences how the barriers and enablers manifest during *future* performance periods. As such, these adaptation processes are dynamic and may influence each other in a bidirectional manner. The factors in this model are discussed in the following section and serve as the theoretical foundation for the research described in this chapter.

Barriers and Enablers to Cross-Cultural Adaptation

For leaders to help team members adapt, they must be aware of the individual, team, or situational factors that may either facilitate or hinder cross-cultural adaptation. Depending on the degree and nature of the cultural change, certain cross-cultural competencies (McCloskey et al. 2010) may be more or less critical to an individual's ability to adapt successfully. Cross-cultural competencies can be cognitive (e.g., perspective taking, sensemaking), affective (e.g., openness, uncertainty tolerance), or behavioral in nature (e.g., self-monitoring, relationship building).

Associated with these competencies is a variety of factors that help or hinder efforts to adjust to new cultures. We refer to the factors that help an individual adapt successfully across cultures as "enablers," while those factors that prevent or hinder successful adaptation are labeled "barriers." Awareness of these barriers and enablers can empower leaders to monitor for and help others overcome the challenges of adapting to new cultures.

A helpful summary of barriers and enablers to cross-cultural adaptation is provided in Table 9.1. Past research suggests that cognitive, affective, and behavioral/skill factors can help and hinder the speed and quality with which one adjusts to new cultures. Behaviors and skills are largely driven by cognitive and affective factors, and thus join with these categories in Table 9.1 (e.g., perspective taking is a cognitive skill, while dehumanizing others is an affective behavior). *Cognitive* factors describe the knowledge bases, cognitive processes, and cognitive skills that may impact adaptation, whereas *affective* factors relate to attitudes and more stable personality characteristics and behaviors. In addition, *situational* factors describe past experiences with leaders or teams that may have an influence on one's propensity to embrace and adjust to new cultures. We will explore each of these factors in greater detail, including evidence for their importance in guiding cross-cultural adaptability.

Table 9.1 Barriers and enablers to cross-cultural adaptation

Category	Barriers	Enablers
Cognitive	*Knowledge* • Insufficient expertise • Cognitive cultural biases • Ignorant *Skills* • Unable to take others' perspectives • Insufficient task proficiency • Insufficient tactical competence	*Knowledge* • Understanding of big picture • Understanding of own and other cultures *Skills* • Tactical competence • Mental preparation • Contingency planning • Perspective taking • Being observant • Expectation management
Affective	*Individual characteristics* • High strung (Type A) • Prideful • Fearful • Anxious • Emotionally immature • Impatient • Low emotional intelligence *Attitudes* • Low motivation to change • Unwilling to take others' perspectives • Dehumanizing others • Intolerant of other cultures • Affective cultural biases • Disengaged	*Individual characteristics* • Humility • Patience • High emotional intelligence • Empathy *Attitudes* • Acceptance of big picture • Acceptance of the inevitability of change • Respect for others • Openness to other cultures • Adoption of coping strategies • Willingness to adapt
Situational	• Culture—or organization-centric experience • Poor communication among team members • Poor team coordination • Poor guidance from leadership	• Previous experience in similar situations • Previous host national communication • Leader and unit member familiarity • High unit cohesion • High unit trust • High unit efficacy • Appropriate unit staffing

Cognitive Factors

The science of decision-making identifies specific cognitive factors that impact adaptation in a cross-cultural context. At its core, effective decision-making requires knowledge and expertise. Without sufficient expertise, decision-making can be ill-informed or biased. However, evidence suggests that multiple *types* of expertise are important to decision-making and adaptation (Holyoak 1991). The initial type of expertise, *general expertise*, comprises the ability to identify helpful heuristics and employ general problem-solving skills across domains (e.g., Newell and Simon

1972). The reliance upon generalizable heuristics, however, may lead to biases when making context-specific decisions.

In contrast, *routine expertise* focuses on domain-specific expertise that allows individuals to make better decisions and be more effective in well-structured domains or problems. However, over time, evidence indicated that when the decision context is dynamic or ill-structured, routine experts perform no better than novices (Devine and Kozlowski 1995). This finding led to a third type of expertise: *adaptive expertise*. To be an adaptive expert, individuals must not only possess expert knowledge of a domain but also need to be more mindful and aware of their own thought processes in order to identify the limitations of current approaches (Smith et al. 1997). The combination of domain expertise plus *metacognitive awareness* allows adaptive experts to (a) recognize when well-learned procedures or courses of action are no longer appropriate, (b) apply their domain knowledge to *new* situations, (c) adjust their strategies, and (d) create effective solutions to new problems. Attempts to interact with an unfamiliar culture are improved when one is both knowledgeable about the culture and can make more appropriate and fewer biased decisions as conditions change. On the other hand, a lack of cultural knowledge or the inability to employ effective metacognitive strategies when interacting with another culture can serve as barriers to adaptation in cross-cultural situations.

In addition to metacognitive strategies, research identifies other cognitive strategies that are critical to adapting effectively across cultural settings. One of the most frequently discussed variables in regard to promoting cross-cultural competence is *perspective taking* (e.g., Rentsch et al. 2007; Roan et al. 2009). Perspective taking is a skill that allows an individual to imagine a situation from the perspective of another. Perspective taking has been demonstrated to reduce prejudice and improve intergroup relations (e.g., Galinsky and Moskowitz 2000). Galinsky et al. (2005) developed a conceptual model of social perspective taking, which relies on an understanding of the "other" and an understanding of the "self." The creation of mental representations of both the "other" and the "self" allows the individual to recognize commonalities with others. In a cross-cultural context, that understanding of the other and the self would necessarily include an understanding of cultural norms and other culture-related variables. The frequency and accuracy of social perspective taking are positively associated with the ability to choose effective strategies in conflict resolution (Gehlbach 2004). In addition, empathy can promote altruistic behaviors when one takes the perspective of *how the other feels* but can promote personal distress and egoistic motivation when focusing on *how the self feels* (Batson et al. 1997). These findings provide important implications for understanding how individuals may adapt to unfamiliar situations, as well as for the critical role that perspective taking plays in cross-cultural adaptation. If individuals do not engage in perspective taking, they may not be motivated to adapt. Alternatively, these individuals may not realize the impact their behaviors have on others and, as such, may not truly understand the need to adapt.

One other factor that may be an obstacle to effective adaptation is cognitive bias. For example, we naturally have a bias for decisions that require less mental effort

(Kahneman and Tversky 1973; Kool et al. 2010); as a result, individuals may not put in the mental effort needed to make an effective situational assessment or to carefully consider the contingencies and consequences of their behaviors—especially when cognitive demand is high. Such a bias may be particularly problematic when individuals are operating in cultures that contain unfamiliar cultural norms. Additionally, these cognitive biases may lead to reductions or inaccuracies in *situational awareness*, which is a key to interpreting the new environmental contexts (Endsley 1988).

Affective Factors

Motivational factors, including self-efficacy, amount of practice, level of effort, and learning (mastery) orientation all have been shown to contribute to adaptive success (e.g., Bell and Kozlowski 2008; Ford et al. 1998; LePine 2005). Motivational factors such as those listed above influence when, where, and to what extent individuals direct their effort in uncertain and changing situations. When individuals have a learning orientation, they focus their effort on understanding and exploring a task or situation rather than concern for demonstrating high levels of performance. This focus allows individuals to develop a deeper understanding of the task, which is necessary for them to be more adaptable if task conditions change (Bell and Kozlowski 2008). When individuals have a learning orientation, it also makes them more resilient when facing challenging situations. Rather than being defeated and upset when making a mistake or encountering an error, individuals with a learning orientation view them as opportunities to learn and grow (Gully et al. 2002; Keith and Frese 2005). As a result, individuals experience higher levels of self-efficacy and intrinsic motivation, which in turn leads to more effort and ultimately more adaptive performance and behaviors (Bell and Kozlowski 2008). One can imagine such factors as positively influencing performance in cross-cultural settings. By possessing a learning orientation, individuals may be more apt to explore a new area and ask questions about cultures and customs, ultimately facilitating learning cultural nuances.

Additionally, several affective and attitudinal characteristics have received empirical support for both preventing and enabling adaptation. Characteristics such as openness to experience (e.g., LePine et al. 2000), emotional stability (e.g., Pulakos et al. 2002), and tolerance for ambiguity (e.g., Gwinner et al. 2005) have been positively related (i.e., enablers) to adaptation. Conversely, other characteristics including Type A dispositions, neuroticism (e.g., Pulakos et al. 2002), and anxiety (e.g., Bell and Kozlowski 2008) represent barriers to adaptation. For example, Day et al. (2005) propose that Type A individuals can fall into one of two types: achievement striving (*AS*) or impatience irritability (*II*). *AS Type A* individuals are likely to be characterized as hard working, active, and serious; in contrast, *II Type A* individuals are likely to be viewed as impatient, irritable, and angry, with a lack of impulse control. Whereas *AS Type A* individuals are more likely to be successful due to their hard work mentality, *II Type A* individuals are likely to experience more difficulties being effective in interpersonal situations and competitive or high stress situations. This particular Type A behavior overlaps greatly with some of the subscales of emotional intelligence (EI), or the ability to recognize and appraise emotions and subsequently use this knowledge of emotions to enhance thought (Mayer and Salovey 1993). Furthermore, managing emotions is also considered a facet of EI. Emotion management includes activities such as showcasing patience and not becoming inappropriately angry (Kaplan et al. 2014). In cross-cultural settings, emotion management allows individuals to appropriately convey emotions as dictated by emotional norms.

Several theories (e.g., affect-as-information model; Schwarz and Clore 1988) can lend explanations to why and how unmanaged negative affect can degrade judgment and decision-making. Affective biases occur when an individual's emotional state colors or clouds his/her thought processes and reactions to cross-cultural situations. Impediments to adaptability can often arise when one misattributes his/her affect from one cultural experience to another cultural encounter, or when one inappropriately uses affect to interpret a situation (Matthews and Hudlicka 2009; Williams et al. 1997). Specifically, affective biases have been found to diminish cognition and decision-making in a number of ways, including (a) narrowing of, or selective, attention (Williams et al. 1997); (b) over attention to costs over benefits (Matthews and Hudlicka 2009; Raghunatha and Pham 1999); (c) decision errors and more cautious decision-making (Raghunatha and Pham 1999); (4) cue detection bias (Matthews and Hudlicka 2009); (d) high risk behavior (Raghunatha and Pham 1999); (e) threat bias (Bar-Haim et al. 2007; Williams et al. 1997); (f) cognitive or behavioral withdrawal from a task (Kanfer et al. 1996); (g) misappraisal of other's intentions (Matthews et al. 2000); and (h) inaccurate/ineffective self-evaluation (Adomdza and Baron 2013).

When such cultural biases and negative affect remain unmanaged or are encouraged by others, these inflammatory dynamics can lead to a more severe disdain toward a culture and its people. This disdain may result in demeaning actions against that cultural group, which are characteristic of *dehumanization*. Dehumanization is at the core of prejudice, racism, and discrimination, and enables an individual or group to engage in callous, rude, hostile, or aggressive behavior toward another group (Demoulin et al. 2009; Zimbardo 2008). It stems from a lack of empathy toward members of the other group and thwarts the desire to take the perspective of others. In a new and different cultural setting, such attitudes can lead to demeaning, disrespectful, and potentially harmful interactions with those from the other culture. Therefore, it is imperative that leaders intervene and help provide an alternative perspective that can embrace and respect cultural differences.

Situational Factors

Environmental factors such as an individual's team, leader, and surrounding environment can greatly impact the adaptation process. Cultures can vary on several dimensions, and the extent of these differences can greatly affect one's ability to quickly transition from one culture to another. Such cultural dimensions include the individualistic versus collectivistic cultural orientation, the comfort with ambiguity (i.e., uncertainty avoidance) in the culture, and the distribution of power (i.e., power distance) within the culture (e.g., Hofstede 1983). Cultures may also vary in terms of their social structure and political or economic systems (McFate et al. 2012). Situational factors that stand out as notably different in the new culture will help indicate the need for a change in response. However, recognizing situational cues in a culture with less obvious differences may be more of a challenge, particularly for those with cultural biases or simply less cross-cultural experience. In these situations, individuals may miss or misinterpret the more subtle cultural cues that can make or break a successful interaction.

A variety of external factors exist that, over the course of one's career, can influence the desire and ability to adapt to a new culture. In work units operating across cultures, each team member possesses a unique history of experiences that guides his or her approach toward interacting with other cultures. In this section, we discuss four situational factors that can shape how individuals adapt to unfamiliar cultures: *team*, *leader*, *experiential*, and *contextual* factors.

Team factors. Communication and coordination go hand in hand in the adaptability literature, as both have been identified as central components to individual and team adaptation (Burke et al. 2006). Effective communication improves team mental models and situational awareness, provides the ability for individuals to anticipate what other team members need (implicit coordination), and ultimately facilitates adaptive performance (Burke et al. 2006; Entin and Serfaty 1999; Klein et al. 2010). A breakdown in team communication or coordination can serve as a barrier to cognitive and affective adaptation. Additionally, the appropriate staffing of a team is highly important to a team being adaptable. For example, a team on a patrol needs to have the right types of technical expertise to execute a mission, whether that expertise is common or distributed (Burke et al. 2006). It is also critical to consider the "intangibles" when determining how to select a team for particular tasks. The team composition should establish compatibility across members to allow for effective interaction, ensuring success in a cross-cultural situation. The familiarity of the team, along with the extent to which they have a shared mental model and high levels of cohesion, trust, and efficacy, can impact how a team communicates, coordinates, and adapts to situations (e.g., Chen et al. 2005; Rosen et al. 2011).

Leader factors. Research has also clearly demonstrated the role of the leader in an individual's or team's ability to adapt (Burke et al. 2006; Kozlowski 1998; Salas et al. 2004). Generally, leaders can effectively shape their Soldiers' cognitive (learning), motivational (effort), and affective (emotional) responses by employing strategies that have received support in the literature for facilitating adaptive performance. The strategies, which originate from the active learning approach (Baard et al. 2014; Bell and Kozlowski 2008, 2010; Smith et al. 1997), can help create a learning and performance climate that promotes adaptation. In general, leaders should engage in actions that promote cognitive skills such as metacognition and increased expertise; further, they should also facilitate the development of self-efficacy and increased motivation/effort within their team members.

Experiential factors. As mentioned previously, avoiding dehumanizing behaviors and developing perspective taking skills (among others) is essential to successful interactions with individuals from another culture. The *mere exposure effect*, advanced by Zajonc (1968), would suggest that positive regard naturally increases with more exposure to a stimulus, even when the attitude seems implicit. Additionally, Hess et al. (2009) argued that the ease with which a member of one group is able to read the emotions of a member of the other group depends upon the individual's beliefs, attitudes, and stereotypes as well as familiarity with that target group. Harkening back to the role of EI, understanding the emotions of others has significant implications for appropriate coordination of common goals between groups. Increased positive contact has been associated with empathy, and, further, the increased ability to take the perspective of others (see Pettigrew and Tropp 2011). Such research suggests gaining experiences outside of one's culture is a powerful tool in facilitating effective adaptation. Exposure to individuals from other cultures helps to facilitate the reduction of biases (both cognitive and affective) and promote perspective taking and greater cultural awareness, among other factors.

Contextual factors. The contextual cues surrounding cross-cultural interactions are often rich with complexity. For example, being in a dangerous or intimidating situation may cloud an individual's ability to make rational decisions and think critically about a situation. In the military, physical threats diminish an individual's ability to respond analytically to a situation, relying instead on emotions to guide decision-making processes (Gordan and Arian 2001). In other contexts, being surrounded by an abundance of unfamiliar cultural norms may be overwhelming and force one to rely on heuristics, assumptions, and cultural biases to make decisions. Such novel surroundings can cause overload, particularly when one does not have previous cultural frames of reference with which to make sense of this new information.

Summary of Barriers and Enablers

The sections above identified several barriers to and enablers of cross-cultural adaptation. Consistent with Fig. 9.2, these factors are distilled into cognitive, affective, and situational factors (including leaders, teammates, cultural experiences, and surrounding context). Every one of these factors has the potential to both help and hinder one's adaptation to new cultural nuances. The next section presents leader strategies for detecting when team members may struggle with these barriers, or when these individuals are likely to excel at cross-cultural interactions. Additionally, these leader strategies provide useful interventions for leaders to help team members overcome existing barriers and facilitate cross-cultural adaptation.

Leader Strategies for Improving Unit Adaptability

Past research provides insight into the specific actions that enable leaders to strategically improve the adaptability of team members. For example, leaders play an important role in facilitating and assessing the development of knowledge and metacognitive skills. Specifically, leaders should give intent and guidance in terms of their vision, expectations, and objectives. Instead of providing detailed and explicit instructions for each task, leaders should allow team members to come to a deeper understanding of how to apply this guidance in a variety of situations. This strategy is consistent with the inductive learning component of active learning theory. Leaders can provide opportunities for Soldiers to talk through different problem scenarios (past or hypothetical) and explain their rationale for selecting a course of action. Using the leader's guidance, team members can make their assumptions explicit and learn through discussion which actions are preferred. By talking through a variety of situations, individuals can begin to look past the surface similarities of situations and instead make connections among deeper, structural relationships. These deeper connections provide the guidance for selecting effective courses of action (Smith et al. 1997). The team members' responses, in turn, provide the leader with insight into the assumptions, biases, and connections presented by team members, which can be used to provide feedback and additional guidance.

A comprehensive model of leader strategies is provided in Fig. 9.3. As can be seen within the figure, the leader strategies are broken into four major categories: *Monitor Behavior, Prepare, Adjust,* and *Develop. Monitoring Behavior* provides an input for leaders at each of the other three points, as it allows leaders to determine necessary leader strategies. In the *Prepare* stage, the leader is focused on setting the conditions necessary for individual adaptation. A major premise of this stage is communication, in that open communication will allow leaders to understand if subordinates are adapting and can also be used as a leader tool to convey intent and strategy (and thereby develop factors such as increased motivation). In the *Adjust* stage, leaders are focused on quickly adjusting ineffective team member behaviors by identifying opportunities for near real-time intervention. Finally, the *Develop* stage is focused on longer term development by allowing leaders to identify learning and development opportunities based on assessments of personnel strengths and weaknesses. Each of the strategies in Fig. 9.3 is described in detail below.

We conducted a thorough review of the adaptability literature and compiled a set of strategies to help facilitate unit adaptation across cultures.

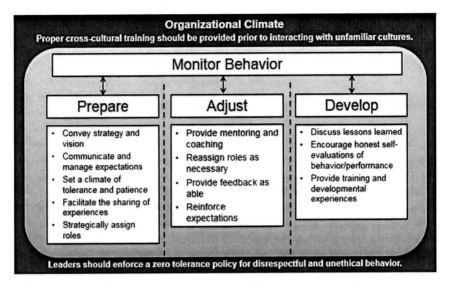

Fig. 9.3 Leader strategies for facilitating unit adaptability

Monitor Behavior

As organizations focus on the development of adaptive individuals, it is important for organizational leaders to be able to recognize whether individuals are engaging effectively in the adaption process. Leaders should be constantly monitoring for team members' behavior across various stages of performance. When monitoring, it is important to look for behaviors that may give clues as to whether certain barriers are keeping team members from adjusting to aspects of the new culture. We refer to these indicators here as *behavioral markers* of maladaptation.

Within the current context, these markers can serve as "warning signs" that individuals may not be adapting effectively and allow leaders to intervene prior to witnessing performance decrements. Recent data collected from experienced U.S. Army Soldiers suggests that these behaviors may be indicators of six of the aforementioned barriers to cross-cultural adaptation: *Ignorance, Bias, Anxiety, Lack of Motivation, Intolerance*, and *Dehumanizing Others*. By connecting the markers to specific barriers, leaders can help identify and mitigate the underlying causes of the troubling behavior. Examples of common markers are linked to these barriers in Table 9.2.

The barriers in Table 9.2 are listed from least challenging to most challenging to overcome. Barriers that are more challenging to overcome, such as *Intolerance* and *Dehumanizing Others*, are those in which the individual remains highly committed to resisting the new culture. In some cases, this commitment can lead one to deliberately degrade another culture. In contrast, *Ignorance* and *Bias* can be more easily overcome by having leaders and teammates correct such fallacies with

Table 9.2 Behavioral markers and barriers to cross-cultural adaptation

Barriers to cross-cultural adaptation	Behavioral markers
Ignorance	• Not showing respect/not performing basic courtesies when interacting with locals • Lack of fundamental understanding of the cultural basics • Dismissive remarks about people/group • Using false facts • Generalizations about "how people are" • Frequent stereotyped jokes
Bias	• Labeling groups based on a single experience • Trouble learning or respecting foreign languages • Not learning names of foreigners with whom they work • Lack of compassion or care for natives of a certain culture • Expressing bitterness toward locals • Unwillingness to learn about cultural differences
Anxiety	• Avoidance of a particular group • Sleep loss • Exhaustion, burnout, overload • Acting skittish when in the presence of local nationals
Low motivation to adapt	• Not completing assignments • Ignores best practices for interacting with locals • Dismissive remarks about cross-cultural training • Repeated refusal to accept certain cultural norms • Does not volunteer for any new tasks
Intolerance	• Actively pushing one's own agenda • Lack of control or discipline • Hostility toward locals • Controlling the conversation to continue with familiar topics • Blatant disregard for host national customs
Dehumanizing others	• Referring to locals as though they have no feelings • Inappropriate jokes or comments • Macho mentality • Being deliberately disrespectful • Refusing to provide assistance to locals

accurate cultural knowledge. And lastly, while the intent is to provide a helpful framework of markers that may indicate certain barriers to cross-cultural adaptation, such relationships are not proposed here to be mutually exclusive. Leaders should use their expertise and consider the information in this chapter to help determine which barrier(s) may be holding back one's adaptation to a different culture.

Prepare

There are several leader strategies associated with preparing individuals to adapt, such as conveying strategy and vision, managing expectations, facilitating the sharing of experiences, and strategically assigning roles. Each of these strategies is elaborated on in this section.

Convey strategy and vision. One of the overall goals with this phase is to have leaders convey their intent and communicate "big picture" information about the vision and mission. This communication is important because it helps motivate and focus the efforts of team members. A lack of motivation to adapt can lead to lower effort learning the new culture and less success when interacting with others from that culture. However, if team members understand the intent and why adapting helps support the mission, they are more likely to be amenable to adapting their behavior.

Manage expectations and set a climate for tolerance and patience. To maintain respect for the nuances of the new culture, it is important for leaders to role model, articulate, and enforce the behaviors that are expected of their team members. By clearly conveying and reinforcing expectations, team members are more likely to engage in culturally appropriate behavior (and adapt their behavior if needed).

Facilitate the sharing of experiences. By sharing experiences related to a previous or expected event, team members will learn about the cross-cultural experiences of their teammates, and perhaps begin to think differently about a specific culture. A discussion about experiences may also help individuals understand their own cultural biases, and learn from their teammates how to overcome those biases.

Strategically assign roles. Finally, once leaders better understand the tendencies and beliefs of their team members, they can use this knowledge to their advantage by assigning cultural stretch assignments to specific individuals. For example, it may be desirable to have a U.S. Army Soldier who is very outgoing and personable to meet with locals, particularly when the interaction is mission critical. In contrast, it is just as important to identify those who have ongoing biases against the culture. While these individuals may be withheld from important interactions in which their bias may jeopardize the mission, leaders should carefully consider finding opportunities for those individuals to learn about the culture—and reduce bias over time—by engaging in positive interactions with locals.

Adjust

Leaders have several strategies at their disposal to facilitate the adjustment of an individual's behaviors. These strategies include providing coaching and developmental activities, reassigning roles as necessary, providing feedback as able, and reinforcing expectations. Each of these strategies is elaborated on in this section.

Provide coaching and developmental activities. Leaders should provide guidance *when needed*—not exclusively following performance—to help team members learn cultural norms and rapidly adjust the ways they interact with locals in a new culture. As a coach or mentor, leaders can recommend developmental activities that allow team members to gain practice in these cross-cultural interactions. These learning opportunities can stretch the individual's capabilities to new levels of complexity.

Reassign roles as necessary. In many operational environments, leaders can strategically assign roles to members of the team. For example, if a U.S. Army Soldier is not adapting due to low motivation or cultural biases, the leader can assign that Soldier to a situation where he or she has to interact with the locals. As noted previously, engaging with the locals and learning more about that culture helps build empathy for the culture, which in turns can produce more positive outcomes.

Provide feedback as able. As the team continues to perform, providing feedback to team members is very important. This ongoing formative feedback can help team members make adjustments on the fly, perhaps during cultural interactions.

Reinforce expectations. Leaders are in the unique position of having the legitimate authority to hold team members accountable for meeting expectations. By rewarding those who adhere to cultural norms and penalizing those who ignore local customs, leaders highlight expected behavior and establish consequences for violating the cross-cultural standards set for the group.

Develop

Learning to adapt to unfamiliar cultures is a long-term challenge. Leaders can help team members become more adaptive over time by discussing lessons learned, encouraging honest self-evaluations of behavior and performance, and providing training and developmental opportunities. Each of these strategies is elaborated on in this section.

Discuss lessons learned. A large part of a team's after action review (AAR) is a discussion of lessons learned. Leaders can learn more about the strategies that worked, those that failed, and how team members can learn vicariously from the diverse experiences of others in this situation.

Encourage honest self-evaluation of behavior and performance. To continue learning about a culture, an honest self-evaluation is necessary. If team members are afraid to be honest about their performance, their behavior will be more difficult to change in the future. Given the importance of honest evaluations, it is essential that the leader set a climate of honesty and openness among team members.

Providing training and developmental opportunities. Finally, the developmental needs of individual team members become more apparent during performance debriefs or feedback sessions. Such insights can point to developmental experiences —such as specific interactions with the culture—that would help improve the individual's perceptions of the culture (e.g. require perspective taking). Oftentimes new training can help provide that new perspective. Such opportunities can directly address problem areas and accelerate cross-cultural adaptability.

Leader Strategies

In order to successfully guide culturally adaptive team members, leaders will need to read the situation to determine the most effective combination of strategies (see Fig. 9.3). It is recommended that leaders employ an active learning approach (e.g., Bell and Kozlowski 2008), in which the learner is an integral part of the learning experience. Active learning increases individuals' control over their own learning (i.e., making them active participants in deciding what and how to learn), and promotes an inductive learning approach; that is, learners are encouraged to explore and experiment in their environment to infer rules, principles, and strategies for effective performance.

In addition, the active learning approach triggers three key self-regulatory processes of learning: exploration (cognitive), training frame (motivational), and emotion control (emotional). This approach moves beyond "learning by doing" to a more strategic approach for designing and manipulating developmental experiences that maximize learning and adaptation. Table 9.3 showcases how specific active learning principles are tied to adaptive outcomes. In sum, leaders should determine which adaptive outcomes are of interest in the current cultural context and use the active learning principles to select the most appropriate combination of leader strategies.

To facilitate higher levels of motivation in their team, leaders should frame learning experiences to emphasize a mastery orientation. After performance episodes or during after action reviews (AARs), leaders should communicate that errors are a natural and positive part of the training process. Errors highlight opportunities to develop a deeper understanding of the situation, which helps reduce errors when adapting to new cultures in the future. Leaders can also

Table 9.3 Active learning principles and adaptive outcomes

	Active learning principles	Adaptive outcomes
Cognitive	• Promote metacognition and self-evaluation • Encourage inductive learning • Provide diverse practice opportunities • Provide intent and guidance but allow team members to determine ways to fulfill intent	• Deeper levels of expertise • Increased metacognitive activity • Increased unit communication • More shared mental models • Improved situation awareness • Improved self-awareness
Affective/motivational	• Structure learning opportunities to emphasize progressive achievement • Help team members set mastery goals • Frame errors and mistakes as learning opportunities	• Increased learning orientation • Increased self-efficacy • Increased effort • Increased psychological safety • Increased cohesion

explicitly link discussions of errors or mistakes to possible strategies or solutions that aid future improvement and learning. Proactive language such as "areas for improvement" or "developmental opportunities" should be emphasized, while discouraging statements such as "weaknesses" or "bad performance" should be reduced. Learning from errors produces gains in future attempts to adapt to new cultural norms, and discussions should emphasize these points. Leaders should also encourage subordinates to reflect on their behaviors and performance, and ask them to generate their own insights into (a) why a mistake was made, (b) what might have been done differently, and (c) what learning opportunities they think may assist in their adaptability to the new culture.

Finally, adaptation to new cultures can be challenging and at times very frustrating. One can quickly become overwhelmed by negative emotion when trying to explain subtle cultural differences. Thus, leaders should engage in emotion management activities to encourage positive emotions and mitigate the impact of negative emotions (Kaplan et al. 2014). Several emotion control strategies have been discussed in the literature, including cue controlled relaxation, cognitive modification, guided mental imagery, rational attitude training, and emotion control intervention (e.g., Kanfer and Ackerman 1990; Keith and Frese 2005). While these strategies have some differences, at the core, most of these strategies encourage an increase in positive self-talk and rational statements (e.g., "*Remember, worry does not help anything*"), while reducing negative self-talk or irrational statements. As leaders hear team members share their experiences or engage in self-reflection during exercises and debriefs, they should listen for negative or self-defeating statements and instead encourage positive and constructive self-statements. Such indications of trouble adapting to new cultures are signs that leaders can intervene and make a difference. In the event that leaders are not always present to witness such behaviors, leaders should routinely encourage team members to conduct their own self-monitoring, so they can recognize their own negative or self-destructive thoughts to improve their own perspective or reach out for help.

Summary

This chapter aims to serve as a practical guide for (a) distilling the cognitive, affective, and situational factors that influence how individuals adapt to unfamiliar cultures; and (b) specify leader strategies for facilitating cross-cultural adaptation throughout the team. An integrated theoretical model of adaptation is offered, which specifies how such factors can combine to influence one's process for adapting to new cultural challenges. Extending this model is a list of individual characteristics that may serve as enablers and barriers to adaptation. These cognitive, affective, and situational characteristics can produce a variety of behaviors that stand in the way of effective cross-cultural adaptation. Monitoring for these behavioral markers can help leaders identify the need to intervene and further support a team member's attempt to work across cultures. To keep team members from struggling to adapt, this chapter summarizes leader strategies to better prepare team members, adjust their behaviors, and develop their readiness for the demands of cross-cultural adaptability. When used in combination, such strategies represent helpful tools by which leaders can monitor and facilitate successful cross-cultural adaptation.

References

Abbe, A., Gulick, L. M. V., & Herman, J. L. (2008). *Cross-cultural competence in Army leaders: A conceptual and empirical foundation (2008-01)*. Arlington, VA: Army Research Institute.

Adomdza, G. K., & Baron, R. A. (2013). The role of affective biasing in commercializing new ideas. *Journal of Small Business & Entrepreneurship, 26*, 201–217.

Baard, S. K., Rench, T. A., & Kozlowski, S. W. J. (2014). Adaptation: A theoretical review and integration. *Journal of Management, 40*, 48–99.

Bar-Haim, Y., Lamy, D., Pergamin, L., Bakermans-M, J., & van Ijzendoorn, M. H. (2007). Threat-related attentional bias is anxious and non-anxious individuals: A meta-analytic study. *Psychological Bulletin, 133*, 1–24.

Batson, C. D., Early, S., & Salvarani, G. (1997). Perspective taking: Imagining how another feels versus imagining how you would feel. *Society for Personality and Social Psychology, 23*, 751–758. doi:10.1177/0146167297237008

Bell, B. S., & Kozlowski, S. W. J. (2008). Active learning: Effects of core training design elements on self-regulatory processes, learning, and adaptability. *Journal of Applied Psychology, 93*, 296–316.

Bell, B. S., & Kozlowski, S. W. J. (2010). Toward a theory of learner-centered training design: An integrative framework of active learning. *Learning, training, and development in organizations, 263–300.*

Burke, C. S., Stagl, K. C., Salas, E., Pierce, L., & Kendall, D. (2006). Understanding team adaptation: A conceptual analysis and model. *Journal of Applied Psychology, 91*(6), 1189–1207.

Chen, G., Thomas, B., & Wallace, J. C. (2005). A multilevel examination of the relationships among training outcomes, mediating regulatory processes, and adaptive performance. *Journal of Applied Psychology, 90*, 827–841.

Day, A. L., Therrein, D. L., & Carroll, S. A. (2005). Predicting psychological health: Assessing the incremental validity of emotional intelligence beyond personality, Type A behavior, and daily hassles. *European Journal of Personality, 19*, 519–536.

Demoulin, S., Poso, B. C., & Leyens, J. P. (2009). Infrahumanization: The differential interpretation of primary and secondary emotions. In S. Demoulin, J. P. Leyens, & J. F. Dovidio (Eds.), *Intergroup misunderstandings: Impact of divergent social realities* (pp. 153–171). New York: Psychology Press.

Devine, D. J., & Kozlowski, S. W. J. (1995). Expertise and task characteristics in decision making. *Organizational Behavior and Human Decision Processes, 64*, 294–306.

Endsley, M. R. (1988). Situation awareness global assessment technique (SAGAT). *Proceedings of the 1988 National Aerospace and Electronics Conference*, pp. 789–795.

Entin, E. E., & Serfaty, D. (1999). Adaptive team coordination. *Human Factors, 41*(2), 312–325.

Ford, J. K., Smith, E. M., Weissbein, D. A., Gully, S. M., & Salas, E. (1998). Relationships of goal orientation, metacognitive activity, and practice strategies with learning outcomes and transfer. *Journal of Applied Psychology, 83*, 218–233.

Galinsky, A. D., Ku, G., & Wang, C. S. (2005). Perspective-taking and self-other overlap: Fostering social bonds and facilitating social coordination. *Group Processes Intergroup Relations, 8*(2), 109–124. doi:10.1177/1368430205051060

Galinsky, A. D., & Moskowitz, G. B. (2000). Perspective-taking: Decreasing stereotype expression, stereotype accessibility, and in-group favoritism. *Journal of Personality and Social Psychology, 78*(4), 708–724. doi:10.1037/0022-3514.78.4.708

Gehlbach, G. (2004). Social perspective taking: A facilitating aptitude for conflict resolution, historical empathy, and social studies achievement. *Theory and Research in Social Education, 32*(1), 39–55.

Gordan, C., & Arian, A. (2001). Threat and decision making. *The Journal of Conflict Resolution, 45*(2), 196–215.

Gully, S. M., Payne, S. C., Koles, K., & Whiteman, J. A. K. (2002). The impact of error training and individual differences on training outcomes: An attribute-treatment interaction perspective. *Journal of Applied Psychology, 87*, 143–155.

Gwinner, K. P., Bitner, M. J., Brown, S. W., & Kumar, A. (2005). Service customization through employee adaptiveness. *Journal of Service Research, 8*, 131–148.

Hess, U., Adams, R. B., & Kleck, R. E. (2009). Intergroup misunderstandings in emotion communication. In S. Demoulin, J. Leyens, & J. F. Dovidio (Eds.), *Intergroup misunderstandings: Impact of divergent social realities* (pp. 85–100). New York: Psychology Press.

Hofstede, G. (1983). The cultural relativity of organizational practices and theories. *Journal of International Business Studies, 14*, 75–89.

Holyoak, K. J. (1991). Symbolic connectionism: Toward third-generation theories of expertise. In K. A. Ericsson & J. Smith (Eds.), *Toward a general theory of expertise* (pp. 301–336). Cambridge: Cambridge University Press.

Kahneman, D., & Tversky, A. (1973). On the psychology of prediction. *Psychological Review, 80*, 237–251.

Kanfer, R., & Ackerman, P. L. (1990). *Ability and metacognitive determinants of skill acquisition and transfer* (Air Force Office of Scientific Research Final Report). Minneapolis, MN: Air Force Office of Scientific Research.

Kanfer, R., Ackerman, P. L., & Heggestad, E. D. (1996). Motivational skills & self-regulation for learning: A trait perspective. *Learning and Individual Differences, 8*, 185–209.

Kaplan, S., Cortina, J., Ruark, G., LaPort, K., & Nicolaides, V. (2014). The role of organizational leaders in employee emotion management: A theoretical model. *The Leadership Quarterly, 25*(3), 563–580.

Keith, N., & Frese, M. (2005). Self-regulation in error management training: Emotion control and metacognition as mediators of performance effects. *Journal of Applied Psychology, 90*, 677–691.

Klein, G., Wiggins, S., & Dominguez, C. O. (2010). Team sensemaking. *Theoretical Issues in Ergonomics Science, 11*, 304–320.

Kool, W., McGuire, J. T., Rosen, Z. B., & Botvinick, M. M. (2010). Decision making and the avoidance of cognitive demand. *Journal of Experimental Psychology: General, 139*(4), 665–682. doi:10.1037/a0020198

Kozlowski, S. W. J. (1998). Training and developing adaptive teams: Theory, principles, and research. In J. A. Cannon-Bowers & E. Salas (Eds.), *Decision making under stress: Implications for training and simulation* (pp. 115–153). Washington, DC: APA Books.

Kozlowski, S. W. J., Gully, S. M., Brown, K. G., Salas, E., Smith, E. A., & Nason, E. R. (2001). Effects of training goals and goal orientation traits on multi-dimensional training outcomes and performance adaptability. *Organizational Behavior and Human Decision Processes, 85*, 1–31.

Laurence, J. H. (2011). Leading across cultures. In P. Sweeney, M. Matthews, & P. Leste (Eds.), *Leading in dangerous situations: A handbook for the armed forces, emergency services and first responders* (pp. 291–310). Naval Institute Press.

LePine, J. A. (2005). Adaptation of teams in response to unforeseen change: Effects of goal difficulty and team composition in terms of cognitive ability and goal orientation. *Journal of Applied Psychology, 90*, 1153–1167.

LePine, J. A., Colquitt, J. A., & Erez, A. (2000). Adaptability to changing task contexts: Effects of general cognitive ability, conscientiousness, and openness to experience. *Personnel Psychology, 53*, 563–593.

Matthews, G., Derryberry, D., & Siegle, G. J. (2000). Personality and emotion: Cognitive science perspectives. In S. E. Hampson (Ed.), *Advances in personality psychology* (Vol. 1). London: Routledge.

Matthews, G., & Hudlicka, E. (2009). *Affect, risk and uncertainty in decision-making an integrated computational-empirical approach*. Pentagon Final Report (A291505); Contract No: FA9550-07-C-0055.

Mayer, J. D., & Salovey, P. (1993). The intelligence of emotional intelligence. *Intelligence, 17,* 433–442.

McCloskey, M. J., Behymer, K. J., Papautsky, E. L., Ross, K. G., Abbe, A. (2010). *A developmental model of cross-cultural competence at the tactical level*. ARI Technical Report 1278, Arlington, VA: United States Army Research Institute for the Behavioral and Social Sciences.

McFate, M., Damon, B., & Holliday, R. (2012). What do commanders really want to know? In J. H. Laurence & M. D. Matthews (Eds.), *The oxford handbook of military psychology* (pp. 92–113). New York: Oxford University Press Inc.

Newell, A., & Simon, H. A. (1972). *Human problem solving*. Englewood Cliffs, NJ: Prentice-Hall.

Pettigrew, T. F., & Tropp, L. R. (2011). *When groups meet: The dynamics of intergroup contact*. New York: Psychology Press.

Pulakos, E. D., Arad, S., Donovan, M. A., & Plamondon, K. E. (2000). Adaptability in the workplace: Development of a taxonomy of adaptive performance. *Journal of Applied Psychology, 85,* 612–624.

Pulakos, E. D., Schmitt, N., Dorsey, D. W., Arad, S., Borman, W. C., & Hedge, J. W. (2002). Predicting adaptive performance: Further tests of a model of adaptability. *Human Performance, 15,* 299–323.

Raghunatha, R., & Pham, M. T. (1999). All negative moods are not equal: Motivational influences of anxiety and sadness on decision making. *Organizational Behavior and Human Decision Processes, 79,* 56–77.

Ratwani, K. L., Horn, Z. N. J., Laurence, J., & Pham, S. (2014, under review). *Adapting Cognitively and Affectively to Cross-Cultural Changes* (Technical Report). Arlington, VA: U.S. Army Research Institute for the Behavioral and Social Sciences.

Rentsch, J. R., Gunderson, A., Goodwin, G. F., & Abbe, A. (2007, November). *Conceptualizing multicultural perspective taking skills* (Technical Report 1216). Arlington, VA: U.S. Army Research Institute for the Behavioral and Social Sciences.

Roan, L., Strong, B., Foss, P., Yager, M., Gehlbach, H., & Metcalf, K. A. (2009). *Social perspective taking (ADA509341)*. Arlington, VA: U.S. Army Research Institute for the Behavioral and Social Sciences.

Rosen, M. A., Bedwell, W. L., Wildman, J. L., Fritzsche, B. A., Salas, E., & Burke, C. S. (2011). Managing adaptive performance in teams: Guiding principles and behavioral markers for measurement. *Human Resource Management Review, 21,* 107–122.

Salas, E., Burke, C. S., & Stagl, K. C. (2004). Developing teams and team leaders: Strategies and principles. In D. V. Day, Zaccaro, S. J., & Halpin, S. M. (Eds.), *Leader development for transforming organizations: Growing leaders for tomorrow* (pp. 325–355). Mahwah, NJ: Lawrence Erlbaum Associates, Inc.

Scales, R. H. (2009). Clausewitz and World War IV. *Military Psychology, 21,* (Supl. 1), S23–S35.

Schwarz, N., & Clore, G. L. (1988). How do I feel about it? The informative function of affective states. In K. Fiedler & J. Forgas (Eds.), *Affect, cognition, and social behavior* (pp. 25–43). Toronto, Ontario, Canada: Hogrefe International.

Smith, E. M., Ford, J. K., & Kozlowski, S. W. J. (1997). Building adaptive expertise: Implications for training design. In M. A. Quinones & A. Dudda (Eds.), *Training for a rapidly changing workplace: Applications of psychological research* (pp. 89–118). Washington, DC: APA Books.

U.S. Department of the Army (2012, May). *Mission command* (ADRP 6-0). Washington, DC.

Vergun, D. (2014, February 12). *Odierno: Leader development No. 1 priority.* Retrieved from http://www.army.mil/article/120024/Odierno__Leader_development_No__1_priority

Williams, J. M. G., Watts, F. N., MacLeod, C., & Mathews, A. (1997). *Cognitive psychology and emotional disorders* (2nd ed.). Chichester, England: Wiley.

Zajonc, R. B. (1968). Attitudinal effects of mere exposure. *Journal of Personality and Social Psychology, 9*(2), 1–27.

Zimbardo, P. (2008). *The lucifer effect: Understanding how good people turn evil.* New York: Random House.

Chapter 10
Twenty Countries in Twenty Years: Modeling, Assessing, and Training Generalizable Cross-Cultural Skills

Michael J. McCloskey and Julio C. Mateo

Consider the following incident reported by a Special Forces Soldier during a data collection for one of our research efforts:

> A 12-person Special Forces squad was assigned to a relatively remote region of an unnamed Central African country to promote pro-US sentiment by building positive relationships with all local clans in their particular region. During one of their routine trips through the region, the Special Forces squad leader was traveling in the third of three vehicles carrying his squad and their interpreter on a rugged road through the dense jungle toward a remote village. The drivers of all vehicles had been hired from local clans, as dictated by the regional minister. This was the first visit of the squad leader to this region, which was not used to the presence of U.S. Forces, and he had only been in-country for less than a month. However, according to the squad leader's own description of his experience, previous deployments had taken him to "twenty countries in twenty years".

> Well into the forty kilometer journey through dense terrain, the lead vehicle came to an abrupt stop, halting the entire convoy. The squad leader saw a gathering of nationals ahead, so he immediately exited the vehicle and moved forward, arriving to a scene of utter chaos. The lead vehicle, which was driven by a local national hired from a neighboring village, had struck and apparently killed a small child who had been too close to the dangerous road. A very hostile crowd of nearly 300 villagers waving machetes and other basic weapons were surrounding the lead vehicle.

The views, opinions, and/or findings contained in this report are those of the authors and shall not be construed as an official Department of the Army position, policy, or decision, unless so designated by other documents.

M.J. McCloskey (✉) · J.C. Mateo
361 Interactive LLC, 400 South Main Street, Springboro, OH 45066, USA
e-mail: mike@361interactive.com

J.C. Mateo
e-mail: julio@361interactive.com

© Springer International Publishing Switzerland 2016
J.L. Wildman et al. (eds.), *Critical Issues in Cross Cultural Management*,
DOI 10.1007/978-3-319-42166-7_10

The squad members were understandably tense and adopting defensive stances (e.g., raising their weapons) as the crowd was drawing nearer. The squad leader deliberately calmed himself down and was able to quickly read the situation, even though he could not understand the local dialect. He immediately ordered his squad members to lower their weapons to prevent potential escalation of hostilities, and he quickly and "intuitively" identified the key decision maker in the mob. He "got the sense" that this mob was mostly concerned with justice and wanted acknowledgement of fault and monetary retribution for the loss of the child. He knew that he needed to quickly and respectfully assume responsibility and request a meeting with the village leader to "make amends" for what had happened.

The squad leader called over his interpreter and addressed the individual he identified as the mob leader to make his request. He expressed genuine remorse over the child's death and ensured the mob that they would not try to escape. Tensions visibly eased slightly as the squad leader's actions showed the mob that the squad and the driver from the neighboring clan were not trying to escape blame. The squad leader also requested that a neutral third party from another village lead all negotiations to prevent a continuation or escalation of hostilities. A series of meetings were then set up with the village leader. After 12 h of meals, heated discussions, and offerings for compensation for the victim's family, the squad leader was able to negotiate an agreement for compensation for the family and the sparing of the driver's life. Ultimately, the situation was resolved amicably and the Special Forces squad was able to continue their mission in the region.

The Special Forces squad leader in this incident found himself in a novel cultural environment, facing a high-uncertainty, high-stakes situation that required his immediate intervention. In spite of his lack of familiarity with the specific language and culture of the region, in a matter of seconds he was able to observe and interpret key pieces of information (e.g., the mob leader), assess the situation (e.g., the mob wanted acknowledgment of fault and/or retribution), and make mission-effective decisions (e.g., remain calm, express remorse over the child's death, request a meeting with the village leader) that prevented a potential bloodbath.

As is often the case when interviewing domain experts, when the squad leader was asked how he knew exactly what to do to prevent an escalation of hostilities, he responded: "*I just knew. I followed my gut.*" Following subsequent probing during multiple follow-on interviews, it became clear to us (and to the squad leader himself) that it was his extensive experience during prior deployments that allowed him to quickly make these mission-effective decisions. That is, drawing upon elements of similar situations he encountered in his "twenty countries in twenty years," he was able to, seemingly unconsciously, recognize parallels that pointed him to the right course of action. This is what *Naturalistic Decision Making* (*NDM*) researchers recognize as *expertise* whether it lies within an aviator, a firefighter, an intelligence analyst, a surgeon, or a Soldier (Klein et al. 1993; Zsambok and Klein 1997). Expertise is borne of extensive experience within one's domain; meaningful, reflective practice in making decisions, and learning from one's successes and mistakes. This experience base becomes a library of analogues that can be quickly drawn upon to point the way to a workable solution.

Summary of the Science

The Special Forces Soldier serving as the squad leader in the incident described above was one of the first of over 500 Warfighters with whom we interacted over the course of our research efforts. Our approach to modeling cross-cultural competence (3C) began in 2007, and has been empirically driven from the start. Then, Abbe et al. (2007) had recently conducted a review of the published literature and developed a framework of 3C in Army leaders by applying constructs from the 3C literature to operational situations. Abbe et al.'s seminal framework provided an excellent foundation for subsequent 3C modeling efforts. However, at the time there was a dearth of research efforts approaching the development of 3C models by directly investigating how cross-culturally competent Warfighters made decisions in novel cultural situations during deployments.

Our work emphasizes the understanding of 3C and how it impacts decision making in operational environments from the perspective of the Warfighter. Beginning with real incidents, involving real Warfighters making real decisions in real uncertain, high-stakes, time-critical operational situations, we have leveraged a wide range of *cognitive task analysis* (CTA) techniques to develop conceptual models, assessment methods, and training tools to promote generalizable cross-cultural skills among Warfighters. Over the past seven years, our research team has worked toward the development of empirically based theoretical models, assessment methods, and training tools to promote generalizable cross-cultural skills among Warfighters (McCloskey and Baxter 2008; McCloskey and Behymer 2012a, b; McCloskey et al. 2010a, b, 2012; Mateo et al. submitted). Incidents like the one presented above represent the data from which we have developed our current understanding of 3C in operational settings.

Modeling General Cross-Cultural Competence

The first step in our quest to develop assessment and training methods to promote general 3C in operational forces was to gain a better understanding of what general 3C is in the first place. What *knowledge, skills, abilities, and aptitudes* (KSAAs) underlie general 3C? How do possessing these KSAAs leads Warfighters to make effective decisions and select successful actions in unfamiliar cultural settings? What stages of development do Warfighters tend to go through as they develop this competence?

Within the last decade, the Department of Defense (DoD) has funded and conducted a substantial amount of research to develop models of general 3C in operational settings (see Abbe 2014). Early efforts (Abbe et al. 2007; McDonald et al. 2008; Selmeski 2007) were characterized by a top-down approach to the development of models of 3C in operational settings. That is, these efforts began by reviewing what was known about 3C in other domains and, based on these findings, developed 3C models about how that knowledge was expected to apply in the military domain. Based on the methodology they used, some later DoD-funded efforts can also described as top-down models (e.g., Caligiuri et al. 2011).

At the time when our research efforts began, existing models of 3C in operational settings had been developed following a *top-down* perspective. The intent of our initial modeling efforts (McCloskey et al. 2010a, b, 2012) was to develop a model of general 3C in operational settings using a more *bottom-up*, empirically driven approach. Bottom-up models are based on the domain-specific data collected from military personnel about their experiences in operational settings. The KSAAs underlying general 3C in operational settings are then derived, through (mostly qualitative) analyses, from these operational accounts. Other models of general 3C in operational settings (e.g., Rasmussen et al. 2013; Ratwani et al. 2014) also followed bottom-up approaches.

Our research effort collected data from Warfighters using a combination of traditional and novel CTA protocols and simulation interviews. This data collection led to 28 key competencies found to impact mission success in novel cultural environments (see McCloskey et al. 2010a, b, for a complete list). Through continued research, this initial set was further developed and refined into a five-factor model that comprised general 3C in operational environments. These five factors were: *interpersonal skills, relationship orientation, cultural relativism, cultural interest,* and *cultural acuity* (McCloskey et al. 2012).

Interpersonal skills include the behavioral aspects of 3C, such as self-monitoring, self-presentation, and rapport-building skills. Self-monitoring, for the purposes of our model, was defined as "the ability to see yourself as others see you and to recognize subtle changes in your own personal affect and adjust outward behaviors accordingly." And related, self-presentation was defined as "the ability to consciously modify overt behaviors and appearances in response to changing demands of the cross-cultural interaction." (McCloskey et al. 2010a, b) An example of self-monitoring and self-presentation can be found in a Company Commander in a Medical Unit from one our data collections. In an attempt to persuade an Iraqi medical director to stop sending patients to dangerous hospitals, the Soldier explained how "*I had to create the image that I cared what he had to say, I cared what he wanted, and it was kind of like playing poker.*" This Soldier leveraged his awareness of how he came across (self-monitoring) and his ability to actively change his behavior to support his goal at the time (self-presentation) to successfully persuade the Iraqi counterpart. An example of rapport building can be found in a transition team Soldier, who explained how what he did was "*just going in and let him* (the Iraqi counterpart) *speak. Some days, in the beginning, I would just sit there ... just listen, just allow him to speak and get everything off his chest, just open himself up, and gain some trust with him. I would bring him something every once in a while I'd get maybe an American CD, give him an American CD to give to his family, ask him about his family, that's a real big thing.*"

Relationship orientation refers to the affective attributes of cross-culturally competent Warfighters, such as emotional self-regulation and emotional empathy. As an example of self-regulation, consider the squad leader in the sample incident presented above, who "*deliberately calmed himself down and was able to quickly read the situation.*" Examples of emotional empathy can be found in the many Soldiers who were able to feel the emotions of local nationals by considering the local national's situation (e.g., death threats, stressful conditions) and thinking about how the Soldiers would feel and act under similar circumstances.

Cultural relativism refers to the ability and willingness to adjust one's cultural interpretations based on new information; attributes including flexibility in novel cultural environments, uncertainty tolerance, and openness to unfamiliar practices contribute to cultural relativism. An example of this openness to unfamiliar practices can be found in a Soldier who, when observing behaviors displayed by members of an Afghan tribal group that were highly questionable by U.S. moral standards, was able to interpret them in the context of the local culture. The Soldier still strongly disagreed with these practices, but being able to understand them within the context of that culture allowed him to build a relationship and work successfully with members of this Afghan tribal group.

Cultural interest involves an awareness of how culture affects a person's perceptions, interpretations, and actions; as well as a desire to learn more about cultural differences. Examples of this desire to learn about cultural differences can be found in a Soldier from our data collections who continuously sought opportunities to understand how their culture influenced Iraqis by studying the differences between tribal roots (e.g., one tribe might have an Egyptian background, and another tribe a Syrian one).

Cultural acuity refers to the ability to accurately assess sociocultural systems, the perspectives of members of other cultures, and the long-term and short-term impact that one's actions may have in a foreign cultural environment. An example of high cultural acuity can be found in a Soldier who reported making a concerted effort to better understand the individual Iraqis working under him to implement policies that respected their cultural and religious traditions and norms (e.g., work breaks for prayer). In response, Iraqi workers were more cooperative, harder working, and faster at finishing their jobs. In terms of assessing the long-term impact of one's actions, one example was a particularly competent Captain who would ensure that, whenever possible, his foreign counterpart would get credit for his own success or ideas. He explained: "*The trick was not to let them believe the Americans made the decision, because if you let them believe the Americans made the decision, then they would come to you for everything. What you have to do is empower the leaders.*"

In addition to identifying the five factors comprising general 3C in operational settings, the model delineated the developmental stages for each factor. That is, it described the expected changes as a Warfighter progressed from novice to expert. These expected changes were based on the collected CTA data, and they represent a generalization of how 3C tended to develop in the Soldiers we interviewed. We noticed interesting parallels to Bennett's model of cultural competency wherein Bennet describes early, ethnocentic stages, where individuals tend to be either unaware of the existence of cultural differences, or otherwise minimize acknowledged differences (Bennett 1993).

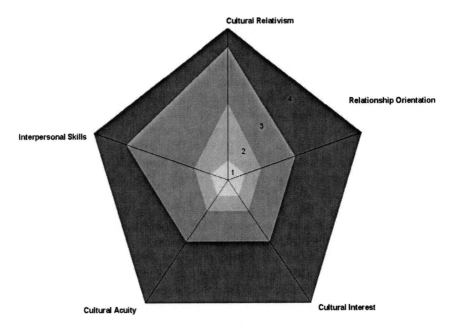

Fig. 10.1 The developmental model of cross-cultural competence (McCloskey et al. 2010a, b)

Developmental stages are represented by numbers increasing outward in Fig. 10.1: the *beginner* stage is represented with a 2, the *intermediate* stage with a 3, and the *advance*d stage with a 4. Compared to other domains in which researchers have studied expertise, this developmental model is unique in that the addition of a *pre-competent* stage (represented with a 1 in Fig. 10.1) was necessary to appropriately capture the development of 3C in operational settings. Individuals at the pre-competent stage typically (a) do not see value of acquiring cross-cultural skills for mission success and/or (b) have strong prejudices and biases against people from other cultures. They embrace stereotypes that are typically simplistic and inaccurate. They further avoid cross-cultural interactions whenever possible. These attitudinal barriers are usually inexistent in other domains: a doctor will not argue against the importance of developing his or her skills, nor will a pilot actively avoid critical training. Yet, the attitudes of pre-competent individuals in the 3C domain can prevent them from acquiring the cultural knowledge and learning the basic guidelines upon which Soldiers depend to operate during deployments. Thus, interventions with pre-competent individuals should focus on addressing these barriers before resources are spent on teaching them the knowledge and skills necessary to increase their 3C (McCloskey et al. 2012). Moving past the pre-competent stage, soldiers at the beginner stage of 3C development:

> ...show variability in empathy levels toward foreign nationals, ranging from lack of sensitivity to some compassion. These Soldiers are dedicated and are willing to engage, but they display a lack of confidence about their abilities. Their understanding of cultures is

superficial. Their ability to take the perspective of others is limited to imagining how they would feel in a specific situation without regard to cultural differences.

Soldiers at the intermediate stage are exhibiting effective cross-cultural skills in most deployment settings. They tend to be:

...effective at relationship-building and persuasion due to displaying interpersonal abilities, empathy, and cultural awareness. However, these skills are not optimized due to limited openness and perspective taking ability. A Level 3 (Intermediate level) Soldier leader takes responsibility for the cultural interactions of his/her Soldiers, and provides effective guidance on how to avoid cross-cultural incidents.

Finally, at the highest development stage in our model, advanced 3C Soldiers:

...possess the highest level of cross-cultural competence levels. These Soldiers integrate true awareness of cultural differences into all aspects of the mission. They display appropriate affect, which supports perspective taking, negotiation, persuasion, and manipulation abilities. They develop genuine relationships with locals. Their pre-deployment preparation efforts include a study of relevant cultural aspects of the region, as well as assessments of subordinates' abilities. (McCloskey et al. 2010a, b, 2012).

In the last few years, the *Defense Language Office* (now the *Defense Language and Security Education Office*, *DLNSEO*) has sponsored efforts aimed at creating a *meta-model* of 3C in operational settings (Reid et al. 2012; Wisecarver et al. 2012). Both of these efforts began with a review of 3C models (including most of the ones cited in this chapter), analyzed the commonalities and differences among them, and proposed a meta-model that synthesizes the findings from previous research on general 3C in operational settings. For example, Reid et al.'s model includes the following six dimensions: *self-awareness, self-regulation, cultural learning, cultural perspective taking, intercultural interaction,* and *cultural reasoning.* Table 10.1 categorizes some of the existing models of general 3C in operational settings based on the approach used to develop them.

Table 10.1 Models of general 3C in operational settings	Modeling approach	Citations
	'Top-down'	Abbe et al. (2007)
		Caligiuri et al. (2011)
		McDonald et al. (2008)
		Selmeski (2007)
	'Bottom-up'	McCloskey et al. (2012)
		Rasmussen et al. (2013)
		Ratwani et al. (2014)
	'Meta-models'	Reid et al. (2012)
		Wisecarver et al. (2012)

Bridging the Gap: Evidence-Based Practices

The 3C model introduced above explicitly acknowledges the importance of inter-personal skills, affective skills (i.e., relationship orientation), and cognitive skills (i.e., cultural interest, cultural relativism, cultural acuity) to general 3C. Existing training tools, however, often place greater emphasis on the development of interpersonal and affective skills than on cognitive skills associated with 3C (Ramsden Zbylut 2013). Yet, as the incident presented above illustrated, the ability to rapidly assess novel cultural environments or diagnose observed behaviors and actions is key and can make the difference between mission success and failure. The cognitive skills underlying this ability are a critical aspect of what distinguishes those Warfighters who excel in novel cultural environments from their peers. Our efforts to develop general 3C assessment methods and training tools have primarily focused on these cognitive skills.

Our approach emphasizes the importance of using cognitively authentic situa-tions capturing the key aspects of the operational tasks and settings when assessing and training general 3C. Rather than deriving tests to train or assess specific 3C constructs from the factors in the 3C model, assessment and training materials and tasks are based on the demands of operational settings. Given that Warfighters develop expertise through repeated exposure to situations with meaningful feed-back on outcomes (akin to the squad leader incident above), training interventions should replicate key aspects of these cognitively challenging situations. For example, novel cultural situations in operational settings almost invariably involve high levels of uncertainty, missing data, high-stakes, and continuously changing circumstances that are affected by the actions of Warfighters. When developing our assessment and training methods, we leverage our knowledge about operational situations to create tasks that faithfully recreate the key demands of operational situations. We further allow students to encounter many situations "on the hot seat," on occasion with little, or no, time to prepare. We let them first experience the situation first hand, making mistakes that sink in. Then, in the debrief, we have them reflect on their experiences, hoping that they will come to their own under-standings versus simply being told where their sensemaking and decision-making went wrong. We further offer opportunities for students to compare their percep-tions and actions to those of 3C experts, and then probe them to consider the differences.

Assessing General Cross-Cultural Competence

Cognitive processes from our model that have been identified as critical to effective cross-cultural mission performance (primarily under the Cultural Acuity factor) include sensemaking, perspective taking, information seeking, and hypothesis formation and modification skills. An assessment method may measure a

Warfighter's ability to recognize basic customs, greetings and taboos, identify underlying cultural norms, and discern governing rules in unfamiliar cultures. Methods to assess cultural cognitive skills should consider both process and outcome.

In recently completed effort sponsored by the U.S. Army Research Institute, we developed six innovative methods to assess Warfighter cognitive skills in unfamiliar cultural environments (Mateo et al. submitted). One of the methods we developed is the *fictional culture exercise*. For this method, we "created" a fictional culture with unique customs, communication norms, and deeper, fundamental characteristics (e.g., low uncertainty tolerance, high emphasis on family). We recruited and trained, over several iterations, actors to portray multiple scenes based on critical incidents describing operational encounters. Respondents completing the fictional culture exercise observe a series of video clips of this critical incident and are queried to assess a wide range of cultural cognitive abilities (e.g., identifying underlying social norms and rules, maintaining awareness of own cultural biases) both between clips and at the end of the incident.

Another method, the *dynamic location exercise*, primarily aims to assess an individual's information seeking strategies and abilities. In this exercise, participants are virtually "placed" in a series of unfamiliar physical environments somewhere in the world and they are given limited time to explore multiple scenes within the computerized environment. They are asked to verbalize their thought processes as they explore the scenes and attempt to determine where in the world they are located. They are assessed not only on the information seeking strategies they use, but also on how they form and adjust hypotheses, the nature and range of the perceptual cues they leverage in their assessments, their ability to apply general cultural knowledge to determine the locations, and several other factors.

In their current form, these performance-based assessment methods require one-on-one administration and are more resource-demanding than traditional paper-and-pencil survey assessment methods. However, they also contain a set of stimuli that better reflect the demands of the operational situations encountered by Soldiers which demand cultural acuity. As a result, these methods elicit similar cognitive processes to those elicited by novel intercultural situations, enable administrators to assess relevant 3C behavior as it happens, rather than relying on self-report responses.

Training General Cross-Cultural Competence

Like the assessment effort described above, our training efforts have focused primarily on enhancing the cognitive aspects of 3C, primarily cultural acuity. NDM research (Klein 1997) suggested that an optimal way to develop expertise is to engage in deliberate repeated practice with opportunities for reflection and meaningful feedback, and this approach has been used successfully in operational settings (Pliske et al. 2001). We follow an NDM approach to training development and leverage operationally relevant materials and tasks to provide trainees with opportunities to encounter relevant cross-cultural situations in a safe environment and with the benefit of feedback tailored to their responses. The operationally relevant feedback provided to trainees incorporates information obtained from experienced Warfighters and cultural trainers.

We are currently leveraging this approach in the development of CultureGear, a computer-based tool that provides guided practice opportunities to develop cultural observation and assessment skills. In CultureGear, whose development is sponsored by the Office of Naval Research, trainees are presented with culturally rich imagery and video in a wide range of environments. They are asked to identify and interpret the critical perceptual cues as they assess political, economic, social, infrastructure and other elements of the scenes. After completing this assessment, trainees are shown assessments of the same scenes or videos made by Warfighters and cultural trainers with extensive knowledge of the region. Rather than simply being told about the critical elements within scenes, trainees first do their own assessment and then compare them to the more experienced assessments (see Fig. 10.2). Other CultureGear modules are focused on further promoting operational skill development based on how experts learn. For example, a deployment preparation module based on the preparation strategies used by culturally seasoned Warfighters supports trainees in learning about unfamiliar, pending deployment locations. Another module is being developed to help trainees become more aware of their own cultural biases to reduce their impact when interpreting novel cultural settings.

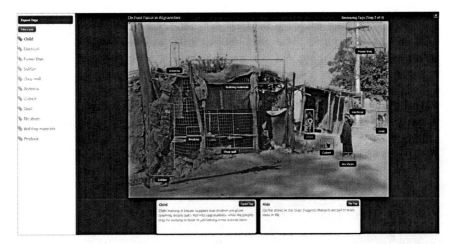

Fig. 10.2 Screenshot of the Observations module in the current version of CultureGear. The three participant tags are represented by the circular icons (e.g., see the goat on the far right), whereas the "expert tags" reported by experienced Warfighters are represented by rectangular boxes. When reviewing the "expert tags," the trainee can compare his or her response to the response of more experienced Warfighters (see the bottom of the screenshot)

Conclusion

General 3C is a complex and multi-faceted phenomenon. Even though it has received increasing attention in recent years, our understanding of exactly what 3C is and how it manifests itself in operational settings is still limited and more research is needed. Cognitive skills, often more subtle and hidden, are critical for optimal mission performance, and they cannot be neglected in favor of interpersonal skills and affective attributes. Rather, all three are essential and overlapping. The ability to build rapport is important in operational environments, but it is useless if a Warfighter cannot determine how and when to leverage that rapport. Positive attitudes toward other cultures and willingness to engage are extremely important as well, but without an ability to interpret, assess, and project, good feelings will not get you far. Cognitive, affective, and behavioral abilities are all critical to different extents, based on the mission type.

One further note; over the years, we have observed a distinct schism within the research community regarding the best approach to approach 3C research and develop assessment methods and training tools. One camp favors an empirically driven, bottom-up approach to studying 3C, leveraging CTA methodologies to collect operational data that informs our models, theories, and applications. The other camp adopts a theoretically driven, top-down approach, wherein models and applications are driven by what theory suggests. While our approach is clearly more aligned with the first camp described above, we recognize the value of both approaches and consider them complementary to each other. As long as both sides of the schism recognize the value of the other, remain flexible in approach, and are willing to work together (or at least, towards the same goals), we consider this to be a healthy debate that can strengthen the field of 3C research and application.

Acknowledgments Research described in the paper was funded by the U.S. Army Research Institute (Contract W91WAW-09-C-0037, W91WAW-08-P-0068, and W5J9CQ-13-C-0006) and the Office of Naval Research (Contract N00014-13-C-0153).

References

Abbe, A. (2014). The historical development of cross-cultural competence. In R. Greene Sands & A. Greene-Sands (Eds.), *Cross-cultural competence for a twenty-first-century military: Culture, the flipside of COIN* (pp. 31–42). Lanham, MD: Lexington Books.

Abbe, A., Gulick, L. M. V., & Herman, J. L. (2007). *Cross-cultural competence in Army leaders: A conceptual and empirical foundation (SR 2008-1).* Arlington, VA: U.S. Army Research Institute for the Behavioral and Social Sciences.

Bennett, M. J. (1993). Towards ethnorelativism: A developmental model of intercultural sensitivity. In R. M. Paige (Ed.), *Education for the intercultural experience.* Yarmouth, ME: Intercultural Press.

Caligiuri, P., Noe, R., Nolan, R., Ryan, A. M., & Drasgow, F. (2011). *Training, developing, and assessing cross-cultural competence in military personnel (TR 1284).* Arlington, VA: U.S. Army Research Institute for the Behavioral and Social Sciences.

Klein, G. A. (1997). Developing expertise in decision making. *Thinking & Reasoning, 3*, 337–352.

Klein, G. A., Orasanu, J., Calderwood, R., & Zsambok, C. E. (Eds.). (1993). *Decision making in action: Models and methods*. Norwood, NJ: Ablex Publishing Corporation.

Mateo, J. C., Branlat, M., McCloskey, M. J., Abbe, A., & Brooks Babin, L. (submitted). *Development of performance-based methods to assess cultural acuity in Army personnel* (Technical Report). Fort Leavenworth, KS: U.S. Army Research Institute for the Behavioral and Social Sciences.

Mateo, J. C., McCloskey, M. J., Grome, A. P., Abbe, A., & Behymer, K. (submitted). *A framework for understanding intercultural perspective taking in operational settings* (Technical Report). Fort Leavenworth, KS: U.S. Army Research Institute for the Behavioral and Social Sciences.

McCloskey, M. J., & Baxter, H. C. (2008). Promoting cross-cultural perspective taking skills in operational environments. *Proceedings of the Interservice/Industry Training, Simulation, and Education Conference*, Orlando, FL.

McClosey, M. J., & Behymer, K. J. (2012a). Methods for capturing cultural lessons learned and training cross-cultural skills. In D. Schmorrow & D. Nicholson (Eds.), *Advances in design for cross-cultural activities Part I* (pp. 86–95). Boca Raton, FL: CRC Press.

McCloskey, M. J., & Behymer, K. (2012b). Modeling and assessing cross-cultural competence in operational environments. *Proceedings of the* 1st *International Conference on Cross-Cultural Decision Making*, CRC Press, Taylor & Francis, Ltd.

McCloskey, M. J., Behymer, K. J., Papautsky, E. L., Ross, K. G., & Abbe, A. (2010a). *A developmental model of cross-cultural competence at the tactical level (TR 1278)*. Alexandria, VA: U.S. Army Research Institute for the Behavioral and Social Sciences.

McCloskey, M. J., Grandjean, A. K., Behymer, K. J., & Ross, K. G. (2010b). *Assessing the development of cross-cultural competence in soldiers (TR 1277)*. Alexandria, VA: U.S. Army Research Institute for the Behavioral and Social Sciences.

McCloskey, M. J., Behymer, K. J., Papautsky, E. L., & Grandjean, A. K. (2012). *Measuring learning and development in cross-cultural competence (TR 1317)*. Alexandria, VA: U.S. Army Research Institute for the Behavioral and Social Sciences.

McDonald, D. P., McGuire, G., Johnston, J., Selmeski, B., & Abbe, A. (2008). *Developing and managing cross-cultural competence within the Department of Defense: Recommendations for learning and assessment*. Regional and Cultural Capabilities (RACCA) Working Group Report.

Pliske, R. M., McCloskey, M. J., & Klein, G. (2001). Decision skills training: Facilitating learning from experience. In E. Salas & G. Klein (Eds.), *Linking expertise and naturalistic decision making* (pp. 37–53). Mahwah, NJ: Lawrence Erlbaum Associates.

Ramsden Zbylut, M. (2013). Preface. In B. E. Strong, L. Brooks Babin, M. Ramsden Zbylut, & L. Roan (Eds.), *Sociocultural systems: The next step in Army cultural capability* (Research Product 2013-02) (pp. vii-xviii). Fort Belvoir, VA: U.S. Army Research Institute for the Behavioral and Social Sciences.

Rasmussen, L. J., Sieck, W. R., Crandall, B. W., Simpkins, B. G., & Smith, J. L. (2013). *Data collection and analysis for a cross-cultural competence model*. Arlington, VA: Defense Language and National Security Education Office.

Ratwani, K. L., Beaubien, J. M., Entin, E. B., Feyre, R. J., & Gallus, J. A. (2014). *Identifying dynamic environments for cross-cultural competencies (TR 1345)*. Fort Belvoir, VA: U.S. Army Research Institute for the Behavioral & Social Sciences.

Reid, P., Kaloydis, F., Sudduth, M., & Greene-Sands, A. (2012). *Executive summary: A framework for understanding cross-cultural competence in the Department of Defense* (Tech. No. 15–12). Melbourne, FL: Defense Equal Opportunity Management Institute.

Selmeski, B. R. (2007). *Military cross-cultural competence: Core concepts and individual development*. Centre for Security, Armed Forces & Society Occasional Paper Series-Number 1. Kingston, Ontario: Royal Military College of Canada.

Wisecarver, M., Ferro, G., Foldes, H., Adis, C., Hope, T., & Hill, M. (2012). *Regional expertise and culture proficiency* (Project Report 2012-01). Arlington, VA: Defense Language and National Security Education Office.

Zsambok, C. E., & Klein, G. (Eds.). (1997). *Naturalistic decision making*. Mahwah, NJ: Lawrence Erlbaum Associates.

Chapter 11
The Way Ahead: Critical Directions for Future Research in Cross-Cultural Management

Kyi Phyu Nyein and Jessica L. Wildman

The chapters in this book have discussed cross-cultural competence, global leadership, multinational teams, and cross-cultural conflict management, not only based on scientific research but also from years of experience, knowledge, and expertise in the field. To the degree that today's world is constantly changing, organizational needs and areas of interests are also changing and evolving. Despite the importance and need for cross-cultural competence and leadership, there is much more that needs to be studied and answered. So, what is next for cross-cultural management?

In this chapter, we identify several key areas that we believe need significantly more research, provide some directions for future research, and provoke thoughts on cross-cultural management. There are eight areas we have identified for future directions: (1) talent management of global leaders; (2) person–environment fit in the cross-cultural context; (3) team-level competence in the cross-cultural context; (4) universal values, processes, and competencies; (5) cross-cultural ethical conflicts; (6) metaphors, languages, and alternatives; (7) cross-cultural trust development, violation, and repair; and (8) cross-cultural bias.

Research Need 1: Talent Management of Global Leaders

Throughout this book, it has been established that leaders play a very important role in developing and managing cross-cultural teams and competence. However, there is a shortage of competent leaders in many fields (Collings and Mellahi 2009).

K.P. Nyein (✉) · J.L. Wildman
School of Psychology and Institute for Cross Cultural Management, Florida Institute of Technology, 150 W. University Blvd, Melbourne, FL 32901, USA
e-mail: nyeink2015@my.fit.edu

J.L. Wildman
e-mail: jwildman@fit.edu

© Springer International Publishing Switzerland 2016
J.L. Wildman et al. (eds.), *Critical Issues in Cross Cultural Management*,
DOI 10.1007/978-3-319-42166-7_11

Given the scarcity of effective leadership, and the complexity of cross-cultural contexts, we need best practices regarding how to select, develop, and maintain global leaders as well as how to share knowledge and talent across them. In other words, effective talent management of global leaders is critical for the future of global organizations.

Global talent management includes attracting, developing, and retaining "individuals with high levels of human capital (e.g., competency, personality, motivation) consistent with the strategic directions of the multinational enterprise in a dynamic, highly competitive, and global environment" (Tarique and Schuler 2010, p. 124). It is an important and significant topic because organizations need diverse talents to be successful, innovative, and adaptive. Talent management is also forward looking and proactive such that it is a continuous process that plans talent needs, builds an image and reputation to attract and retain top talent, and facilitates the continuous movement and strategic integration of talent in places where they can have the most impact. Not only do we need to develop, select, and retain global leaders, but also we need to manage and share their knowledge, expertise, and experiences. Through knowledge management and sharing, individuals, teams, and other leaders can all benefit, and organizations can retain those resources.

Surprisingly, there is little research on talent management of global leaders specifically, although some research has been done to study leadership development in general. Church et al. (2015) found that assessments were used in organizations most commonly for identifying high potential talents and for succession planning for senior executives. The three most commonly used assessments were 360 degree feedback, personality inventories, and interviews. Unsurprisingly, the most commonly used criterion for identifying high potential talents was performance, including both past and current performance. Additionally, Ruvolo et al. (2004) gave a framework for leadership development as follows:

Experience + New Knowledge (with support & feedback) + Reflection +

TIME (more practice/experience) = Leadership Growth and Development (p. 13)

Based on this framework, leadership growth and development is achieved by previous experience, gaining new knowledge, getting feedback, learning from others and reflection, and more experience over time. Additionally, leadership development activities must be ingrained in the organizational culture because without the organizational support, resources, and emphasis on leadership development, these activities would not be successful.

However, more research is needed to examine whether what we know from the literature regarding domestic leadership development and talent management can also be applied in the global context. Not only is global leadership identification and development important, but also retaining these global leaders and their knowledge management are also necessary. After all the investments in selecting and developing global leaders, if we do not retain and manage them, the investments will be a waste. The followers can also face more difficulties in achieving their goals without the support from leadership and with constant changes in leadership. Therefore, the following topics are suggested for future research on global leader talent management:

• Tools and methods to identify, develop, and select global leaders
• Motivational and reward systems to retain global leaders
• Global leadership knowledge sharing and management (e.g., establishing systems and procedures).

Research Need 2: Person–Environment Fit in the Cross-Cultural Context

Once global employees are selected, decisions must be made in terms of what cross-cultural teams, leaders, and environments they will be assigned to. Then, the question becomes how we select them to fit with the leaders, teams, environments, and goals in the cross-cultural context. A lot of research has been done on person–environment fit and on the outcomes when there is a person–environment fit. Person–environment fit is the extent to which an individual is matched or compatible with work environmental characteristics. The premise is that both individuals and the environment they are in account for their behaviors and performance. Person–environment fit has five dimensions: person–vocation fit, person–job fit, person–organization fit, person–group fit, and person–supervisor fit (Kristof-Brown et al. 2005). Person–vocation (P–V) fit happens when one has a career or occupation that fits with one's interests and goals. Person–job (P–J) fit happens when one has knowledge, skills, and abilities that can meet demands and requirements of the job (demands-abilities fit) and when one's needs and values are met by the job (needs-supplies or supplies-values fit). Person–organization (P–O) fit occurs when one's personality, goals, and values fit with those of the organization one is in. Person–group (P–G) fit and person–supervisor (P–S) fit happen when there is compatibility between one's personality, goals, and values and those of the group and supervisor, respectively.

A meta-analytic study of Kristof-Brown et al. (2005) examined the outcomes when there was a person–environment fit at the workplace. Job satisfaction was most strongly related to P–J fit, and organizational commitment to P–O fit closely followed by P–J fit. As expected, satisfaction with coworkers was highest with P–G fit, and satisfaction with supervisors with P–S fit. Organizational attraction was moderately influenced by P–J and P–O fits. In addition, there were moderate to small correlations between overall performance and P–J, P–G, and P–S fits. Finally, P–J, P–O, and P–G fits had moderate, negative relationships with intent to quit. Thus, individual attitudes and behaviors are influenced by the perception of the person–environment fit, and both individuals and organizations can benefit from the person–environment fit.

To compare fit cross-culturally, in their recent meta-analysis, Oh et al. (2014) examined the effects of person–environment fit on a number of organizational outcomes across cultures, and these outcomes included job satisfaction, organizational commitment, intent to quit, organizational citizenship behavior, and job performance. They found that P–J fit and P–O fit had stronger effects in North American and Europe to a less extent than in East Asia, whereas P–G fit and P–S fit had stronger effects in East Asia than in North America because of the value of collectivism and high power distance in East Asia. On top of that, person–environment fit could be found across all cultures, and the higher the fit, the more likely it would lead to positive organizational outcomes.

These studies indicate that fit matters and that when it happens, it leads to positive outcomes. Nevertheless, a lot of research on this topic is conducted to understand the relationship between fit and its outcomes. There is little research on strategies or approaches to ensure fit and on fit particularly in the cross-cultural context. Given all these benefits, more insights are needed to understand:

- How to determine and select individuals to ensure fit particularly in the cross-cultural context
- Factors, including individual, organizational, and situational characteristics, which can be beneficial or detrimental to the cross-cultural fit.

Research Need 3: Team-Level Competence in the Cross-Cultural Context

Throughout this book, we have discussed the individual-level cross-cultural competencies needed to be successful when working in a different culture or with people from different cultures and how to best develop these competencies. Given the complexity of the cross-cultural context, it is unclear if individual-level cross-cultural competence is enough to attain success in global teams and organizations as a whole. At the same time, organizations are using teams more and more to accomplish goals, and technology also allows them to form teams and groups from different geographical locations and cultures. Since teams can accomplish more than individuals, we need to know more about what it means to be cross-culturally competent as a team or organization, and whether or not team-level cross-cultural competence can produce better results than individual-level competence alone.

This is based on the concepts of isomorphism and discontinuity in the multilevel model theory of Kozlowski and Klein (2000). Isomorphism assumes that knowledge, skills, and abilities are more or less similar for all individuals in the team. On the other hand, discontinuity assumes that what individuals contribute to the team is different, not shared in terms of overlapping, but compatible. To put it in another way, team-level competence is a higher level construct and emerges from a lower level construct individual competence. These two levels of construct have similar meanings, influence each other, and can occur simultaneously (Kauffeld 2006). Team-level competence, however, is more than the sum of individual team members because through interactions, knowledge, skills, behaviors, and attitudes can be changed and complemented, hence changing the entire team as a system.

Kauffeld (2006) studied the competence of self-directed teams by group-level analysis and compared it to the competence of traditional teams in completing organizational tasks. Four facets of competence were also examined: professional competence, methodological competence, social competence, and self-competence. Professional competence was the sum of specific professional skills and knowledge that team members had. Methodological competence was the ability to find and apply resources and means to accomplish goals, and social competence was the ability to communicate and collaborate with each other in a self-organized, proactive way. Self-competence concerned with the willingness to create situations for growth and improvement. It was found that self-directed teams were more competent than traditional teams in completing tasks. Moreover, self-directed teams showed greater professional, methodological, and self-competence than traditional teams.

In order to enhance team-level cross-cultural competence, Brandl and Neyer (2009) propose cross-cultural training using the cognitive adjustment theory especially in global virtual teams that have to deal with uncertain situations and behaviors. Based on the cognitive adjustment theory, when individuals are in an uncertain situation, they have to adjust their way of thinking and learn to interpret the situation correctly. They also need to adapt their behaviors to the highly diverse, technologically-mediated situation and be sensitive to the various beliefs, values, and norms in the situation. In contrast, culture orientation programs only teach them general theories of differences in self-identity, relationships, communication, and conflict management across cultures. However, culture is such a broad concept that there is no best theory to completely capture and understand all aspects of a culture. Therefore, Brandl and Neyer (2009) call for the seemingly more effective cross-cultural training based on the cognitive adjustment theory. This theory provides one useful first step toward exploring cross-cultural competence at higher levels, but more research is still needed in:

- Understanding the concept of cross-cultural competence at higher levels of analysis (i.e., what does it mean to be a cross-cultural competent team or organization?)
- Theory and evidence on cross-cultural competence at a higher level
- Benefits or drawbacks of higher level cross-cultural competence
- Conditions and constraints in the emergence of higher level cross-cultural competence
- Training and development for higher level cross-cultural competence.

Research Need 4: Universal Values, Processes, and Competencies

One of the obvious thoughts when it comes to discussing cultures is the difference across them. Differences—small and big—do exist, and conflicts can happen due to these differences. However, in conflict management as well as working in teams, establishing common ground in terms of, for example, goals, values, and processes, is essential for a mutual understanding, conflict resolution, and effective teamwork (e.g., Cramton 2002).

Although many studies focus on what the cultural differences are and how to overcome them, there are a few studies that have been conducted related to universal values, processes, and competencies across cultures. As previously mentioned, Oh et al. (2014) found that regardless of which cultures individuals were in, person–environment fit was a phenomenon, and if a person achieved fit with their environment, it led to positive outcomes. Gentry and Sparks (2012) also studied leadership competencies that were valued across 40 countries and that were perceived by managers at different levels in organizations as necessary for the success in organizations. They found that three types of leadership competencies—resourcefulness, change management, and building and mending relationships—were globally valued and needed for organizational success; however, no such value or need was found for balancing personal life and work. Peterson (2007) claimed that due to the globalization, senior executives increasingly shared similar experiences, for example, experiencing similar market demands and complexities in their organizations and even reading the same books and journals. Moreover, many countries were also adopting Western leadership styles in the emergent global culture. Thus, although there is some promising research examining universal elements of culture, the following areas are suggested for continuing future research:

- The emergence of global culture
- Values, processes, and competencies that are universally respected and needed for the success and effectiveness of cross-cultural teams and organizations.

The social identity theory of intergroup behaviors explains that we strive to achieve a positive social identity by favoring those who are in the same social group or share the social identity (in-group) than those who are not in the same social group (out-group; Jackson et al. 1999). In other words, we tend to like more and give more favorable ratings to in-group members than out-group members. In the cross-cultural context, if groups from different cultures share something and consider each other as in-group members, they are more likely to come together and work collaboratively. Therefore, future research on the suggested areas will help understand and achieve perceptions of in-group membership.

Research Need 5: Cross-Cultural Ethical Conflicts

Cultural conflicts can take different forms including interpersonal, legal, and ethical. One type of conflict that can be especially problematic, but is relatively underdiscussed in the cross-cultural management literature, is ethical conflict. Ethical conflicts refer to disagreements over what is right and wrong or moral and immoral, whereas legal conflicts are about laws and institutional procedures and policies (Sanchez-Runde et al. 2013). Individuals and organizations in different cultures have different values and definitions of ethical and unethical behaviors that often result in ambiguous situations and uncomfortable conflicts. For instance, bribery might be considered unethical and unfair in Western cultures whereas it may be considered acceptable and even desirable and necessary in building professional relationships in many other cultures. Moreover, culture also plays a role in using different approaches to resolving ethical conflicts. For example, Chinese prefer that someone from the senior management gets involved and solves the ethical conflicts, whereas Americans prefer egalitarianism in terms of ethical decision making (Pan et al. 2010).

While there is a relative lack of empirical research on cross-cultural ethical conflicts, Sanchez-Runde et al. (2013) give some useful suggestions to deal with cross-cultural ethical conflicts. To being with, individuals and organizations have their own preferences over business practices, and they find that most of the time, disagreements over these preferences lead to ethical conflicts. So, it is important to discuss and agree on the practices that they will use. Additionally, it is recommended to discuss and negotiate their level of tolerance for different values. Through understanding of the values and practices and tolerance of each other, the ethical conflicts can be reduced and resolved. Likewise, based on how Google, Yahoo, and MSN handled censorships in China, Hamilton et al. (2008) give six heuristic questions as guidelines in solving ethical dilemmas. They suggest weighing ethical implications and the values and benefits added to the host country by following a particular practice.

As research regarding cross-cultural ethical conflicts has been conducted in clinical psychology (e.g., Knapp and VandeCreek 2007; Strom et al. 2012), more research—both theoretical and empirical—is needed in more traditional organizational settings. Hence, we call for more research in the following areas:

- Cross-cultural ethical values and conflicts in global organizations
- Cross-cultural ethical conflict management and resolution.

Research Need 6: Novel Approaches to Cross-Cultural Communication

When there are differences and conflicts within cross-cultural relationships, not everyone has the same reactions or approaches to solve them. To make the matter more complicated, the same word often has different meanings and implications in different cultures, which can cause miscommunication and misunderstanding. Therefore, it is important not only to understand different metaphors and languages used by different cultures, but also to identify approaches that all individuals from different cultures can use to mitigate these linguistic difficulties.

Stories, metaphors, and storytelling have been found to be effective strategies for communicating ideas as well as making sense of different environments. In particular, Yost et al. (2015) found that in the U.S., when people shared work-related stories, such as career challenges, crossroads, and leading successful and unsuccessful projects, their underlying motivation focused on achievement and responsibilities. In other words, they consistently strived for goal achievement and personal mastery. When sharing positive stories, they exhibited internal locus of control where they took responsibilities of the outcomes and focused on personal strengths. When sharing negative stories, they separated themselves from negative outcomes and focused on their positive roles in the situations and personal growth. In other words, the stories that were shared reflected the underlying values without explicitly naming those values. In this way, storytelling can be an effective way to connect people across cultures by illustrating underlying similarities or differences in beliefs, values, and norms.

In addition, Gibson and Zellmer-Bruhn (2001) studied the use of the following five metaphors in the U.S., France, Puerto Rico, and Philippines in describing team-related concepts (e.g., teamwork, team motivation, mental images of teams, and the cultural impact on teams): family, sports, community, associates, and military. They found that the higher the power distance in the national and organizational culture, the more use of metaphors with clear role content. When there was more emphasis on performance, metaphors, such as sports and military, were used more. Individualistic cultures used the metaphors of sports and associates more. In comparing four countries, the community metaphor was used more in Philippines than in the U.S., the military metaphor more in Puerto Rico than in the U.S., and the associate metaphor more in France than in Puerto Rico. In other words, while the concepts of teams and teamwork were cultural universal to some extent, the metaphors used to describe them differed, and also revealed underlying differences in values and perspectives.

von Glinow et al. (2004) studied emotional conflicts—experiencing negative emotions such as anger and frustration—in multicultural teams and how to resolve these conflicts. Emotional conflicts occurred in teams because of members' differences in values, beliefs, mental models, and language interpretations. In resolving emotional conflicts, a typical way, or the Western style, was to talk because the lack of talk, such as withdrawal, avoidance, and stonewalling, was not seen as effective. However, talking in conflict resolution was not always the best method, especially in multicultural teams. When experiencing these conflicts, individuals could not verbalize their thoughts, express their feelings well, or communicate effectively. Therefore, von Glinow and colleagues suggested the use of visual aids (e.g., drawing) and aesthetic activities (e.g., music; also see Nissley 2002) as alternative or additional methods to talking in conflict management. For example, in 2002, to commemorate the first anniversary of the 9/11 disaster, a moment of silence and choral singing occurred worldwide to communicate the emotional conflicts caused by the 9/11 disaster and its memories. Another example was from the study of Gibson and Zellmer-Bruhn (as cited in von Glinow et al. 2004) where they asked individuals from different cultures to use metaphors to explain what teamwork meant to them. Using both visual and verbal processes helped in understanding different cultural meanings of teamwork.

Taken together, these studies suggest that although individuals in different cultures tend to use different story themes and metaphors to describe the same concepts, the use of stories and metaphors could be effective strategies for improving cross-cultural communication and understanding. Moreover, there are non-verbal alternatives, such as drawing and music, which everyone can understand despite cultural differences. Therefore, more research is needed to understand:

- The use of metaphors and storytelling for communication across cultures
- Effective alternative (e.g., visual, musical) approaches in resolving conflict
- The role of technology in the use of stories, metaphors, and non-verbal communication techniques.

Research Need 7: Cross-Cultural Trust Development, Violation, and Repair

Trust, defined as the willingness to be vulnerable to another individual based on positive expectations of their behavior, is a critical element to success interpersonal interactions, especially cross-cultural interactions (Dirks and Ferrin 2001; Lewicki and Bunker 1996). While trust is the foundation of all types of relationships, the dynamics of trust development can vary widely across cultures (Doney et al. 1998; Fehr and Gelfand 2010; Ren and Gray 2009).

In a study using an investment game, Chinese were found to show higher trust and reciprocity towards other players in the game, whereas Japanese had lower trust and reciprocity (Buchan et al. 2002). Americans showed higher trust but lower reciprocity while Koreans showed lower trust but higher reciprocity. Interestingly, Yuki et al. (2005) found that when interacting with strangers, Americans showed higher trust in in-group members, who shared the same membership with them, than out-group members. Japanese, on the other hand, showed higher trust in those who had direct or indirect interpersonal connections (e.g., knowing someone personally or through a friend) regardless of in-group or out-group membership. However, the reason for the difference in Americans and Japanese was unclear as Buchan et al. (2002) found that similarity in identity did not play a role in such difference.

Beyond these differences in trust propensities and development across cultures, conflicts are nearly inevitable in cross-cultural relationships, and as a result, trust violations are a likely occurrence. Trust violation occurs when the violated party's or the victim's positive expectations and perceptions of the offender or the violator are challenged or disconfirmed by the violator. Nonetheless, there are only a few studies on the dynamics of trust violation, strategies of repairing trust, and the differences in their effectiveness across cultures.

One of the few empirical studies conducted to understand cross-cultural differences in trust repair and restoration was the study of Kuwabara et al. (2014). They examined the relationships between generalized trust and the timing of violations across participants from the United States and Japan. Generalized trust was the general tendency to trust people, including strangers. The U.S. has a high-trust culture because the long-term relationships are mobile. Japan, on the other hand, has a low-trust culture because it is a collectivistic culture with stable social connections. They found that trust violation in the early establishment of relationship was more damaging to the relationship only among Americans but not among Japanese. Trust violation was more damaging to the relationship if it happened at a later time only for Japanese because the violation threatened the stability of the relationship. In addition, generalized trust not only was higher among Americans, but also mattered more for them. In early trust violation, the higher the generalized trust, the more likely that Americans could fully cooperate.

Ren and Gray (2009) also present a theoretical framework of the effectiveness of trust restoration depending on violation types and culture. Two types of violation are identity violation and violation of control. Identity violation happens when the victim's identity is challenged or threatened, and the victim loses face because the violator breaks the expectations of being respectful and considerate of the victim. Violation of control occurs when the victim's ability to influence over something or someone is challenged. Violation of control breaks the expectancy and equity norms and challenges the expectations that resources will be fairly allocated and distributed. In addition to the types of violation, individualistic and collectivistic cultures also play a role in trust restoration. Individualistic culture emphasizes having a unique, independent self from the group, one's own achievements, and needs. Collectivistic culture emphasizes relatedness to the group, conformity, and meeting others' needs.

Hence, Ren and Gray (2009) propose that the collectivistic violator is more likely to suppress negative emotions after trust violation and to use indirect means of communication because direct confrontations will challenge the stability of the relationship. Moreover, after identity violation, an explanation and apology through a third party as well as a demonstration of concern and consideration toward the victim will be more effective for the collectivistic violator to repair trust than for the individualistic violator. Similarly, after violation of control, not only reframing the situation and giving a genuine explanation though a third party but also showing guilt and offering redemption privately will be more effective for the collectivistic violator than for the individualistic violator. Although this study is not an empirical study, Ren and Gray (2009) explore possible cultural differences in the effectiveness of strategies to repair trust. As we still have a lot to understand and learn in terms of trust development and repair in the cross-cultural context, more research is needed in the following areas:

- Initial trust and trust development in cross-cultural interpersonal relationships
- Types of violation and the differences in their consequences across cultures
- Effectiveness of trust repair activities and restoration in different cultures.

Research Need 8: Cross-Cultural Bias

As we know, culture is an inherently multilevel phenomenon that can manifest at the individual, team, organizational, and national levels. Methodological issues in cross-cultural management research are important because there is a limited generalizability across different levels and cultures (Taras et al. 2009). Bias can occur not only in measurements themselves, but also in interpretation of scores from the studies (van de Vijver and Poortinga 1997). Based on their analysis of 121 instruments, Taras et al. (2009) present methodological biases in cross-cultural equivalence. First, they find that self-report questionnaires are commonly used in cross-cultural studies, but the results from these self-reports are individual-level. Data aggregation from the results does not always represent higher levels of culture such as the national cultural context within which the research is embedded. Second, reliability and validity of scales cannot always be generalized across levels and cultures. For example, a reliable and valid educational test given to American test takers was found to be inadequate for non-American test takers (van de Vijver and Poortinga 1997). Last, but not least, measurement scales and wording in these scales as well as test questions can have different meanings and result in different interpretations across cultures, making comparative research difficult to execute and interpret.

Although the focus of this book is not on methodological or psychometrics issues, it is important to be aware of the various cross-cultural biases that could be influencing research results as we strive to study cross-cultural management issues and apply them in global organizations. Thus, future research needs to explicitly consider the potential cross-cultural biases in measurements and applications so that study results can be more reliable and valid and result in desirable outcomes for individuals, teams, and organizations involved.

Final Thoughts

We hope that the research findings, practices, and experiences by academic scholars, practitioners, and military experts in this book will help you better understand and manage these cross-cultural topics and issues. We also hope that this book serves as an integration of cross-cultural research and practices as well as a source for new areas of interest and best practices. If you, your team, or your organization encounters cross-cultural issues or has creative insights, please let us know. As always, our team at the Institute for Cross Cultural Management is eager and ready for new ideas, learning, practices, and challenges.

References

Brandl, J., & Neyer, A.-K. (2009). Applying cognitive adjustment theory to cross-cultural training for global virtual teams. *Human Resource Management, 48*, 341–353. doi:10.1002/hrm.20284

Buchan, N. R., Croson, R. T. A., & Dawes, R. M. (2002). Swift neighbors and persistent strangers: A cross-cultural investigation of trust and reciprocity in social exchange. *American Journal of Sociology, 108*, 168–206. doi:10.1086/344546

Church, A. H., Rotolo, C. T., Ginther, N. M., & Levine, R. (2015). How are top companies designing and managing their high-potential programs? A follow-up talent management benchmark study. *Consulting Psychology Journal: Practice and Research, 67*, 17–47. doi:10.1037/cpb0000030

Collings, D. G., & Mellahi, K. (2009). Strategic talent management: A review and research agenda. *Human Resource Management Review, 19*, 304–313. doi:10.1016/j.hrmr.2009.04.001

Cramton, C. D. (2002). Finding common ground in dispersed collaboration. *Organizational Dynamics, 30*, 356–367. doi:10.1016/S0090-2616(02)00063-3

Dirks, K. T., & Ferrin, D. L. (2001). The role of trust in organizational settings. *Organization Science, 12*, 450–467. doi:10.1287/orsc.12.4.450.10640

Doney, P. M., Cannon, J. P., & Mullen, M. R. (1998). Understanding the influence of national culture on the development of trust. *Academy of Management Review, 23*, 601–620. doi:10.2307/259297.

Fehr, R., & Gelfand, M. J. (2010). When apologies work: How matching apology components to victims' self-construals facilitates forgiveness. *Organizational Behavior & Human Decision Processes, 113*(1), 37–50. doi:10.1016/j.obhdp.2010.04.002.

Gentry, W. A., & Sparks, T. E. (2012). A convergence/divergence perspective of leadership competencies managers believe are most important for success in organizations: A cross-cultural multilevel analysis of 40 countries. *Journal of Business and Psychology, 27*, 15–30. doi:10.1007/s10869-011-9212-y

Gibson, C. B., & Zellmer-Bruhn, M. E. (2001). Metaphors and meaning: An intercultural analysis of the concept of teamwork. *Administrative Science Quarterly, 46*, 274–303. doi:10.2307/2667088

Hamilton, J. B., Knouse, S. B., & Hill, V. (2008). Google in China: A manager-friendly heuristic model for resolving cross-cultural ethical conflicts. *Journal of Business Ethics, 86*, 143–157. doi:10.1007/s10551-008-9840-y

Jackson, L. A., Sullivan, L. A., Harnish, R., & Hodge, C. N. (1999). Achieving positive social identity: Social mobility, social creativity, and permeability of group boundaries. *Journal of Personality and Social Psychology, 70*, 241–254. doi:10.1037/0022-3514.70.2.241

Kauffeld, S. (2006). Self-directed work groups and team competence. *Journal of Occupational and Organizational Psychology, 79*, 1–21. doi:10.1348/096317905X53237

Knapp, S., & VandeCreek, L. (2007). When values of different cultures conflict: Ethical decision making in a multicultural context. *Professional Psychology: Research and Practice, 38*, 660–666. doi:10.1037/0735-7028.38.6.660

Kozlowski, S. W. J., & Klein, K. J. (2000). A multilevel approach to theory and research in organizations: Contextual, temporal, and emergent processes. In K. J. Klein & S. W. J. Kozlowski (Eds.), *Multilevel theory, research and methods in organizations: Foundations, extensions, and new directions* (pp. 3–90). San Francisco, CA: Jossey-Bass.

Kristof-Brown, A. L., Zimmerman, R. D., & Johnson, E. C. (2005). Consequences of individuals' fit at work: A meta-analysis of person-job, person-organization, person-group, and person-supervisor fit. *Personnel Psychology, 58*(2), 281–342.

Kuwabara, K., Vogt, S., Watabe, M., & Komiya, A. (2014). Trust, cohesion, and cooperation after early versus late trust violations in two-person exchange: The role of generalized trust in the United States and Japan. *Social Psychology Quarterly, 77*, 344–360. doi:10.1177/0190272514546757

Lewicki, R. J., & Bunker, B. B. (1996). Developing and maintaining trust in work relationships. In R. Kramer & T. Tyler (Eds.), *Trust in organizations: Frontiers of theory and research* (pp. 114–139). Thousand Oaks, CA: Sage Publications.

Nissley, N. (2002). Tuning-into organizational song as aesthetic discourse. *Culture and Organization, 8*, 51–68. doi:10.1080/14759550212104

Oh, I.-S., Guay, R. P., Kim, K., Harold, C. M., Lee, J.-H., Heo, C.-G., & Shin, K.-H. (2014). Fit happens globally: A meta-analytic comparison of the relationships of person-environment fit dimensions with work attitudes an performance across East Asia, Europe, and North America. *Personnel Psychology, 67*, 99–152. doi:10.1111/peps.12026

Pan, Y., Song, X., Goldschmidt, A., & French, W. (2010). A cross-cultural investigation of work values among young executives in China and the USA. *Cross Cultural Management: An International Journal, 17*, 283–298. doi:10.1108/13527601011068379

Peterson, D. B. (2007). Executive coaching in a cross-cultural context. *Consulting Psychology Journal: Practice and Research, 59*, 261–271. doi:10.1037/1065-9293.59.4.261

Ren, H., & Gray, B. (2009). Repairing relationship conflict: How violation types and culture influence the effectiveness of restoration rituals. *Academy of Management Review, 34*, 105–126. doi:10.5465/AMR.2009.35713307

Ruvolo, C. M., Peterson, S. A., & LeBoeuf, J. N. G. (2004). Leaders are made, not born: The critical role of a development framework to facilitate an organizational culture of development. *Consulting Psychology Journal: Practice and Research, 56*, 10–19. doi:10.1037/1061-4087.56.1.10

Sanchez-Runde, C. J., Nardon, L., & Steers, R. M. (2013). The cultural roots of ethical conflicts in global business. *Journal of Business Ethics, 116*, 689–701. doi:10.1007/s10551-013-1815-y

Strom, T. Q., Gavian, M. E., Possis, E., Loughlin, J., Bui, T., Linardatos, E., et al. (2012). Cultural and ethical considerations when working with military personnel and veterans: A primer for VA training programs. *Training and Education in Professional Psychology, 6*, 67–75. doi:10.1037/a0028275

Taras, V., Rowney, J., & Steel, P. (2009). Half a century of measuring culture: Review of approaches, challenges, and limitations based on the analysis of 121 instruments for quantifying culture. *Journal of International Management, 15*, 357–373. doi:10.1016/j.intman.2008.08.005

Tarique, I., & Schuler, R. S. (2010). Global talent management: Literature review, integrative framework, and suggestions for further research. *Journal of World Business, 45*, 122–133. doi:10.1016/j.jwb.2009.09.019

van de Vijver, F. J. R., & Poortinga, Y. P. (1997). Towards an integrated analysis of bias in cross-cultural assessment. *European Journal of Psychological Assessment, 13*, 29–37. doi:10.1027/1015-5759.13.1.29

von Glinow, M. A., Shapiro, D. L., & Brett, J. M. (2004). Can we talk, and should we? Managing emotional conflict in multicultural teams. *Academy of Management Review, 29*, 578–592. doi:10.2307/20159072

Yost, P. R., Yoder, M. P., Chung, H. H., & Voetmann, K. R. (2015). Narratives at work: Story arcs, themes, voice, and lessons that shape organizational life. *Consulting Psychology Journal: Practice and Research, 67*, 163–188. doi:10.1037/cpb0000043

Yuki, M., Maddux, W. W., Brewer, M. B., & Takemura, K. (2005). Cross-cultural differences in relationship- and group-based trust. *Personality and Social Psychology Bulletin, 31*, 48–62. doi:10.1177/0146167204271305

Index

© Springer International Publishing Switzerland 2016
J.L. Wildman et al. (eds.), *Critical Issues in Cross Cultural Management,*
DOI 10.1007/978-3-319-42166-7

CPSIA information can be obtained
at www.ICGtesting.com
Printed in the USA
LVOW09*1654070117

520137LV00007B/67/P

9 783319 421643